ITALIAN CRIME FICTION

EUROPEAN CRIME FICTIONS

ITALIAN CRIME FICTION

Edited by

Giuliana Pieri

UNIVERSITY OF WALES PRESS
CARDIFF
2011

www.uwp.co.uk

British Library Cataloguing-in-Publication Data
A catalogue record for this book is available from the British Library.

ISBN   978-0-7083-2431-8 (hardback)
         978-0-7083-2432-5 (paperback)
e-ISBN 978-0-7083-2433-2

Typeset in Wales by Eira Fenn Gaunt, Cardiff
Printed in Great Britain by CPI Antony Rowe, Chippenham, Wiltshire

Contents

Acknowledgements   vii
Notes on Contributors   ix

1 Introduction
   Giuliana Pieri   1

2 The Emergence of a New Literary Genre in Interwar Italy
   Jane Dunnett   6

3 Founding Fathers: Giorgio Scerbanenco
   Jennifer Burns   27

4 Literature and the *Giallo*: Gadda, Eco, Tabucchi and Sciascia
   Joseph Farrell   48

5 The Mysteries of Bologna: On Some Trends of the Contemporary
   Giallo
   Luca Somigli   73

6 Crime and the South
   Mark Chu   89

7 Italian Women Crime Writers
   Giuliana Pieri and Lucia Rinaldi   115

8 *Milano nera*: Representing and Imagining Milan in Italian *Noir*
   and Crime Fiction
   Giuliana Pieri   132

9 Annotated Bibliography
   Lucia Rinaldi   151

Index   155

Acknowledgements

Three conferences were important stages in my growing academic interest in Italian crime fiction. In March 1998, I was invited to present, to my knowledge, the first-ever paper in the UK on Andrea Camilleri, at a conference devoted to the 'Cross border *policier* – the European crime novel', at the University of Edinburgh. In April 2002, Claire Gorrara and I co-organized a conference at the Institute of Germanic and Romance Studies devoted to 'Cultural intersections: *noir* fiction and film in France and Italy'. This was in many ways the starting point of the Italian crime fiction project and was also a very important moment in the conception of the European Crime Fiction series. Finally, in July 2004, I attended a conference co-organized by my fellow series editor, Shelley Godsland, on 'Murder and mayhem in the *Mare Nostrum*: contemporary configurations of Mediterranean detective fiction', in Prato, which provided much needed insight into the place of contemporary Italian fiction in the European scene.

I would like to thank the School of Modern Languages, Literatures and Cultures at Royal Holloway, for help in the form of sabbatical leave and especially colleagues in the Italian department who covered for my absence. I am also very grateful for the assistance I received from staff of the Biblioteca Nazionale, Florence, and the British Library. A very special thanks goes to Claire Gorrara, whose support and passionate intellectual engagement with European crime fiction over the past decade has been crucial to me on an academic and personal level. Special thanks go also to Sarah Lewis, commissioning editor of University of Wales Press, who offered us the opportunity to develop the series, for her invaluable advice and enthusiasm for the Italian crime fiction project, to Elin Nesta Lewis, whose editing has been superb, and to my Royal Holloway colleague, Professor Jane Everson, who provided much appreciated help with some of the translations into English of Italian *giallisti*.

Lastly, I would like to dedicate this book to my family and to my children in particular, who were born as this project unfolded. If they caused some delay to the project, the final result is also due to the incredible focus that motherhood has afforded me.

London
August 2011

Notes on Contributors

Jennifer Burns is Associate Professor in the department of Italian at the University of Warwick. Having published a monograph on notions of political commitment in contemporary Italian narrative in 2001, entitled *Fragments of impegno*, she developed from this project an extended programme of research into the literary works of immigrant writers appearing in Italy since 1990. She has published a number of articles on ethical, thematic and stylistic issues in this emerging area of Italian literature, and has a monograph on the topic forthcoming. Her most recent research turns towards the late nineteenth century and the work of the *Scapigliatura*, focusing on notions of transgression – including criminality – in the cultural context of discourses of progress and modernity.

Mark Chu is Senior Lecturer in Italian and head of Italian at University College Cork. His main areas of research are Sicilian literature since 1870, and Italian crime fiction in its European and global context. He is particularly interested in the ethico-political engagement with the text and its intended and unintended meanings, with a deconstructionist method. His research on Sicilian literature focuses on the very nature of the representation of the region by authors working predominantly in a realist mode and frequently referring to aspects of the island's history. He has published studies on, among others, Camilleri, Lucarelli, Sciascia, Vittorini and Consolo.

Jane Dunnett is Lecturer in Italian at Swansea University and an associate editor of *Romance Studies*. Her research focuses on the literature and cultural history of twentieth-century Italy, with a particular interest in translation studies. She is currently completing an AHRC-funded monograph on the production and reception of interwar Italian detective novels. Recent publications include: 'Translating under pressure: the censorship of foreign fiction in Italy between the wars' (Dublin: Four Courts, 2008), '*Il mestiere di uomo*: meditazioni, delitti e buone maniere nel primo Scerbanenco' (Rome: Menghini, 2009) and 'Crime and the critics: on the appraisal of detective novels in 1930s Italy', *Modern Language Review*, 106 (2011).

Joseph Farrell is Professor Emeritus of the University of Strathclyde. His main research interests are in the fields of Sicilian culture and theatre history. He is author of *Leonardo Sciascia* (Edinburgh: Edinburgh University Press, 1995) and *Dario Fo and Franca Rame: Harlequins of the Revolution* (London: Methuen, 2001). He co-edited, with Paolo Puppa, *History of Italian Theatre* (Cambridge: Cambridge University Press, 2006), and has edited volumes of essays on Carlo Goldoni, Dario Fo, Primo Levi, Carlo Levi, Ugo Betti and on the mafia. He has also produced editions of Fo's *Accidental Death of an Anarchist*, Pirandello's *Six Characters in Search of an Author* and Goldoni's *Servant of Two Masters*, all for Methuen, London. His translations include novels by Leonardo Sciascia, Vincenzo Consolo, Daniele Del Giudice, as well as plays by Fo, Baricco, De Filippo and Goldoni. He is currently translating a series of detective novels by Valerio Varesi. He is a frequent contributor to radio arts programmes both in London and Scotland, and reviews regularly for several newspapers, including *The Herald* and *The Times Literary Supplement*.

Giuliana Pieri is Senior Lecturer in Italian and the visual arts at Royal Holloway, University of London. Her main research interests are in the fields of post-war Italian crime fiction, Anglo-Italian artistic and cultural relations and the visual arts in Italy in the nineteenth and twentieth centuries. Her monograph, *The Influence of Pre-Raphaelitism on Fin-de-siècle Italy* (Oxford: Maney, 2007), formed part of a number of studies on Anglo-Italian cultural relations in the late nineteenth century and the work of Gabriele d'Annunzio. She has also published a number of studies on Italian crime writers, including Scerbanenco and contemporary crime writers (Camilleri, Lucarelli, Fois). As co-investigator in the AHRC research grant on The Cult of the Duce: Mussolini and the Italians 1915–2010, she has worked on the iconography of Italy's dictator Benito Mussolini and the role of the visual arts in the construction of the cult of the Duce and the fall of the regime. The latter was also the subject of the exhibition, co-curated by her, *Against Mussolini: Art and the Fall of the Regime*, Estorick Collection of Modern Italian Art, London, in 2010.

Lucia Rinaldi is Teaching Fellow in Italian at University College London. Her research interests are twentieth-century Italian literature and culture, in particular crime and *noir* fiction. Her publications include: *Assassinations and Murder in Modern Italy. Transformations in Society and Culture*, co-edited with S. Gundle (New York and Houndsmills: Palgrave, 2007); 'Bologna's *noir* identity: narrating the city in Carlo Lucarelli's crime fiction', *Italian Studies*, 64/1 (2009); 'Location and identity in contemporary Italian crime narrative. The case of Fois's *Gialli*', in L. Rorato and A. Saunders (eds), *The Essence and the Margin: National Identities and Collective Memories in Contemporary European Culture* (Amsterdam and New York: Rodopi, 2009). She is currently working on a monograph based on her doctoral thesis entitled *Contemporary Italian Crime Fiction: Postmodernity, Identity and Representation* and on a volume on Andrea Camilleri.

Luca Somigli is Associate Professor of Italian studies at the University of Toronto. His research interests are in the areas of European modernism and the avant-garde, Italian genre fiction and visual media, especially comics. He has written and co-edited several books, including *Legitimizing the Artist. Manifesto Writing and European Modernism, 1885–1915* (Toronto and London: University of Toronto Press, 2003; winner of the best book award of the American Association for Italian Studies in 2004). In the field of genre fiction, he has published a monograph on Italy's premier science-fiction writer, Valerio Evangelisti (2007), edited a special issue of the journal *Symposium* on Italian detective fiction (2005) and written articles on Augusto De Angelis, Loriano Macchiavelli and the representation of Fascism in contemporary mysteries. He is currently working on theoretical and historical issues in the definition of Italian modernism.

1

Introduction

GIULIANA PIERI

In Italy, crime fiction had a relatively late and slow start. The so-called *gialli*, which take their name from the distinctive yellow cover of the crime series by the Milanese publishing house Mondadori in the 1930s, consisted at the time of vast quantities of translated British, French and American detective and *noir* novels. The immense popularity enjoyed by this genre led Italian novelists to try their hand at writing their own crime fiction during the 1930s and the early 1940s. Italian readers, however, still showed a marked preference for foreign crime fiction: a trend that continued in the immediate post-war decades. Despite this xenophilia, Italian crime fiction has been growing steadily in importance and, since the late 1980s, has been enjoying unprecedented popularity. The success of the *gialli*, now a short-hand term for any type of detective fiction and more widely any story that has a mystery element, has transformed the Italian literary scene at the turn of the new millennium and has been sustained by a number of prestigious Italian publishing houses and increasing critical interest. Detective novels, procedural novels, *noir* fiction and true crime writing are all testimony to an unquenched appetite of the Italian public for home-grown crime fiction which extends also to cinema and television, with a plethora of film adaptations and television series and the often close involvement of Italian crime writers in the scriptwriting and production of these series.

The present volume is the first study in the English language to focus specifically on Italian crime fiction, weaving together a historical perspective and a thematic approach, with a particular focus on the representation of space, especially city space, gender and the tradition of *impegno*, the social and political engagement which characterized the Italian cultural and literary scene in the post-war period and resurfaced as the leading element in the work of the new generation of Italian crime writers in the 1990s. Although a number of studies have been published in Italy on the history of this literary genre, most have been rich in history and poor in analysis.[1] They have approached the development of crime fiction by providing their readers with a first mapping of the chief Italian contributors to the crime genre but have overlooked the socio-historical and literary elements present in what is by now a substantial body of works. One of the reasons behind these critical shortcomings in the analysis of the Italian *gialli* is linked to the way in which crime fiction, and especially the home-grown variety, has been viewed by the Italian literary establishment until very recently. If not with open hostility, it would be fair to say that Italian crime fiction has been systematically met with indifference and suspicion by literary critics who, even when confronted with established writers such as Carlo Emilio Gadda or Leonardo Sciascia, whose work is analysed in chapter 4, have treated their crime fiction as an example of the subversion of the genre and reinstated their overall negative view of this popular genre. Whilst in the post-war period, British, American and French literary critics and theorists were engaged in studies of the crime fiction traditions of their respective countries, Italian critics for decades ignored home-grown examples.[2] Giuseppe Petronio, who has worked extensively on the Italian *giallo*, as late as 1978 pointed towards the bias against this popular narrative form in Italy.[3] Petronio emphasized especially the prejudice and snobbism of the Italian academic and literary establishment against the detective novel.[4] This attitude changed very little in the following decade when Italian critics still seemed to view the *giallo* in terms of the literature versus popular literature binary, with the implicit denial of proper literary status to the latter. Antonio Gramsci had posed a similar question, in 1930, in a long note on crime fiction, in which he had argued that: 'in detective fiction there have always been two strands: a mechanical one focused on the plot, and an artistic one'.[5] Gramsci, by shifting the focus on to the issue of artistic merit, unwittingly paved the way for the dismissal of this popular genre in Italy. Italian culture in the post-war period was still primarily dominated by the so-called *critica idealista* which focused on purely literary and stylistic matters and was thus not best suited to analyse a genre which thrives on its connections with socio-historical and political issues. Besides, as Umberto Eco noted in 1964, when it came to popular culture, Italian critics were overall sceptical about applying the same critical tools that were used for the study of high-brow literature to its more popular counterpart.[6] The lack of critical interest in Italian crime fiction had, however, one positive result: it made Italy more open to seminal foreign works on the theory of crime fiction which would eventually influence a veritable renaissance of crime fiction in Italy in the last decade of the twentieth century.

The year 1980 was in many ways a turning point for the fortunes of Italian crime fiction. Umberto Eco, after having spent the previous two decades writing a number of influential essays on the theory and practice of popular fiction, published his first novel, *The Name of the Rose*, a historical crime novel, which became a best-seller in Italy and abroad, and, many would argue, marked the beginning of a rebirth of novel writing in Italy. Eco's work on mass culture, popular literature, semiotics and postmodernism gave strong theoretical credentials to his own open defence of the choice of the crime genre in his novel.[7] The year 1980 saw also the publication of a collection of several seminal essays on the theory of crime fiction by two Italian literary critics, Renzo Cremante and Loris Rambelli, which had never appeared in Italian translation before.[8] This collection, which fostered a reappraisal of the theoretical underpinnings of this popular genre, included Edmund Wilson's 'Who cares who killed Roger Ackroyd?', W. H. Auden, 'The guilty vicarage', and essays by, among others, G. K. Chesterton, Richard A. Freeman, J. L. Borges, Tzvetan Todorov and Gadda. Todorov's 'The typology of detective fiction' was particularly influential in Italy: this was the proof that one could apply the same stringent analytical models of high literature to a genre that was still viewed by the majority of literary critics as unworthy of literary status. Yet, when Todorov claimed that in high literature the mark of quality is to break the canon (whilst in mass literature the best novel is that which does not go beyond the canon, otherwise from *roman policier* it becomes literature), he reinforced, at least in the eyes of Italian literary critics, the fundamental oppositional view of literature proper versus popular literature as mere entertainment.[9] The question that critics should have been posing at the time, and should certainly do in the new millennium, is whether we still need to redefine this genre or whether we can simply accept that in our postmodern age the boundaries between different literary genres are constantly being crossed and re-defined. As Italo Calvino noted in the essay 'Cibernetica e fantasmi', the value of an artistic work is that it is able to give shape to the ghosts that lie dormant in every society.[10] Calvino, voicing one of the central principles of postmodern narrative, argues that the emphasis should not be placed on the author but on the act of reading; the reader's reaction is the ultimate test of the actual significance of an artistic work. Leaving aside the complex theoretical implications inherent in the analysis of texts from the point of view of the reader's response, Calvino shifts the focus towards the impact of the literary work on its readers and the dialogue that the writers are able to establish with their readership. If we were to look at Italian narrative, especially in the post-war period but also in the interwar years, as Jane Dunnett argues in chapter 2, from Calvino's perspective with the aid of book sales figures, the Italian literary scene would appear as almost entirely dominated by Italian and foreign crime fiction, with a marked upsurge of interest in this genre since the early 1990s, as will be discussed in chapters 5 and 6 in particular. The chapters in this book, in highlighting the contribution of Italian crime fiction to the most important social and often political debates of the time, as well as showing the literary and stylistic innovations brought about by Italian crime writers, argue strongly in favour of reinserting Italian crime fiction into the nation's literary canon. They consider the Italian *giallisti* as some of the most interesting protagonists of the renewal of Italian narrative in the second half of the twentieth century.

The case of established writers such as Gadda, Sciascia and Antonio Tabucchi (see chapter 4) is revealing since their openly declared and obvious engagement with this literary genre has overall been marginalized by literary critics, who have often discussed the use of crime fiction by these writers with a degree of unease and as an 'aberrant' example rather than as a central narrative model especially suited to convey complex philosophical, ethical and moral issues. As the new generation of Italian crime writers who started their literary career in the 1990s shows, the blueprint of the new Italian *giallo* is a complex mix of the narrative and thematic models provided by these established literary figures and the work of a number of writers who can be considered the real founding fathers of Italian post-war crime fiction, namely Giorgio Scerbanenco (whose work will be discussed in chapter 3) and Loriano Macchiavelli who had a great impact on the bourgeoning

Bologna school (see chapter 5). The common thematic focus of the new generation of crime writers who emerged in Italy in the 1990s is a new commitment to the portrayal of the new Italy. Crime writers held up the mirror and showed their readers a country that was striving to leave behind the violence and social and political turmoil that characterized the so-called Leaden Years; a country that struggled, after the fall of the Berlin wall, with the faltering of its long-standing communist and socialist past ideologies, and that was confronted, in the early 1990s, with the political and administrative scandals of *Tangentopoli* and *Mani Pulite* and some of the worst mafia killings in recent memory.[11] In the course of the 1980s and 1990s, Italy was also transformed by continual and consistent immigration which has turned a country of migrants into one of mass immigration confronted with the new challenges of a global, multi-ethnic and multicultural society. These transformations affected big and small urban centres and paved the way for the Italian provinces to become as effective an object of scrutiny as the old metropolis of the foreign and home-grown *noir* tradition. In the postmodern world, crime fiction has been transformed by Italian writers into a new powerful vehicle to express Italy's discontents and to deal with the new challenges posed by the social and political changes of the new millennium. One of the strongest messages to come from Italian crime fiction is the need to re-engage with the time-honoured tradition of *impegno*, the social and political commitment that we strongly associate with Italian post-war literature and culture. As we shall see in this volume, this is the common denominator of most contemporary crime writers in Italy, and is especially evident in the writers associated with the Bologna School, whose work is analysed in chapter 5, and in the work of Andrea Camilleri, Marcello Fois and Gianrico Carofiglio (see chapter 6). Italian women crime writers also emerge from the analysis in this volume as central protagonists in this renewed *impegno*; their stance is often less overtly political but more firmly ethical than their male counter-parts. In their investigation of the many forms of violence towards women in con-temporary society, these writers show that Italy still retains all the marks of a patriarchal society.

The overt social and political critique that can be found in the work of con-temporary *giallisti* echoes the socio-political and often ethical and philosophical commitment of more established writers. The result is a body of works that, when viewed without the artificial distinction between high and popular literature, shows a remarkable insight into Italy's post-war history, tracking its societal and political troubles and changes as well as often also engaging with metaphorical and philo-sophical notions of right or wrong, evil, redemption and the search for the self.

Notes

[1] The only studies specifically dedicated to Italian crime fiction are: Loris Rambelli, *Storia del giallo italiano* (Milan: Garzanti, 1979); Massimo Carloni, *L'Italia in giallo. Geografia e storia del giallo italiano contemporaneo* (Reggio Emilia: Diabasis, 1994); Luca Crovi,

Delitti di carta nostra. Una storia del giallo italiano (Bologna: Punto Zero, 2000); Luca Crovi, *Tutti i colori del giallo. Il giallo italiano da De Marchi a Scerbanenco a Camilleri* (Venice: Marsilio, 2002); and Maurizio Pistelli, *Un secolo in giallo. Storia del poliziesco italiano (1860–1960)* (Rome: Donzelli, 2006), the only volume to focus on the nineteenth-century beginnings of the genre in Italy.

[2] Some of the initial interest in the genre was within broader studies on crime fiction. See for instance: Alberto del Monte, *Breve storia del romanzo poliziesco* (Bari: Laterza, 1962). Ernesto G. Laura, *Storia del giallo. Da Poe a Borges* (Rome: Studium, 1981).

[3] Giuseppe Petronio, 'Sulle tracce del giallo', *Delitti di carta*, 1 (1997), 54–9.

[4] G. Petronio and U. Schulz-Buschhaus (eds), *Trivialliteratur?* (Trieste: Lint, 1979).

[5] 'in questa letteratura poliziesca si sono sempre avute due correnti: una meccanica, d'intrigo, l'altra artistica': Antonio Gramsci, 'Sul romanzo poliziesco', in *Letteratura e Vita Nazionale* (Torino: Eiunaudi, 1974), p. 116.

[6] Eco noted this attitude in the reception of his book *Apocalittici e integrati*, explaining that of one of his critics 'vede con molto sospetto questo uso degli strumenti della cultura Alta per spiegare e analizzare la cultura Bassa' (views with great suspicion the use of instruments of high culture in order to explain and analyse low culture), in *Apocalittici e integrati* (Milan: Fabbri, 1964; Bompiani, 1988), p. vi.

[7] See Eco's postscript in *The Name of the Rose Including the Author's Postscript*, trans. William Weaver (New York: Harvest Books, 1994). On Eco and popular culture see, in particular, U. Eco, *Apocalittici e integrati* and *Il superuomo di massa. Retorica e ideologia nel romanzo popolare* (Milan: Bompiani, 1978), which includes Eco's famous essay on Ian Fleming.

[8] Renzo Cremante and Loris Rambelli, *Teoria ed analisi del racconto poliziesco* (Parma: Pratiche editrici, 1980).

[9] T. Todorov, 'The typology of detective fiction', *The Poetics of Prose* (Oxford: Blackwell, 1977), 42–52.

[10] Italo Calvino, 'Cibernetica e Fantasmi', in *Una pietra sopra* (Torino: Einaudi, 1980), pp. 164–81.

[11] For a historical analysis of this complex period of Italian recent history see, Stephen Gundle and Simon Parker (eds), *The New Italian Republic: from the Fall of the Berlin Wall to Berlusconi* (London: Routledge, 1996) and Paul Ginsborg, *Italy and its Discontents: Family, Civil Society, State 1980–2001* (London: Allen Lane, 2001).

2

The Emergence of a New Literary Genre in Interwar Italy

[handwritten: → between WWI and WWII (1920s – early 40s)]

JANE DUNNETT

The proliferation of crime fiction in Italy between the wars represented a publishing phenomenon of unprecedented scale. Indeed, it took many writers and critics by surprise, and polarized opinion sharply. If detective novels enjoyed a massive following amongst readers, they encountered considerable critical resistance, at times even hostility. Regarded as products of low cultural value, they were seen by some as an assault on belletrism, on the very idea of literature as art, in a country where 'literature' was still conceived of narrowly in terms that, today, inevitably strike us as conservative and, above all, elitist. Here was a genre that challenged all the conventional canons according to which works of prose had for so long been judged, a genre that, perhaps more than any other, appealed to people from different classes and backgrounds. The vogue for stories about murder and mystery had been imported from abroad, and this too fuelled much of the criticism levelled at it, given the Fascist regime's policy of promoting national literature. But it also added to the attraction of such stories which people associated automatically with Britain and the United States where it had been born. Like many contemporary commentators, the writer Alberto Savinio (1932) maintained that

[handwritten: why not set in italy]

> The detective novel is quintessentially Anglo-Saxon. The English or the American metropolis, with its sinister overcrowded slums – dark, damp and squalid – its gangs of organised and militarised criminals, its masses as black as sewer water, the ghostly appearance of its buildings, offers the most favourable setting, the most appropriate stage for the scene of the crime. It is difficult to imagine a detective novel taking place within the city walls of Valenza or of Mantua, of Avignon or of Reggio Emilia.[1]

Nevertheless, the 1930s saw the first collective attempt by Italian authors to produce Italian detective novels. This chapter discusses the work of the pioneering crime writers who paved the way for the genre to establish itself in post-war Italy. Whilst the majority of critics would probably not classify as crime fiction Carlo Emilio Gadda's *Quer pasticciaccio brutto de Via Merulana* (1957, but first serialized in the journal *Letteratura* in 1946) however one might wish to categorize the novel, there is no doubt that it owes much to the new trend that had gained ground over the previous decade. In order to appreciate fully the distinctiveness of the detective novel in Italy it is necessary to have some understanding of its earliest origins and subsequent development into a recognizable literary form. To that end, a brief publishing history will be traced before providing a more detailed discussion of the context and constraints of production under Fascism, based on archival research. After examining the relevant background material and surveying the range of crime writing that was available in translation in interwar Italy, this essay will then focus on the work of writers such as Alessandro Varaldo, Ezio D'Errico, Augusto De Angelis and Giorgio Scerbanenco.

Importing crime fiction

Although the detective story had made its first appearance in Italy in the late nineteenth century, with occasional translations of works by, amongst others, Edgar Allan Poe (*Storie incredibili*, 1863), Émile Gaboriau (*Il signor Lecoq*, serialized in a newspaper in 1869) and Wilkie Collins (*La pietra della luna*, 1870), it was not until the 1920s that a market began to be created for this type of literature. Signs of things to come could have been detected, however, in the enormous success enjoyed by Arthur Conan Doyle, who was introduced to the Italian public in 1895 through a collection of his short stories (*Le Avventure di Sherlock Holmes*). Their subsequent serialization in the *Corriere della Sera*'s weekly magazine *La Domenica del Corriere* (7 May–5 November 1899) led to a marked increase in its sales. As a result, the proprietors of the newspaper seized on other stories by Conan Doyle, translating them as soon as they came out and publishing them in instalments over the next fifteen years: *Le ultime avventure di Sherlock Holmes* (1900–1), *La maledizione dei Baskervilles* (1902–3), *Il ritorno di Sherlock Holmes* (1904– 5) and *La valle della paura* (1915).[2] These stories were later republished in the illustrated instalments of the 'Romanzo Mensile' (1903, 1904, 1907, 1907–8, 1918), which gives a clear indication of their popularity. By the end of the First World War, Sherlock Holmes had become a familiar figure for most Italians. If the appeal of the detective genre was never in question in Italy, the publishing potential that it represented would not be fully realized for another decade or so, as we shall see shortly.

Generally speaking, before the First World War, French writers dominated the catalogues of Italian publishers in areas of so-called *letteratura amena*, and this applied no less to crime fiction (the best-known writers included Émile Gaboriau, Ponson du Terrail, Pierre Souvestre and Marcel Allain). In 1914, Sonzogno launched the series 'I romanzi polizieschi', which carried on well into the 1920s and can claim to be amongst the very first 'dedicated' detective series in Italy. Twenty-four out of the thirty-one books published were by the French novelist Georges Meirs, and featured the 'Avventure di William Tharps, il celebre poliziotto inglese'. Between 1921 and 1924, Sonzogno brought out a weekly series entitled 'Il romanziere poliziesco' which ran to 134 issues (with frequent reprints). There were other, similar initiatives to capture a popular audience, all of which consisted of producing pamphlet-like publications containing translations of French writers: one such series was 'Il romanzo poliziesco' (1921–2) published by Varietas. The early 1920s saw Bemporad joining in the trend by publishing a series called 'Collezione di avventure poliziesche'. All the novels, of which there were twenty-one in total, were written by a single author, Gustave Le Rouge, and had the same protagonist, 'Il misterioso Dr. Cornelius'. In 1930, Sonzogno also devoted a series to Gustave Le Rouge's novels, which was called 'Le meravigliose avventure del miliardario Todd Marvel'.

A noteworthy, and altogether neglected, exception to the ubiquity of imported crime fiction can be found in a series published by Bietti between 1914 and 1920: it appears to have been the first series devoted entirely to Italian detective novels. Entitled 'Le avventure del poliziotto americano Ben Wilson', it comprised a total of twenty-four books in magazine format, all written by Ventura Almanzi. The fact that the stories were set in the USA was often highlighted in the titles of individual issues: 'Gli schiumatori di Nuova York', 'I giustizieri della California' and 'I creditori della sedia elettrica'. This setting is not without significance – given the time-span of the series – anticipating as it does the fascination with all things American that would become so striking a feature of Italy's cultural landscape throughout the Fascist era and beyond.[3]

Foreign authors continued to supply the lion's share of detective stories published during the interwar years, the only difference being that French authors began to be supplanted by Anglo-American authors. Demand grew steadily in the course of the 1920s as publishers brought out these books in ever greater numbers, several even devoting entire series to crime fiction. Despite the titles often given to such series – for example, Varietas's 'Il Romanzo Poliziesco', mentioned earlier – they consisted not of books but of periodicals. The authors who wrote for this particular series were in fact almost all Italians, 'albeit presented mainly by means of improbably "exotic" pseudonyms'.[4]

The turning-point in the fortunes of the detective novel in Italy came in September 1929, with the launch of Mondadori's legendary 'I Libri Gialli', a series that was to catapult the genre to the forefront of contemporary culture. It is instructive to note the titles of the four books that the series opened with and which appeared in quick succession: *Il Mistero delle due cugine* (*The Leavenworth Case*, 1878) by Anna Katherine Green, *La strana morte del Signor Benson* (*The Benson Murder Case*, 1926) by S. S. Van Dine, *L'uomo dai due corpi* (*Captain of Souls*, 1923) by Edgar Wallace, and *Il Club dei suicidî* (*The Suicide Club*, 1878) by Robert Louis Stevenson. These are all translations of works by major writers from Britain and the USA, works that can be considered classics of the genre, with the sole exception of *The Suicide Club*.[5] Books came out every two months, then monthly, and before long, fortnightly. They were sold mainly by subscription, had distinctive yellow covers[6] – hence the name given to the series – and were immensely popular; indeed, they proved to be one of the most commercially successful of all Arnoldo Mondadori's ventures. Whilst Mondadori was not the sole publisher operating in the sector, his firm played a decisive role in shaping perceptions of crime writing and in giving it a quasi-literary status.[7]

Conceived by one of Mondadori's closest collaborators Luigi Rusca, the series 'I Libri Gialli' was entrusted to Lorenzo Montano (the pseudonym of Danilo Lebrecht, 1893–1958). A refined intellectual, poet and a writer who had been a founder member of *La Ronda*, his editorship guaranteed a degree of professionalism and an attention to detail rarely accorded to this type of book. The standards that Montano set for the series emerge clearly from a letter he wrote to Mondadori shortly after being put in charge and in which he stressed the need for texts to be well translated; hitherto, he argued, the widespread circulation of detective novels had been greatly hampered by the poor quality of the translations.[8] Commenting on the first four novels in the series that were published simultaneously (and which he had not in fact chosen himself), he reported that he had to overhaul three of them substantially. He went on to explain:

> A series of this nature certainly does not require great linguistic or stylistic sophistication, but it does need fluent, lively translations which can be read easily and with pleasure. I took the necessary action immediately, and trust that the translations done under my supervision will be more satisfactory.[9]

Montano appears to have had a fairly precise idea of the kind of readership that Mondadori was aiming to build up, a readership that would include educated Italians who up until then might have baulked at the idea of buying detective novels, not least because of their poor prose style. A concerted attempt to turn crime fiction into a more respectable genre seems to be at work here, as is evinced by Montano's editorial emphases in this and in further correspondence with Mondadori. In his role as series editor Montano had responsibility for selecting what to publish in 'I Libri Gialli', finding translators and revising translated texts so as to ensure that a certain standard was maintained in the writing.[10] A dynamic and able negotiator, he was active in establishing contacts with publishers abroad. Crucially, he was alert to the importance of obtaining maximum publicity for the books under his editorship, affording them especially the critical attention that they might not otherwise have received.

Edgar Wallace was amongst the most popular of the authors published by Mondadori, dominating their catalogue for over a decade: during the period 1930–1941, an average of ten novels by the Anglo-American writer came out in the 'I Libri Gialli' series, contributing in large measure to its viability. Two million copies of Wallace's novels alone were sold in the course of the 1930s. Other best-selling foreign crime writers published by Mondadori included Margery Allingham, Agatha Christie (for whom the firm had acquired exclusive rights), Alfred E. W. Mason, Freeman Wills Crofts, Rex Stout, Ellery Queen, and S. S. Van Dine – all authors who assured their Italian publisher excellent sales figures.

It is important to bear in mind that *gialli* (whether or not they were translations) were subject to various restrictions imposed by the censorship authorities – restrictions that applied to all books published under Fascism – including a ban on references to suicide, abortion, incest, rape and anything else that might offend
against religion

9

what official documents refer to as 'Fascist morality', a category that largely co-incided with Catholic morality. In the case of detective novels, however, pressure was periodically applied to publishers to reduce their output, considered to be unhealthy reading for the nation. Moreover, novelists were actively discouraged from portraying Italians as criminals in their books (although exceptions to this rule can be found), which is why, as we shall see, so many of the country's writers would choose to set their detective novels abroad, in foreign locations that only added to their exotic lustre. Public demand for this new literary genre was such, however, that even with these limitations, the books continued to circulate in large numbers until the early 1940s.

The 'I Libri Gialli' series ran until October 1941, when it was forced to close on account of Fascist censorship. Before long, another of Mondadori's series would be targeted: in 1942, the periodicals in the 'I Gialli Economici' series were also banned. After the war a new series was launched, the 'Giallo Mondadori' (1946–96) whose longevity speaks for itself; it outlived all its competitors, surviving for half a century. A fitting testament to the extraordinary success achieved by Mondadori's various crime fiction series is the currency that the term *giallo* gained within a very short space of time, replacing the calque coinage *romanzo poliziesco* (derived from *roman policier*). Today, the word *giallo* is used not only to refer to the crime fiction genre but also to any unsolved murder case, or mystery in general, much favoured by newspaper headline writers in Italy.

Home-grown crime writers

Witnessing the explosion of a new literary vogue for crime fiction, Italian authors too were stimulated to try their hand at writing in this genre. Clearly, they did not wish to lose out on such a promising publishing opportunity, and may even have hoped to equal the sales figures achieved by imported detective novels. They would almost certainly have been heartened in their endeavour by the introduction in 1931 of government measures aimed at curbing what some nationalist critics referred to as the 'excessive' quantity of translations circulating in Italy. Quotas were apparently set to restrict the number of books by foreign writers that could appear within a given series, stipulating that at least 15 per cent had to be written by Italians. (In the case of detective-novel series, this move naturally produced somewhat paradoxical results for the regime, given its disapproval of the genre, as outlined above.) Thus spurred, countless would-be crime writers competed for a place in this potentially lucrative market and, before long, Montano was being inundated with unsolicited – and largely un-wanted – manuscripts. The extent to which this posed a problem for Montano emerges from a letter he wrote to Mondadori, dating from 1932, in which his exasperation is palpable:

Authors who want to write for the *Gialli* series are becoming a real nuisance. Would it not be possible to set up a small committee of readers with the job of doing a first reading? It could be made up, for instance, of your son and two or three of his friends. All Italian *Gialli* manuscripts sent in by unknown authors would go to them for consideration. They would then pass only the best ones on to me, thereby saving me a lot of the valuable time I am wasting at the moment reading an endless amount of nonsense.[12]

Whether Mondadori took up Montano's suggestion is not known. What is certain, however, is that not all Italian authors who experimented with the crime genre were churning out 'nonsense'. Among the earliest Italian contributions it is worth mentioning Alessandro De Stefani's *La crociera del 'Colorado'* (1932), Armando Comez's *L'uomo dei gigli* (1933), Vasco Mariotti's *L'uomo dai piedi di fauno* (1934) and Franco Vailati's *Il mistero dell'idrovolante* (1935).

One author, in particular, whose contribution to 'I Libri Gialli' had been welcomed, indeed sought out, was Alessandro Varaldo (1878–1953), an established writer of romantic novels and plays. Approached by Arnoldo Mondadori himself who was keen to have on board writers noted for the quality of their prose, and with whom readers were already familiar, Varaldo took up the challenge and attempted to adapt to the prevailing taste of modern readers. The result was a book regarded as the first proper Italian detective novel, *Il sette bello*, which came out in 1931, followed the same year by *Le scarpette rosse*. In these and in the other books that Varaldo went on to produce, he created two detective characters: Ascanio Bonichi, a police chief (*Commissario di Polizia*) who appears in his first novel, and Gino Arrighi, a private investigator who appears (together with Bonichi) in his second novel. Bonichi is the protagonist of seven other novels that Varaldo wrote between 1931 and 1938: *Tre catene d'argento* (1931), *La gatta persiana* (1933), *La scomparsa di Rigel* (1933), *Circolo chiuso* (1935), *Casco d'oro* (1936), *Il segreto della statua* (1936), *Il tesoro dei Borboni* (1938) and a collection of short stories, *La trentunesima perla* (1938). Gino Arrighi is the protagonist of two other books: *Le avventure di Gino Arrighi. Novelle poliziesche* (1939) and *Il signor ladro* (1944). A prolific writer, Varaldo also composed plays about detection, so-called *drammi gialli*, including 'Il tappeto verde', published in the magazine *Il Dramma* in 1933.[13]

Varaldo set his detective stories in a Rome redolent of the pre-war past, a Rome still laden with objects from an age that no longer existed but that was re-evoked through the memories of the living. In Varaldo's descriptions of Rome with its baroque and neo-baroque buildings, the Italian capital emerges at times as a sort of metaphysical city, according to the literary critic Loris Rambelli. He argues that the fountains or bridges of Rome themselves assume an emblematic character when, in the silence of the night or at dawn, the silhouette of a figure is illuminated, for instance.[14] The theatrical quality of such a backdrop is self-evident, and further imbues Varaldo's novels with an atmosphere that suggests an irretrievable past.

The detective-protagonist Bonichi, referred to in familiar terms as Sor Ascanio, is an old-fashioned honest policeman, armed only with a cigar, who happens to be a habitual reader of crime fiction. He may not be a fully fleshed-out character, yet he manages to come across as a reassuring figure. Maurizio Pistelli believes that Bonichi already embodies

> the perfect example of the future national literary policeman: an institutional cop, inclined to action but not to violence, courageous but not foolhardy, understanding, meditative, ironic. A single man, with no family ties, he lives for his work alone, and has earnt the affection and admiration of his most faithful collaborators. He is instantly likeable, easy to talk to, and sensitive to the suffering of his fellow human beings.[15]

Varaldo's novels do not have the tight plotting typical of classic detective stories; instead, they contain a mixture of comic effects, misunderstandings and melodrama. Pistelli has pointed out that the action 'often veers towards the kind found in romantic or adventure novels'.[16] The much-vaunted 'scientific' or logical approach associated with Anglo-American crime fiction is nowhere to be seen, indeed it is scorned by Bonichi who has none of the traits of the traditional infallible detective. A great admirer of the novels of Simenon, it was Varaldo who introduced Italian readers to the Belgian writer in an article of his dating from July 1932 in which he asserts that the crime genre implicitly contains a form of social commentary, containing as it does information about the mores of a given nation.[17] For Rambelli Varaldo's novels paint a picture of an indolent, superficial bourgeoisie that wants to enjoy itself at all costs as a reaction against pre-war austerity. Nevertheless, it perpetuates the customs of its class and remains incapable of regeneration.[18]

Aware of the need to persuade the public that home-grown crime fiction also merited attention, Mondadori stressed Varaldo's literary credentials from the outset, mounting an advertising campaign that sought to reassure the public that his novels were 'quality products', not mere potboilers. However, promotional material also described Varaldo as the 'Wallace italiano', a claim clearly intended to bolster his reputation as the foremost Italian detective-story writer. Initially intrigued by the novelty of a *giallo* 'made in Italy', readers responded well to Varaldo's books. *Il sette bello* was reprinted three times, with a total print run of 23,000 copies, whereas *Le scarpette rosse* was reprinted three times, with a total print run of 17,000 copies.[19] But subsequent novels were not to fare as well.

This would have come as no surprise to Montano who, at an early stage, had spotted difficulties in the attempt by this writer of romances to reinvent himself as a fully fledged crime writer. Explaining his misgivings to Mondadori, he enclosed the letter he had sent to Varaldo concerning his latest *giallo*, the *Casco d'Oro*. It is worth quoting at length from this letter:

> It struck me as being one of your most dazzling detective novels, full of energy, the one perhaps that best pushes forwards to its conclusion without anything getting in the way. The raw and realistic depiction of character is excellent, though that is no less than one would expect from a book by you. I must admit, however, to being a little taken aback that the crime and thriller elements are less pronounced and the romantic aspects more dominant than in your previous detective novels (despite the murder

victim!) . . . Please view this concern in the context of the ever-increasing preferences of our readers for excitement and the strongest possible sensations. That's the reason we have had to opt for Americans such as Queen, etc. who are far more sensational than the English.[20]

Whilst Montano is clearly at pains to be diplomatic, he does not conceal his opinion of the novel. Despite his reservations, publication went ahead. But, as he suggests, the taste of the public was rapidly evolving.

One can sense the impact that crime writing was already beginning to have in Italy during the early 1930s if one examines the contribution to the genre made by Arturo Lanocita (1904–83), a journalist who worked for one of Italy's leading newspapers, *Corriere della Sera*.[21] His first detective novel *Quaranta milioni* (1932) is set in the Dolomites and features a Brazilian millionairess, Maria Quinones, who is holidaying in a mountain resort with her adoptive daughters. One of them, Isotta, is found spread-eagled on the carpet of her hotel room with a bloodied stiletto knife beside her; the director of the hotel goes to fetch the doctor but on returning to the room discovers that Isotta's corpse has been removed. The murder investigation is carried out by a Milanese journalist called Silvio Melius and a woman called Rosetta Martale who each follow different lines of enquiry, and at times even come to suspect one another. A romantic undertone is also occasionally hinted at. With a story that takes place in different locations between Italy (Alto Adige) and Austria (Graz), Lanocita creates a fairly convoluted plot where, amid comic conjectures on the fate of the corpse, eventually it transpires that Isotta was not killed but kidnapped, and has experienced some extraordinary adventures.

The book contains a number of self-referential remarks. For example, a bookseller tells Melius: 'Today's detective novels are risible . . . Suspense, true suspense, believe me, is something that Poe knew how to create.'[22] Moreover, in constructing his work, Lanocita has revisited some of the topoi of the classic detective novel (the hotel as the scene of the crime, wealthy foreigners, etc.), which he then distorts. For Rambelli, this constitutes no less than a parody of the genre;[23] he highlights the work's comic aspects and its transgression of the rules of crime writing, as set out famously by Van Dine in his 'Twenty rules for writing detective stories'.[24] At any rate, 14,000 copies of *Quaranta milioni* were sold. But demand for detective novels by foreign authors was such that thereafter Italian *gialli* would no longer achieve print runs of this size.[25] Indeed, Lanocita's subsequent detective novels, *Quella maledettissima sera* (1939) and *Otto ore di angoscia* (1945), encountered far less commercial success than the first one.

Another journalist who ventured into crime writing was Tito Antonio Spagnol (1895–1979). Curiously, his first detective novel was published in a French translation during the early 1930s. At the time, Spagnol was living in Paris and initially he succeeded in getting his work serialized in the *Nouvelle revue française*; subsequently, it appeared in book form with the title *La griffe du lion* (1932) as part of Gallimard's 'Collection Détective' (no. 54), before an Italian edition was eventually brought out by Mondadori in 1934.

13

L'unghia del leone features an American detective called Alfred Gusman who works as a crime reporter on the New York *Evening Sun*. It revolves around a gruesome double murder that took place in the city in June 1927; as the public clamours for justice, the police are on the point of arresting Ned Sterbing, a criminal involved in alcohol smuggling. Only Gusman and the lawyer Jim Sullivan are convinced of his innocence. One can readily detect the influence of Sherlock Holmes on the character of the American sleuth; equally, the narrative technique employed is traditional (the story is related by a close friend of the detective, the lawyer Sullivan, who is not directly involved in the case), yet the investigation unfolds in an unpredictable manner and the plot is engaging.

The depiction of the USA gains much of its force from the fact that the author had first-hand knowledge of the country, having spent a few years there (notably in New York and in Hollywood where he worked as a screenwriter) before moving to Paris. In order to make his account more realistic and hence more credible, Spagnol describes contemporary American manners and mores during the Prohibition era, evoking the criminal underworld that accompanied it; to further enhance the veracity of his narrative he peppers his story with American terms that are specific to the environment described and which are translated in footnotes (e.g. 'speakeasy', p. 8; 'bootleggers', p. 10). At other times, he simply inserts everyday words such as 'building' (p. 9), 'reporters' (p. 11), 'gangs' and 'racketeers' (p. 19) into the text and italicizes them to signal their foreignness (but without explaining them). This is clearly done to give the account an air of authenticity, although the narrative style itself remains a traditional literary style, with long, well-structured sentences and no attempt made to imitate more innovative modes of writing that were being developed at that time.

Spagnol drew on his experience to produce a number of short stories with an American setting also; these reflect a negative view of US society as motivated by money and success, a cynical and heartless society where violence is the inevitable outcome (a view shared by many Italian travel writers and newspaper correspondents at the time). As such, they take the form of thrillers as opposed to conventional detective stories, and are probably the closest any Italian writer came to experimenting with the hard-boiled genre before the post-war period.[26]

In addition, Spagnol wrote a couple of detective novels with Italian settings, novels for which he remains best known: *La bambola insanguinata* (1935) and *Uno, due, tre* (1936) use the Veneto (the author's own region) as the backdrop for narratives which exploit the topos of a murder that disturbs the serenity of a sleepy countryside community (here, the village of Cozzuolo in the province of Treviso). They feature a character called Don Poldo, an octogenarian priest and student of natural sciences who occasionally takes on the mantle of amateur detective. Although he is clearly based on Father Brown, Don Poldo represents a rather diluted version of Chesterston's Catholic priest who is famous for his ability to solve criminal cases; the stories themselves, whilst mildly entertaining, lack sufficient tension to create suspense. The narrator Celso Rosati is the nephew of Don Poldo, a young married country doctor who is only marginally involved in the investigations.

Once again, this conventional technique of the detective novel is deployed, yet in this instance it feels particularly artificial, and slows the pace too much for any sense of real drama.

Fortunately, Spagnol's earlier invention, the New York sleuth Gusman, makes several other appearances in his work: for example, in a short story entitled 'La collana di smeraldi' (1935), published in *Il Cerchio Verde* (a weekly magazine devoted to crime fiction that had recently been launched by Mondadori); in a somewhat less felicitous novel entitled *La notte impossibile* (1937), set this time in France, and subsequently in the novella 'L'ombrellino viola' (1938) as well as in the novel *Sotto la cenere* (1938), which both mark a return to form for Spagnol who seems more at home when recreating American scenarios.[27]

Ezio D'Errico (1892–1972), a multi-talented playwright, essayist, poet, film set designer and artist, proved equally energetic in so far as crime writing was concerned, producing a total of nineteen detective novels. The first of these, entitled *Qualcuno ha bussato alla porta*, was published in 1936. Set in a Paris teeming with foreigners, it provides an appealingly cosmopolitan backdrop to the adventures of its protagonist Emilio Richard, a French chief of police whose Christian name has, however, been Italianized in accordance with the usage of the times (similarly, the murder victim, an artist living in Montmartre, is referred to as Carlo Boyer). Moreover, with its carefully reconstructed old-fashioned ambience that drew on stereotypes about the behaviour and customs of the Gallic petty bourgeoisie, the novel would have felt reassuringly familiar to readers. It paved the way for a whole series of detective stories by D'Errico that take place in the French capital, which is sketched out through frequent passing references to the names of streets as well as to Notre-Dame and La Seine, both of which, the reader is informed, are visible from the window of Richard's office at the Paris Sûreté.

Richard, a retired civil servant who has been called back into service, lives in a small apartment with his sister Genoveffa; a combination of housekeeper and nagging wife, she attends to his practical needs and generally looks after his welfare. She is a sort of Madame Maigret, according to Rambelli who draws parallels between D'Errico and Simenon.[28] *Qualcuno ha bussato alla porta* has amongst its cast members of the Spanish and French aristocracies, and also the aspiring middle classes as represented by the notary Villeneuve. Allusions to important families, to chateaux, to inheritances and to dowries complete the rather conventional social characterization of the novel where the bourgeoisie emerge from the story as fundamentally grasping and motivated solely by pecuniary interests.

The novel was followed by books that include *Il fatto di Via delle Argonne* (1937), *La famiglia Morel* (1938), *Il quaranta, tre, sei, sei non risponde* (1939), *L'uomo dagli occhi melanconici* (1939), *Il naso di cartone* (1940), *La notte del 14 luglio* (1941). In these novels, D'Errico describes Richard as 'a typical Frenchman, or rather a typical Parisian . . ., something of a sceptic and also a bit of a grumbler, a lover of good food and drink which he savours slowly between puffs of his cigarette'.[29] Not surprisingly, perhaps, Richard is dismissive of his opposite numbers at Scotland Yard with whom, on occasion, he has had to collaborate:

Good people but too placid [. . .] you need patience, naturally, and also some flair, and then you need to understand people . . . not people as they are described in books, where they are all either heroes or scoundrels, but people as they are in real life, that is part-hero and part-scoundrel . . . that's the secret. The difficulty lies in understanding the proportions of this mixture; once you have understood the formula, you can guess what reactions there might be [. . .] When the ratio between heroism and knavery leans towards the second ingredient, then there is a precipitate of criminality. This is the true chemistry, not that of Sherlock Holmes.[30]

Thus, Richard rejects so-called scientific methods of detection, as used traditionally by Anglo-American investigators, and employs a more personal approach that leads him to seek to understand the 'wider picture', instead of focusing on minutiae and placing great importance on a minor physical detail (say, a hair on a jacket or a misplaced handkerchief) from which a positivist detective might extrapolate a solution. To that end, he immerses himself in the atmosphere of places associated with cases he is working on, trying to absorb the thoughts and feelings of characters from their physical environment. His investigations are therefore the fruit of a slow and patient process that needs time to mature. Allied to this aspect of the plot, Richard's fundamental humanity makes D'Errico's books attractive and highly readable, despite their underlying melancholy.

Whatever the merits of the authors discussed so far, one crime writer in particular stands out during this period. Augusto De Angelis (1888–1944) is universally regarded as the finest Italian detective novelist of his generation. A journalist by profession, he wrote for prestigious newspapers such as *La Stampa*, *Il Secolo XIX*, *Il Resto del Carlino* and *L'Ambrosiano*, but his real passion lay in the theatre. For over twenty years, until 1934, he wrote plays which were performed but did not bring him the success he had hoped to achieve. Luckily for the history of Italian crime fiction, in 1931 he was appointed co-editor of a magazine called *I Misteri Polizieschi*, and within a few years he was turning out detective novels to which he now dedicated himself with new-found passion, not to mention professionalism. He had published fourteen novels by the time of his premature and shocking death, following an incident in which he was beaten up by a Fascist thug.[31] By way of example, one might cite *Il candeliere a sette fiamme* (1936), *La barchetta di cristallo* (1936), *Il do tragico* (1937), *Il mistero delle orchidee* (1942) and *L'impronta del gatto* (1943).

Apart from the consistent quality of the writing in these books, the work of De Angelis differs from that of contemporary detective novelists in one fundamental respect. His is a more complex, tragic vision of the world, a vision that emerges through the compelling figure of the Commissario Carlo De Vincenzi. De Angelis presents us with an unusual chief constable: a contemplative character, he is a man of considerable culture, an avid reader of, amongst others, Plato and Freud, Oscar Wilde's *De Profundis* and *The Epistles* of Saint Paul, and hence a student of human nature. Although still a fairly young man (in his mid-thirties), he already feels old, as we learn from one of his first novels, *Sei donne e un libro*; in college they nicknamed him the poet, and indeed he is much given to reflecting on life.[32] He is a sensitive man who sees the extent of the evil around him and, by means of his chosen career, seeks to combat it. Unmarried, he devotes himself tirelessly to his job, and spends every night at police headquarters working or reading. A solitary man, he has for sole company his elderly housekeeper Antonietta, who used to be his nanny.

This figure of an intellectual who relies more on instinct and the imagination than on logic has something in common with the Commissaire Richard. Like D'Errico, De Angelis sets out deliberately to distance himself from the deductive methods of British literary detection. In *L'albergo delle tre rose* he pays homage to Van Dine's character Philo Vance (like De Vincenzi, he is a refined intellectual, with a passion for collecting art) in an explicit reference to the American detective's conviction that one should look at psychological rather than material clues in order to find the truth.[33]

Uniting poetry with perspicacity, De Vincenzi tries to uncover the mystery of human nature by means of a psychoanalytical approach. *Il mistero di Cinecittà* (1941), for example, finds De Vincenzi grappling with what appears to be a crime of passion. In the course of his investigations, he analyses what kind of mind the person who has committed this crime is likely to have and reflects that, if his theory was correct,

> He was dealing with a particularly dangerous type of criminal, who was at once cerebral and passionate, someone driven by an unstoppable and aberrant impulse. A lucid madman. All murders are carried out by madmen. In the case of a crime of passion, the murderer's psychic equilibrium is deeply disturbed, even if their actions follow a strict logic.[34]

Of considerable interest are De Angelis's own reflections on the detective novel and, more especially, on its status in Italy. His novel *Le sette picche doppiate* (1940) included a preface in which he asserted the value of this new literary genre – a genre that still needed defending against the continuing criticism that it was both immoral and of poor quality. De Angelis argued that there was no reason why a detective novel could not be a work of art: Poe, Simenon, Chesterton and Van Dine had all raised the form to the highest level, and this was what De Angelis also intended to do:

> I was determined – and I still am – to write a real Italian detective novel, though it is an extremely difficult thing to do. Here in Italy, we do not have in everyday life the ingredients necessary to devise an American- or English-style detective novel. We do not have detectives, we do not have policemen, we do not have gangsters; we do not, to our misfortune, even have those frail heiresses or old fools whose wealth makes them a target for schemers or murderers. Not that we are short of crime unfortunately, even if it is on a relatively small scale. Not that we are short of tragedies.[35]

At first sight, De Angelis's comments would appear to endorse the view put about by the regime that crime was no longer a problem under Fascism since it had forcibly disappeared from the pages of newspapers. In reality, however, he is acknowledging that there was a darker side to Italian society, one that could provide material for his novels. De Angelis penned several other short pieces on the subject of the *giallo*, justifying his decision to set his detective novels in Italy and to people them with Italian characters, an increasingly unpopular choice from the point of view of the censors.[36]

The last author from this period who merits serious attention is Giorgio Scerbanenco (1911–69), justly regarded as the father of the Italian *noir* because of his Duca Lamberti series published in the 1960s (see chapter 3 in this volume by Jennifer Burns). A prolific writer who worked for a variety of magazines during the 1930s turning out romantic stories, by the end of the decade he was already experimenting with the *giallo*. Within the space of several years he had produced five detective novels set in the United States, all of which featured an investigator by the name of Arturo Jelling: *Sei giorni di preavviso* (1940), *La bambola cieca* (1941), *Nessuno è colpevole* (1941), *L'antro dei filosofi* (1942) and *Il cane che parla* (1942).[37]

Scerbanenco's first, little-known foray into crime fiction has as its protagonist an unlikely detective. He is a quiet, retiring family man who works in the archives at Boston's police headquarters and who, periodically, gets called upon to help solve crimes. Yet, far from being an intrepid investigator, he often seems reluctant to leave his desk and get involved in cases. Initially, he even questions his own ability to deal with difficult or dangerous situations. Thus, in the first novel *Sei giorni di preavviso*, we are presented with a timorous character who does not appear to relish the prospect of adventure; indeed, he is seriously concerned about where his investigation might lead him: 'Why on earth had he, Jelling, got himself into this mess? He vowed that if the Vaton case was resolved successfully he would never venture out of his archive again, not even if they offered him a fortune.'[38]

Self-doubt comes across, too, in Jelling's apologetic and unconfident manner which strikes an almost amusingly discordant note, given the professional role he is required to perform. When he goes to the homes of suspects to interrogate them late at night, for instance, he apologizes profusely. He never takes advantage of his position of power to intimidate others (it is hard not to read a coded reference here to the kind of attitude inculcated by Fascist ideology), but is consistently courteous and considerate. Since this is not the kind of behaviour that criminals are accustomed to, they find it quite disarming. More generally, his candour and apparent ingenuousness allow him to gain the confidence of people who would otherwise be more reticent with the police.

Behind this modest demeanour lies a subtle and brilliant mind, and despite Jelling's propensity to daydream (he is often caught drawing on a sheet of paper or gazing out of the window of his office, oblivious to those around him), he succeeds in getting to the root of problems that have defeated others through a patient process of methodical analysis. He is depicted as slow and meditative, traits that exasperate his superior Sunder who complains: 'You always know everything, but you get there so terribly late!'[39] When necessary, however, he has the ability to be decisive: 'That morning Jelling was terrifically active. It was as if he were driven by the silent tenacity of a mastiff; he talked, thought and acted without wasting a second, rapidly, but also methodically.'[40] Throughout the novels, there is an underlying tension between the imperative to act, and the need to ponder questions first.

Jelling's method is essentially an anti-method in which he rejects traditional methods of detection, based on physical clues, traces, handprints, etc.[41] It consists of following his own nature, 'made up entirely of psychology and logic'.[42] Ultimately, he uses logical reasoning to defeat crime, and it is this obstinacy and determination to follow his own methods and not those of the police that makes Jelling such a compelling figure. A sort of anti-hero, he gains confidence and self-belief as the stories unfold, losing his timidity in the face of aggressiveness and learning to stand up for himself.[43] His indignation at injustice is offered as the plausible explanation for his gradual transformation, although he never loses his idealism and faith in human nature. In the course of the five novels, we witness this change as Jelling learns to adapt intelligently to circumstances.

This is an interesting use of character development, a feature rarely found in the depiction of detectives whose fixed identity tends to be an intrinsic part of the serial formula and the reader recognition that ensues. Initially, the stories were narrated by Jelling's confidant, a certain Signor Tommaso Berra (not the Watson-like fall guy but someone more self-assured and certainly more educated than Jelling himself), whom he visits intermittently to discuss cases with, but by the third novel Scerbanenco no longer employs this device, possibly because Jelling has now assumed a more independent role, and his stature has grown as he gains recognition from his colleagues.

Whilst the America that Scerbanenco depicts is a virtual one (unlike Spagnol, he never visited the country), his narratives are, on the whole, psychologically convincing and, consequently, of strong human interest. Critics have often overlooked Scerbanenco's earliest detective novels, yet the Jelling stories are not only well written and extremely enjoyable to read, they offer insights into the author's trajectory and stylistic evolution. Their essential optimism forms a fascinating counterpoint to the cynicism of Scerbanenco's later, more famous novels.

If, as we saw earlier, an editor such as Montano considered Anglo-American crime fiction to be far superior to the new domestic variety, he was nevertheless compelled to include it in Mondadori's catalogue because of the protectionist measures introduced by the Fascist regime at the beginning of the 1930s. Despite the questionable quality of many of these first attempts at producing home-grown detective novels, the proliferation of such books bears witness to the sheer excitement that surrounded the new literary vogue. For the *giallo* to emerge fully from the shadows of its illustrious foreign models and to develop its own sense of identity would inevitably require time.

The contribution to the early development of crime fiction made by Italian writers whose names have largely been forgotten is, as this essay has sought to demonstrate, well worth revisiting, and not merely for historical reasons. A careful examination of the plethora of Italians who attempted to work within the genre during the interwar years, often producing what were undoubtedly derivative and unsatisfactory results, reveals a handful of authors whose work has in some cases been unjustly neglected, and not only outside Italy.[44] In the cases of D'Errico, De Angelis, Tito Spagnol and the early Scerbanenco, one finds stories of indisputable charm, narrative skill and an unsuspected degree of originality.

* * *

Extract from Augusto De Angelis's *La barchetta di cristallo*

'Bravo, De Vincenzi! This is the first truly interesting point, indeed, more interesting than the crime itself. The dagger! Let me have it, Kruger.'

The flaxen-haired Teuton held out the dagger, holding it by the blade, with two fingers, and placing it on the palm of the professor's hand.

'Magnificent! Quite a startling weapon. To the uninitiated, it could seem authentic, an object fit for a museum . . . but it isn't . . . It doesn't belong to any particular time or period . . . It has a serpent on it, and a ball grip. It's the work of a crackpot or someone with a sick imagination. But it's made of gold, and the steel blade is exotically ornamented. The very idea that a murderer would carry such a weapon to commit his crime is inconceivable . . . There's got to be another reason. What I mean is that there must be another explanation for this. The victim may have owned the weapon. That is possible but there's also another problem: why, if it belonged to him, did the murderer leave the weapon in the wound and not bother to pull it out and take it with him? Do you follow me?'

'Perfectly.'

The professor adjusted his glasses that kept sliding down his aquiline nose.

'Observe that the corpse has not been searched. Bargelli has all the objects that were found in the dead man's pockets . . . You can ask for them and you'll see that there's a wallet with a five-thousand lira note in it, there's the gold watch . . . some letters . . .' The professor's eyes were shining, he had to hold on to his glasses again, halting them in their slippery descent. 'Read the letters! They're very interesting . . . Some of them would explain the murder, if the murderer was their author trying to get them back . . .'

'Blackmail?'

'There's plenty of blackmail material. But the letters haven't been touched. So?'

De Vincenzi looked around.

'What about in here?'

'Yes. I thought of that too. That display cabinet . . . with the Chinese vases . . . But those vases have nothing in common with the dagger, you know – they're genuinely authentic!'

'So I've been told and for a number of reasons I didn't doubt it.'

'Well, the cabinet was opened and someone looked inside it . . . But do you know whose fingerprints were found on the vases and the other objects, all of them, as you'll see, worth hardly anything . . . just bric-à-brac?'

Augusto De Angelis, *La barchetta di cristallo* (1936; Palermo: Sellerio, 2004), pp. 56–7.

Translated by Jane Dunnett.

Notes

[1] 'Il romanzo poliziesco è essenzialmente anglosassone. La metropoli inglese o americana, con i suoi bassifondi sinistri e popolati come gli abissi marini di mostri ciechi, le sue squadre di delinquenti disciplinati e militarizzati, le sue folle nere come l'acqua delle fogne, l'aspetto spettrale delle sue architetture, offre il quadro più favorevole, la messinscena più adatta al quadro del delitto. S'immagina male un romanzo poliziesco dentro la cinta daziaria di Valenza o di Mantova, di Avignone o di Reggio Emilia': Alberto Savinio, 'Romanzo poliziesco', in *Souvenirs* (Palermo: Sellerio, 1976), pp. 193–9, p. 196. The reception of the new genre is discussed in Jane Dunnett, 'Crime and the critics: on the appraisal of detective novels in 1930s Italy', *Modern Language Review*, 106 (2011), 746–65. All translations into English are my own.

[2] In addition, *Corriere della Sera* published some in book form: see bibliography.

[3] See, for example, Jane Dunnett, 'Anti-fascism and literary criticism in post-war Italy: revisiting the *mito americano*', in Guido Bonsaver and Robert Gordon (eds), *Culture, Censorship and the State in Twentieth-century Italy* (Oxford: Legenda, 2005), pp. 109–19.

[4] 'seppure proposti per lo più mediante fantasiosi pseudonimi "esotici"': Maurizio Pistelli, *Un secolo in giallo: Storia del poliziesco italiano (1860–1960)* (Rome: Donzelli, 2006), p. 91.

[5] Stevenson's inclusion as a crime writer is somewhat surprising; the stories in question are in fact tales of the fantastic. Loris Rambelli believes that it was intended to give lustre to the nascent series since Stevenson would have been held to be an author whose work belonged to the category of 'highbrow' literature. Loris Rambelli, *Storia del 'giallo' italiano* (Milan: Garzanti, 1979), p. 10.

[6] Critics have suggested a number of explanations for Mondadori's choice of colour, often tracing the origin of its use to foreign publishers; see, in particular, Rambelli, *Storia del 'giallo' italiano*, pp. 15–19.

[7] Most accounts of Italian crime fiction refer almost exclusively to Mondadori; it should be borne in mind that many other publishers also operated in the sector during this period (see Dunnett, '*Supergiallo*. How Mondadori turned crime into a brand', *The Italianist*, 30/1 (2010), 63–80), thereby contributing to the growing popularity of the genre. But there is no denying the centrality – and uniqueness – of the role performed by Arnoldo Mondadori's firm, hence the space accorded it in the present chapter.

[8] Lorenzo Montano to Arnoldo Mondadori, 25 September 1929, Fondazione Arnoldo Mondatori (hereafter FAM) ('Montano', ARN B. 70).

[9] 'Una collezione di questo genere non domanda certo grandi raffinatezze di lingua o di stile, ma vuole tuttavia delle traduzioni sciolte e vivaci, che si facciano leggere facilmente e piacevolmente. Io me ne sono preoccupato immediatamente, e spero che le traduzioni fatte sotto la mia sorveglianza siano più soddisfacenti': ibid.

[10] Montano's editorial duties are stipulated in a letter (dated 12 May 1931) which Arnoldo Mondadori wrote to Montano, FAM ('Montano', ARN B. 70).

[11] On the structure of the various censorial bodies as they evolved in the course of the twenty-year dictatorship, and their impact on translated texts in particular, see Jane Dunnett, 'Foreign literature in fascist Italy: circulation and censorship', *TTR (Traduction Terminologie Rédaction. Études sur le texte et ses transformations)*, 15/2 (2002), 97–123.

[12] 'gli aspiranti autori ai *Gialli* stanno diventando una vera afflizione. Non si potrebbe impiantare un piccolo comitato di prima lettura, costituito p.es. dal suo figliuolo e da due o tre amici o amiche sue, cui venissero sottoposti tutti i ms. italiani per *Gialli* di autore incognito? Essi poi mi passerebbero soltanto quelli migliori, risparmiando a me

un tempo prezioso che oggi perdo a leggere un'infinità di scemenze': handwritten letter from Montano to Mondadori, dated 4 August 1932, and sent from Albergo Parco, Monte San Primo (Como), FAM ('Montano', ARN B. 70).

[13] In this connection, see Varaldo's essay, 'Dramma e romanzo poliziesco', *Comoedia*, 14/5 (1932), 9–10.

[14] Rambelli, *Storia del 'giallo' italiano*, p. 42.

[15] 'il perfetto esempio del futuro poliziotto letterario nazionale: uno sbirro istituzionale, incline all'azione ma non alla violenza, coraggioso ma non temerario, comprensivo, riflessivo, ironico. Scapolo, privo anzi di qualsiasi legame familiare, vive solo per il lavoro, circondato dall'affetto e dall'ammirazione dei suoi più fedeli collaboratori; un uomo insomma che suscita un'immediata simpatia, disponibile al dialogo, sensibile verso le sofferenze umane': Pistelli, *Un secolo in giallo*, p. 168.

[16] 'spesso tornano a scivolare nel versante della narrativa sentimentale e d'avventura': ibid., pp. 167–8.

[17] Varaldo, 'Dramma e romanzo poliziesco'.

[18] Rambelli, *Storia del 'giallo' italiano*, p. 46.

[19] Ibid., p. 36 and p. 42, respectively.

[20] 'Mi ha fatto l'effetto d'essere uno dei tuoi "gialli" più brillanti e pieni d'*entrain*, e forse quello che corre più dirittamente al suo termine. La pittura dei caratteri al naturale è ottima, come in libro tuo del resto non potrebbe essere altrimenti. Mi dà per contro un po' da pensare il fatto che il colore giallo non è molto carico, e che la parte sentimentale predomina a spese di quella emozionante più che non sia avvenuto nei tuoi precedenti (nonostante il morto!) . . . Questa mia preoccupazione devi metterla in relazione col gusto del nostro pubblico, che si va orientando sempre più risolutamente verso le cose a tinte molto forti, emozionanti quanto più è possibile. Per questa ragione ad es. è stato necessario orientarsi di preferenza verso gli americani tipo Queen ecc. assai più sensazionali degl'inglesi': letter dated 25 June 1935, FAM ('Montano', ARN B. 70).

[21] Lanocita had worked for a number of publications including *L'Ambrosiano* and *La Stampa* before moving to the *Corriere della Sera* where he would remain for nearly forty years (1930–69). Initially, he reported on local news stories, before turning to film criticism and politics.

[22] 'I romanzi polizieschi d'oggi fanno ridere i pulcini . . . Il brivido, il vero brivido, lo sapeva dare Poe, creda a me': Arturo Lanocita, *Quaranta milioni* (Milan: Mondatori, 1932), p. 190.

[23] Rambelli, *Storia del 'giallo' italiano*, p. 48.

[24] *American Magazine*, September 1928. Translated as 'Venti regole per chi scrive romanzi polizieschi', appendix to Joseph Smith Fletcher, *Il motto rivelatore* (Milan: Mondadori, 1938). It is worth mentioning here a book that appeared in 1934 that was a full-blown parody of the contemporary vogue for detective novels: Luciano Folgore's *La trappola colorata* is subtitled *Romanzo extragiallo umoristico*. (This is the pseudonym of Omero Vecchi.) Luciano Folgore, *La trappola colorata* (Milan: Corbaccio, 1934).

[25] Rambelli, *Storia del 'giallo' italiano*, p. 50, n. 2.

[26] For a discussion of the earliest of Spagnol's short stories, one of the most successful, which is entitled 'Una sigaretta' (*L'Italiano*, 8/20, 1933), and set in Chicago, see Rambelli, *Storia del 'giallo' italiano*, pp. 78–9; Pistelli, *Un secolo in giallo*, p. 189. This and other stories, which critics have described as 'thrillers', were collected in the volume *Bassa marea* (Milan: Mondadori, 1941).

[27] 'L'ombrellino viola', published in the sixth volume of Mondadori's 'Supergiallo' series (Milan: Mondadori, 1938); *Sotto la cenere* (Milan: Mondadori, 1938).

28 Rambelli, *Storia del 'giallo' italiano*, p. 82.

29 'il vero tipo del francese, anzi del parigino . . ., un po' scettico e un po' brontolone, amante della buona tavola e del bicchierino d'alcool, centellinato con calma fra una boccata e l'altra di sigaretta': Enzo d'Errico, *Il fatto di Via delle Argonne* (Milan: Mondadori, 1937), p. 43.

30 'Brava gente, ma troppo calma [. . .] pazienza ci vuole; naturalmente, anche un po' di fiuto, e poi conoscere gli uomini . . . non gli uomini come li descrivono sui libri, che sono o tutti eroi o tutti farabutti, ma gli uomini come sono nella vita reale, ossia mezzo eroi e mezzo farabutti . . . ecco tutto il segreto. Il difficile è capire la proporzione della miscela, una volta capita la formula, si intuiscono le reazioni . . . Quando quella tale proporzione fra eroismo e farabutteria pencola a favore del secondo ingrediente, si ha un precipitato di criminalità. Questa è la vera chimica, non quella di Sherlock Holmes': Ezio D'Errico, *Qualcuno ha bussato alla porta* (Milan: Mondadori, 1936), pp. 22–3.

31 These biographical details are taken from Pistelli, *Un secolo in giallo*, pp. 198–9.

32 *Sei donne e un libro* (Milan: Minerva, 1936), p. 12.

33 'I soli veri indizi sono psicologici e non materiali': *L'albergo delle tre rose* (Milan: Mondadori, 1936), p. 162.

34 'aveva a che fare con un criminale di una specie particolarmente pericolosa: il passionale cerebrale mosso da un impulso incoercibile e aberrante. Lo squilibrato lucido. Tutti gli omicidi sono opera di squilibrati. Quando poi il delitto è passionale, l'equilibrio psichico è profondamente turbato, anche se le azioni del soggetto si svolgono rigidamente secondo logica': *De Vincenzi e il mistero di Cinecittà* (Milan: Sonzogno, 1974), p. 136. Tellingly, chapter eight of the novel is entitled 'Psicanalisi' (Psychoanalysis).

35 'ho voluto fare, e continuo a volerlo, un *romanzo poliziesco italiano*. Impresa ardua. Da noi manca tutto, nella vita reale, per poter congegnare un romanzo poliziesco del tipo americano o inglese. Mancano i *detectives*, mancano i *policemen*, mancano i gangsters, mancano persino, poveri a noi!, gli ereditieri fragili e i vecchi potenti di denaro e di intrighi disposti a farsi uccidere. Non mancano – sebbene in scala ridotta – purtroppo i delitti. Non mancano le tragedie'. Augusto De Angelis, preface to *Le sette picche doppiate. Romanzo poliziesco. Con una prefazione sul romanzo "giallo", 'Il romanzo "giallo". Confessioni e meditazioni'* (Milan: Sonzogno, 1940), p. 18.

36 The most accessible and complete version of his observations was reprinted, with the post-humous title 'Conferenza sul giallo (in tempi neri)', in *La Lettura* (March 1980), 27–44.

37 The entire series was republished in one volume in the 1990s: *Cinque casi per l'investigatore Jelling* (Como: Frassinelli, 1995). For ease of consultation, all quotes refer to this edition. Since 2008, Sellerio has been republishing the Jelling stories in individual volumes, the last of which came out in 2011.

38 'Dio mio, ma perché lui, Jelling, si era ficcato in questo impiccio? Promise solennemente a se stesso che se il caso Vaton fosse finito felicemente, non avrebbe messo il naso fuori del suo archivio, neppure per un milione': Scerbanenco, *Cinque casi per l'investigatore Jelling*, p. 61.

39 'Lei sa sempre tutto, ma arriva terribilmente in ritardo!': ibid., p. 329.

40 'Quella mattina Jelling fu un campione di attività. Era come preso dal silenzioso furore del mastino, parlava, pensava, agiva, senza perdere un tempo, con rapidità, ma anche con metodo': ibid., p. 292.

41 Ibid. See, for example, p. 415.

42 'tutta psicologia e logica': ibid., p. 308. Regarding the nature of Jelling's logic, see also p. 338; on his faith in logic, see p. 367.

43 See, for example, ibid., p. 386, p. 423.
44 Unfortunately, the majority of these books have long been out of print, some since the interwar period, and can be consulted only in libraries. Recent years have seen an increasing interest in the history of the detective novel in Italy and the desire to rediscover lost 'classics' of the genre such as De Angelis and Scerbanenco. Many books by both authors have been republished by Sellerio and are still available. To my knowledge, none of the detective novels produced during the interwar years has been translated into English.

Bibliography

Primary sources

Collins, Wilkie, *La pietra della luna* [no translator indicated] (Milan: Treves, 1870).
Comez, Armando, *L'uomo dei gigli* (Milan: Mondadori, 1933).
De Angelis, Augusto, *Sei donne e un libro* (Milan: Minerva, 1936).
——, *Il candeliere a sette fiamme (Le imprese poliziesche di De Vincenzi)* (Milan: Minerva, 1936; Milan: Feltrinelli, 1989).
——, *La barchetta di cristallo* (Milan: Minerva, 1936; Palermo: Sellerio, 2004).
——, *L'albergo delle tre rose* (Milan: Mondadori, 1936; Palermo: Sellerio, 2002).
——, *Il canotto insanguinato (Le imprese poliziesche di De Vincenzi)* (Milan: Minerva, 1936).
——, *Il do tragico (Le imprese poliziesche di De Vincenzi)* (Milan: Minerva, 1937).
——, *Il mistero di Cinecittà* (Milan: Mondadori, 1941), reprinted as *De Vincenzi e il mistero di Cinecittà* (Milan; Sonzogno, 1974).
——, *Le undici meno uno* (Milan: Sonzogno, 1940).
——, *Le sette picche doppiate* (Milan: Sonzogno, 1940).
——, *Il mistero delle orchidee* (Milan: Mondadori, 1942; Palermo: Sellerio, 2001).
——, *L'impronta del gatto* (Milan: Sonzogno, 1943; Palermo: Sellerio, 2007).
——, 'Conferenza sul giallo (in tempi neri)', *La Lettura* (March 1980), 27–44.
D'Errico, Ezio, *Qualcuno ha bussato alla porta* (Milan: Mondadori, 1936).
——, *Il fatto di Via delle Argonne* (Milan: Mondadori, 1937).
——, *La famiglia Morel* (Milan: Mondadori, 1938).
——, *Il quaranta, tre, sei, sei non risponde* (Milan: Mondadori, 1939).
——, *L'uomo dagli occhi melanconici* (Milan: Mondadori, 1939).
——, *Il naso di cartone* (Milan: Mondadori, 1940).
——, *La notte del 14 luglio* (Milan: Mondadori, 1941).
De Stefani, Alessandro, *La crociera del 'Colorado'* (Milan: Mondadori, 1932).
Doyle, Arthur Conan, *Le avventure di Sherlock Holmes: romanzo illustrato* [no translator indicated] (Milan: Verri, 1895).
——, *Le ultime avventure di Sherlock Holmes* (Milan: Corriere della Sera, 1904).
——, *La maledizione dei Baskervilles: avventure di Sherlock Holmes* (Milan: Corriere della Sera, 1907).
——, *Il ritorno di Sherlock Holmes: nuove avventure del poliziotto dilettante* (Milan: Corriere della Sera, 1907).
Dunnett, Jane, '*Supergiallo*. How Mondadori turned crime into a brand', *The Italianist*, 30/1 (2010), 63–80.

——, 'Crime and the critics: on the appraisal of detective novels in 1930s Italy', *Modern Language Review*, 106 (2011), 746–65.

Folgore, Luciano, *La trappola colorata. Romanzo extragiallo umoristico* (Milan: Corbaccio, 1934).

Fletcher, Joseph Smith, *Il motto rivelatore* [no translator indicated] (Milan: Mondadori, 1938).

Gaboriau, Émile, *Il signor Lecoq*, *Il Pungolo* (30 June–29 September 1869).

Gadda, Carlo Emilio, *Quer pasticciaccio brutto de Via Merulana* (Milan: Garzanti, 1957).

Green, Anna Katherine, *Il mistero delle due cugine* (Milan-Verona: Mondadori, 1929).

Lanocita, Arturo, *Quaranta milioni* (Milan: Mondadori, 1932).

——, *Quella maledettissima sera* (Milan: Corbaccio, 1939).

——, *Otto ore di angoscia*, Il Romanzo per Tutti, 6 (Milan, 1945).

Mariotti, Vasco, *L'uomo dai piedi di fauno* (Milan: Mondadori, 1934).

Poe, Edgar Allan, *Storie incredibili*, trans. Guido Cinelli (Milan: G. Daelli e C., 1863).

Scerbanenco, Giorgio, *Sei giorni di preavviso* (Milan: Mondadori, 1940).

——, *La bambola cieca* (Milan: Mondadori, 1941).

——, *Nessuno è colpevole* (Milan: Mondadori, 1941).

——, *L'antro dei filosofi* (Milan: Mondadori, 1942).

——, *Il cane che parla* (Milan: Mondadori, 1942).

——, *Cinque casi per l'investigatore Jelling* (Como: Frassinelli, 1995).

Spagnol, Tito Antonio, 'La sigaretta', *L'Italiano*, 8/20 (1933); reprinted in *Bassa marea* (1941).

——, *L'unghia del leone* (Milan: Mondadori, 1934).

——, '*La collana di smeraldi*', *Il Cerchio Verde*, 7 (1935).

——, *La bambola insanguinata* (Milan: Mondatori, 1935).

——, *Uno, due, tre* (Milan: Mondatori, 1936).

——, *La notte impossibile* (Milan: Mondatori, 1937).

——, *Sotto la cenere* (Milan: Mondadori, 1938).

——, 'L'ombrellino viola', in *Supergiallo 6* (Milan: Mondadori, 1938).

——, 'Avventura americana', *Omnibus* (17 April 1937), 9.

——, 'Chiamata notturna', *Omnibus* (12 June 1937), 7.

——, *Bassa marea* (Milan: Mondadori, 1941; Vittorio Veneto: De Bastiani, 2003).

Stevenson, Robert Louis, *Il club dei suicidî* (Milan-Verona: Mondadori, 1929).

Vailati, Franco, *Il mistero dell'idrovolante* (Milan: Mondadori, 1935).

Van Dine, S. S., *La strana morte del Signor Benson* (Milan-Verona: Mondadori, 1929).

Varaldo, Alessandro, *Il sette bello* (Milan: Mondadori, 1931).

——, *Le scarpette rosse* (Milan: Mondadori, 1931).

——, *Tre catene d'argento* (Milan: Ceschina, 1931).

——, 'Dramma e romanzo poliziesco', *Comoedia*, 14/5 (1932), 9–10.

——, *La gatta persiana* (Milan: Mondadori, 1933).

——, 'Il tappeto verde', *Il Dramma*, 171 (1933).

——, *La scomparsa di Rigel* (Milan: Mondadori, 1933).

——, *Circolo chiuso* (Milan: Mondadori, 1935).

——, *Casco d'oro* (Milan: Mondadori, 1936).

——, *Il segreto della statua* (Milan: Mondadori, 1936).

——, *Il tesoro dei Borboni* (Milan: Mondadori, 1938).

——, *La trentunesima perla* (Milan: Ceschina, 1938).

——, *Le avventure di Gino Arrighi. Novelle poliziesche* (supplement to *La Scena Illustrata*, January 1939).

——, *Il signor ladro (Avventure di Gino Arrighi)* (Rome: Romana, 1944).

Wallace, Edgar, *L'uomo dai due corpi*, trans. T. Marchesi (Milan-Verona: Mondadori, 1929).

Secondary sources

Crovi, Luca, *Tutti i colori del giallo: Il giallo italiano da De Marchi a Scerbanenco a Camilleri* (Venice: Marsilio, 2002).

Dunnett, Jane, 'Foreign literature in fascist Italy: circulation and censorship', *TTR (Traduction Terminologie Rédaction. Études sur le texte et ses transformations)*, 15/2 (2002), 97–123.

——, 'Anti-fascism and literary criticism in post-war Italy: revisiting the *mito americano*', in Guido Bonsaver and Robert Gordon (eds), *Culture, Censorship and the State in Twentieth-century Italy* (Oxford: Legenda, 2005), pp. 109–19.

Pistelli, Maurizio, *Un secolo in giallo: Storia del poliziesco italiano (1860–1960)* (Rome: Donzelli, 2006).

Rambelli, Loris, *Storia del 'giallo' italiano* (Milan: Garzanti, 1979).

Savinio, Alberto, '*Romanzo poliziesco*', in *Souvenirs* (Palermo: Sellerio, 1976), pp. 193–9. First published in *L'Ambrosiano* (23 August 1932), 3.

3

Founding Fathers: Giorgio Scerbanenco

- over 100 novels...
- 4 crime fiction classics

JENNIFER BURNS

The notion of a 'founding father' carries connotations of centrality and tradition, as well as of innovation, and in these senses the label does not fit Scerbanenco well. Born outside Italy (in Kiev), of a Russian father and Italian mother, educated only to compulsory level, trained in jobs from turning brass clock components to ambulance assistant, and with a history as a professional writer which resides in women's magazines and *romanzi rosa*, he is absolutely not a canonical literary figure in Italy. Crime fiction in Italy has a history that dates back to the late nineteenth century, and Scerbanenco's first experiments with this genre date from the early 1940s, when the *giallo* was already an established – albeit, under Fascism, restricted – category within the Italian publishing industry.[1] The novels on which I shall focus here, and which earned Scerbanenco his reputation as a *giallista*, date from the late 1960s, when a number of illustrious names in Italian literature, such as Carlo Emilio Gadda and Leonardo Sciascia, had already marked significant notches in the development of Italian crime fiction. In what ways, then, and to what degree can Scerbanenco be judged to have had a distinctive and inaugural impact on the development of the *giallo*?

The factor that underlies most of the answers to my question is precisely the life experience sketched above. It is Scerbanenco's intimate and immediate understanding of 'ordinary' Italian society in his *gialli* set in Italy which makes them compelling, individual, and which allows the reader to witness the emergence of a branch of crime fiction which is rooted in contemporary Italian society and its moral and social functions and malfunctions. In order to demonstrate how this is achieved, this chapter will explore key themes and issues in the four novels that gained the author his reputation as a *giallista*, or crime writer, with particular attention paid to the first novel. The four novels are set in Milan and feature the detective Duca Lamberti, and were published in rapid succession in the late 1960s: *Venere privata* (1966), *Traditori di tutti* (1966), *I ragazzi del massacro* (1968) and *I milanesi ammazzano al sabato* (1969).[2] The second of these novels earned him the *Gran Prix de la littérature policière* in 1968,[3] and is his only work translated into English.[4] In necessarily narrowing my focus I am excluding important texts by an extremely prolific writer, in particular his early initiative in crime writing, the 'Arthur Jelling' novels of the early 1940s, and his vast and compelling production of short stories, often crime-related.[5] These manifestly merit close critical attention, but in the ambit of this chapter and of this volume, it is the Duca Lamberti series which reveals the breadth and the significance of Scerbanenco's contribution to the development of crime fiction in Italy.

The novels

For the sake of clarity, it is useful first to outline the plot of each of these four novels. *Venere privata* opens with a prologue featuring a dead female body, but when Duca Lamberti is introduced in the first chapter, the investigation he is being asked to undertake is a psychological/medical one: he is asked to cure a young man of his alcoholism. Only later is the connection between the illness and the crime established. Through the process of treating Davide Auseri, the wealthy and direction-less son of a successful Milanese industrialist, Lamberti discovers that his psychological crisis was precipitated by an encounter with a woman: a Milanese shop assistant and occasional 'private' prostitute, whose murder, disguised as suicide, provides the body in the novel's prologue. The investigation at this point turns into a criminal rather than psychological one, and leads to the discovery of an international network of sexual exploitation of women, specializing in recruitment of 'ordinary' young women to pose for nude photographs. The inquiry brings Lamberti into contact with Livia Ussaro, a former student of sociology with expertise in the area of prostitution, who becomes Lamberti's partner (the ambiguity of their relationship will be discussed below) for the remainder of the series of novels. In this novel, Lamberti is in part responsible for the brutal slashing of her face in a punishment ritual enacted when it is suspected that she is acting undercover on behalf of the police.

Traditori di tutti features a sequence of connected murders disguised as accidents, in which three couples are drowned when their cars roll into the waterways of Milan: the River Lambro and the Alzaia Naviglio Pavese, a canal (twice). What lies behind the first and third of these double murders is discovered to be the settling of scores and elimination of potential weak links in a complex network of organized crime, with interests in prostitution and particularly the trafficking of arms to terrorists in the Alto Adige region. At the centre of the network (perpetrator of the first drowning and victim of the second) is a corrupt lawyer who, together with his female partner, expertly played both sides in the struggle between Resistance and Fascist/Nazi forces which characterized the 1943–5 period. The investigation leads to the discovery that one of those they exploited was an American army officer, acting as an intelligence gatherer, whom the couple befriended, pretended to protect and support over a long period, and then tortured to death. His daughter is the perpetrator of the second of the drownings, she in turn having befriended the couple in order to kill them, in revenge for her father's unjust death.

I ragazzi del massacro recounts the investigation into the gang rape and murder of a young female teacher in an evening school for 'problem' students. Eleven male students were present at the time of the crime, but each one of the eleven insists, under questioning, that he had nothing to do with the crime and cannot

28

identify who was the perpetrator. Lamberti's investigation affords the opportunity to investigate the lives and environments of some of the boys/young men, whose activities inhabit the boundaries between legal and illegal behaviour. He takes one of the boys into his personal care for ten days, having identified him as most likely to capitulate to benevolent psychological pressure, and this is effective in leading him to the truth, though the boy is severely injured in the process. Ultimately, as Lamberti intuits early in the investigation, the elaborate murder operation which took place in the classroom turns out to have an external instigator – a woman – who was in fact present at, directed and participated in the murder. Her motive was revenge, since the young teacher's professional zeal and human compassion in taking care of her students had led her inadvertently to incriminate her and her partner, both of whom were sentenced to a period in prison which led indirectly to the partner's death.

In *I milanesi ammazzano al sabato*, Lamberti investigates the disappearance of a young woman who is mentally handicapped, physically much larger than average and also exceptionally attractive. Her widowed father approaches Lamberti to investigate this disappearance thoroughly since other officers over the course of the months his daughter has been missing have brushed him off. Shortly after Lamberti agrees to pursue this, the body of the young woman is found burnt in a pile of agricultural waste by the side of the main road leading from Milan to Lodi. The investigation explores the rich world of prostitution in Milan, and uncovers a network of procurement and sexual exploitation of women run by two men and a woman whom the bereaved father knows well: one works in the bar he visits daily and the others frequent the same bar. A chain of events at the close of the novel leads to the murder – in part in self-defence – of the three perpetrators of the crime at the hands of the father, whose anger and pain on behalf of his abused daughter lend him the strength and resolution to drown and beat to death the three criminals, though he is himself severely injured in the process.

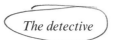

The detective

Duca Lamberti is not – initially at least – a professional detective, nor even a private investigator. His background is closely associated with the police force: his father was a life-long police officer whose legacy to his son is a deep familiarity with the principles and procedures of police work and some close contacts and friends within the Milanese *Questura* (police headquarters). This legacy also bears a strong component of cynicism regarding the profession. Lamberti's father was injured during an investigation into mafia-based criminal activity, and was subsequently relegated to a desk job in the Milan headquarters. Bitterness at being bureaucratically prevented from attacking crime directly taints both father's and son's attitudes to the police service, and prompts the father to ensure that his son builds a career in a different area: the medical profession.

Neither is Lamberti a practising doctor, however. When he is introduced to the reader at the beginning of *Venere privata*, he has just been released from a three-year prison sentence for euthanasia: he had helped a suffering elderly woman to die. This act also resulted in his exclusion from medical practice. The detective in these novels is therefore a private individual (initially) who has significant expertise, gained both vicariously and directly, in police work and medical practice.[6] This combination is a crucial one that informs Lamberti's detective work in a number of ways. First, the novels posit and promote a high regard for expertise of any kind and Lamberti's knowledge of the workings of the human body is repeatedly displayed and proven to be instrumental in solving crime.[7] His understanding of human anatomy allows him to administer physical violence as an investigative technique sometimes with minimum visible impact and always with maximum effect. His experience in diagnosing disease enables him to identify the physical weak points of witnesses or interviewees and so to piece together a profile of their lifestyle.

Physical and psychological flaws and weaknesses are often conflated, exposing further significant factors of Lamberti's professional expertise. There is a strong sense that he is especially knowledgeable in psychology and psychiatric treatment, and this proves a valuable tool in unhinging the vulnerable connections in a criminal's or witness's psychological constitution. By means of a perhaps premature sort of criminal profiling, Lamberti succeeds in solving crimes because his multi-level expertise allows him to identify both perpetrators and victims, and the motivations and circumstances that bring them together. In short, experience in criminal detection facilitates understanding of when human individuals (and society) break down morally, and experience in medicine facilitates understanding of when human individuals break down physically and psychologically. With this background, Duca Lamberti is optimally equipped to investigate crime.

This dual expertise in medicine and in policing also informs the characterization of the detective protagonist. His experience of the police service is, as noted above, coloured with a degree of cynicism and resentment which manifests itself in impatience, arrogance, anger and sometimes controlled cruelty. Violence is a key element of his investigative practice, and he demonstrates little respect for the rules associated with police procedure and the law. The role of the doctor is, however, conventionally viewed as compassionate and nurturing, and Lamberti is indeed shown to feel and to demonstrate a deep empathy for other individuals, including, on occasion, those involved in criminal activity. Again, his conviction for euthanasia is an important marker: he has broken the law, committed a crime, and has experienced life in prison as a result, but this was a crime of compassion, motivated by the will to release another human being from suffering.

In personal relationships, Lamberti is shown also to shift between poles of ruthless indifference and profound compassion. Perhaps the best example of this is his relationship with his sister, Lorenza, who is an unemployed single mother. Lamberti provides both financially and emotionally for his sister and small niece, and takes great care to ensure their physical and emotional health. However, when the 2-year-old child, Sara, falls ill in the third novel of the series, *I ragazzi del massacro*, Lamberti ignores Lorenza's repeated requests for him to go home and attend to the child, because he is at a crucial point in his investigation. He does not neglect the child completely: he contacts a former colleague who is a paediatrician and asks him to attend to her, but when the illness results in the death of the child, the reader is clearly asked to question whether Lamberti assessed the balance between professional dedication and private compassion correctly on this occasion. His calculation in this episode is shown to be supremely rational, and is implicitly endorsed in the text, but it is interesting that anxiety about his sister's well-being is allowed gently to undermine this rationalist conclusion.

The individual upon whom Lamberti relies to take his place during this episode, supporting his sister practically and emotionally, is Livia Ussaro, the partner whom he meets during the course of the investigation in *Venere privata* and who remains at his side throughout the four novels. She is indeed 'at his side': whilst clearly the centre of his emotional experience and well-being, she is an ancillary in his professional and personal life. She assists in his investigations as driver, co-interviewer, co-custodian and assists as well in his domestic life, buying and preparing food, attending to and accompanying his sister, etc. Though she enters the investigation in the first novel by virtue largely of her academic expertise – she is a sociologist who has done extensive research into female sexuality and the sex trade – and her presence in all the texts is punctuated by references to her rational and academic bent, she is by no means an equal partner in the relationship, but appears to act rather in a supporting role. This refers, however, to what she does in the novels: in terms of what she is, and what she signifies to Lamberti, she is, as stated above, at the centre. Though their relationship, and particularly its physical aspect, remains ambiguous throughout the novels, she is figured clearly as the protagonist's primary point of reference, giving him moral and emotional well-being and a sense of purpose in an environment which otherwise engenders pessimism and moral emptiness.

There is a great deal more to be said about the portrayal of Livia in these novels, but this is best discussed below, in the ambit of a wider discussion of gender and sexuality in Scerbanenco's work. In terms of the figuration of the detective in these novels, it is sufficient here to stress that, whilst again, Duca Lamberti fits a certain mould in being single, not in a formally committed relationship, and apparently having little time for emotional or sexual activity, his relationships with his sister and with Livia in particular expose the fault-lines in his rational and cynical persona and allow the reader to experience an individual who is emotionally dependent and, on occasion, emotionally generous. This figure of the cold cynic with a warm heart is, of course, a stereotype of the detective, and perhaps owes some debt to Scerbanenco's extensive experience of writing romantic fiction.

The environment

Milan is the environment that Scerbanenco's crime fictions inhabit, functioning not merely as a backdrop but genuinely as the habitat which engenders, nurtures and occasionally overmasters the criminals and their crimes. The *noir* is generally identified as a metropolitan genre, and Milan in the Duca Lamberti novels figures precisely as a twentieth-century metropolis, bristling with industry and commercial enterprise, clogged with vehicular traffic, choked with pollution, alternately infested with or bereft of people. It is also, however, an Italian city, and precisely Milan, and it is partly in this distinctive national, regional and local texture that the author's inauguration of a specifically Italian brand of popular crime fiction lies.[8]

It is a popular Milan that Scerbanenco re-creates in these novels, not a tourist's Milan or a historical Milan. The Duomo, the Castello Sforzesco and other prominent monuments feature only as topographical locations for orientating the action, and have no intrinsic meaning. The names of streets, squares and the gates of the city are repeated, car journeys delineate traceable routes through the city, and addresses place markers in an imaginary map which enables the reader to see and to experience the topography of a city s/he may never have encountered. Luca Doninelli, in his preface to the 1998 edition of *Venere privata*, argues that the novel has no framework whatsoever – moral, social, geographical – and that the naming process described above evokes nothing: 'He talks of Piazza Cavour, and we do not see it. He talks of via Manzoni, and we do not see it.'[9] Whilst I agree that the novel certainly disrupts certain frames of reference, I would dispute Doninelli's extension of this principle to include the depiction of urban space. Whether the reader has or has not ever seen *piazza Cavour* or *via Manzoni*, Scerbanenco's novels will lead him/her progressively to assemble if not an image of those places then at least a sense of them. This sense will suggest to the reader that *via Manzoni*, for example, is at the heart of the city, in an area occupied largely by shops and businesses of some distinction, by the clients of this sort of enterprise and by those in turn who feed off these wealthy consumers. In other words, Scerbanenco's system of punctilious topographical referencing serves not to locate his fictions in historical terms but to locate them according to the moment. It is a synchronic, rather than a diachronic, notion of the city that he enables his reader to assemble.

The urban peripheries are a location par excellence for crime narratives. Scerbanenco duly deploys in his Duca Lamberti novels the outer edges of Milan, where city seeps into featureless, tainted countryside. In *Venere privata*, for example, the rough ground in Metanopoli where the body of the young woman, Alberta Radelli, is found is a starkly modern wasteland between industrial installations and motorways. An alternative sense of the region is offered, however, by the villa north of Milan, towards Lake Como, owned by the Auseri family. The emphasis here is on the crisp clarity of the air and the fresh odour of the earth. It is an environment that crystallizes the elite lifestyle of the new aristocracy of the times, the capitalist-industrialist bourgeoisie who can afford this kind of escape from the city, provided that the city on which they and their privileged escape depend is close enough to be immediately accessible. The economic and geographical poles of the novel come together in the chase in which the criminals are apprehended towards the end of this novel (see the passage at the end of this chapter). The criminal activity takes place in a large, dazzlingly new condominium, with attached parking area, which is situated in open countryside and approached by a combination of wide new roads and potholed tracks. Giuliana Pieri refers to this, and other buildings like it in Scerbanenco's novels, as 'the cathedrals in the desert of the new secular society'.[10] The incongruity of this shard of modernity embedded in the rural environment is underscored when the car chase originating at the condominium irrupts into a farmyard, scattering livestock and stunning the human onlookers into silent immobility. The composite picture elaborated in this novel, then, is of a city which is changing with such rapidity that its own wider environment is incapable of keeping pace with its demands on space, resources and on the human imaginary.

The times

In discussing the physical environment of the novels above, I have stressed that Scerbanenco depicts a Milan (and environs) of the moment, almost entirely detached from any historical or cultural lineage. This principle informs also Scerbanenco's representation of Italian society: history appears to be absent, and the primary, maybe unique, frame of reference for the actions of individuals and groups is the present. The society we see is an aggressively entrepreneurial one, in which everyone aspires to move ahead and upwards, and this movement is identified in terms of financial wealth as expressed in material goods and professional and private pursuits.[11] It is the society of the economic 'miracle'.[12] Scerbanenco allows us, of course, to view the capitalist onslaught through the particular lens of criminality, so we see the entrepreneurial spirit manifested in the systematic and pitiless neutralization of all obstacles to individual success and wealth creation. It is the dogged, dirty underside of capitalism that Scerbanenco exposes, where the value of the human becomes not a moral or ethical one but a commercial one, and human desire and human fallibility are a source of profit.

Traditori di tutti is different from the other novels in the nature of the crimes it narrates, and also in that it is the only one of these four novels in which, contrary to my thesis here, history has a place. As outlined in the synopsis of the novels above, the root of the sequence of crimes that the novel explores is a crime which took place in the 1940s, during the period of Nazi and Fascist occupation of northern Italy. The factor that is most interesting about Scerbanenco's recourse to the (relatively recent) past here is one that supports my thesis, in fact: he makes reference to a significant moment in modern Italian history in order to reveal the absence of values even in this period characterized by posterity as being profoundly engaged with moral and ideological principles. It is a grim continuity, rather than a breach, which Scerbanenco identifies between the closing years of the Second World War and the Italy of the economic boom. Hence the title of the novel: underlying the stories of Italians in the 1940s through till the 1960s is a principle of betrayal, of offering and withdrawing allegiance to others on the basis of sheer opportunism, according to the reward they can momentarily offer to the individual.

This judgement of contemporary Italian society is underpinned by the fact that the individual who determines to resolve the crime which encapsulates this endemic criminality is the daughter of the murdered serviceman, a foreigner from the 'new' world, rather than an Italian or European imbued with the dreary hues of a complex history.[13] The figure of Susanna Paganica is also distinctive, however, in the fact that what she seeks to achieve by means of her crime is justice, and justice is a notion which is all but absent from Scerbanenco's Duca Lamberti novels. It is useful at this point to refer to Leonardo Sciascia, who also published a number of crime novels in the 1960s, and for whom the quest for justice is perhaps the principal motivation of his crime writing.[14] In Sciascia's work, despite the often obstructive nature of the law and the widespread corruption in society, justice is a concept that retains an immense moral value. In Scerbanenco's novels, however, it is a meaningless term. Susanna Paganica's sense of justice is so pronounced – and so misguided, in Lamberti's view – that she insists on returning to Italy to be tried and punished for the murders she committed. There is something perhaps Sciascia-esque in the absurdity of her being punished for an action that in many ways delivered rather than denied justice, but in Scerbanenco's work, this absurdity does not acquire meaning through irony, but remains simply meaningless. In this climate, Duca Lamberti becomes a member of the police force (by default), but appears to have no conviction whatsoever that to identify the perpetrators of crime and see them punished by the law is an achievement. His motivation in investigating crime is simply to stop suffering immediately and perhaps only temporarily. His is not a mission to clear contemporary society of criminality but an effort to manage criminality in contemporary society; he is not a crusader but a fire-fighter.

In Scerbanenco's Milan, then, history is absent and justice is absent. Religion is apparently absent too. As discussed in my section on the detective, and under-scored in the discussion of justice above, it is a profoundly cynical world that Scerbanenco portrays, for the most part, and faith seems to be a luxury which ordinary individuals have no time or energy to entertain. Compassion constitutes the only positive in this moral wasteland, and it appears in a number of places. With Lamberti himself, it is manifested in relation to certain criminals, to his family, to colleagues, to Livia and, in the iconic act of euthanasia which encapsulates his identity, to a suffering patient. In other characters and episodes, the same sort of profound and life-affirming fellow feeling manifests itself within the family (Donatella and her father in *I milanesi ammazzano al sabato*), between lovers, even temporary (Davide Auseri and Alberta Radelli in *Venere privata*), between friends or acquaintances (a black prostitute and Donatella in *I milanesi ammazzano al sabato*), between professionals and those whose well-being they are responsible for (the schoolteacher, Matilde Crescenzaghi, and a social worker, Alberta Romani, in *I ragazzi del massacro*), and between individuals whose paths cross accidentally (Donatella and the 'good' cousin in *I milanesi ammazzano al sabato*).[15]

There are two important qualifications to be made here, however. The first is that such compassion is neither universal nor guaranteed: family members, friends, colleagues, carers, lovers and spouses are also frequently seen in these novels to betray and hurt each other, both physically and psychologically. The second regards the term itself: compassion, rather than love, is the appropriate term because it indicates a feeling of affection and support towards another who merits it in part because s/he is struggling against an affliction which s/he has no capacity to vanquish. This crippled version of love appears to be the only one that can exist and have any meaning in the world Scerbanenco depicts.

It is part of the pitilessness of urban, northern Italian society in the 1960s, as depicted by Scerbanenco, that no one in these novels succeeds simply by being good. In *I milanesi ammazzano al sabato*, Donatella's father, Amanzio Berzaghi, is a striking example of a decent man who is reduced by the aggressive criminality that targets him, via his daughter, to the level of a criminal himself. Similarly, innocence is a de-valued concept, even though many of the victims in these novels are children or young people, and it is instead a disabling quality of inexperience which is operative. For example, the young women in *Venere privata* – the main victim, Alberta Radelli, for example – are not in any conventional sense innocent: indeed they are casual prostitutes. But this very activity, and their being drawn into the network of sexual exploitation which brings about their deaths, is evidence of a deadly disingenuousness whereby they lack the capacity effectively to recognize and manage the power and commercial value of their own sexuality, and therefore become the direct victims of others who do understand their 'value' in this sense. Davide Auseri's conversations with Alberta Radelli in the few hours they spend together before her murder reveal to the reader her child-like simplicity in perceiving the world: she wishes to help her sister with household bills and her wages as a shop assistant do not always cover these costs so, as and when she needs to, she engineers encounters with men who will pay for sex with her. That these are older, middle-class *signori* (gentlemen) whom she accosts in the affluent streets of the city centre represents for her some sort of guarantee that they and her commerce with them are harmless.

By means of plots in which women such as this are consistently betrayed, injured and killed, Scerbanenco suggests strongly that there are fatal inconsistencies in the ways in which economics, society and culture are changing in contemporary Italy. Economic change has mobilized changes in social attitudes such that young, bright women like Alberta Radelli expect economic and personal independence, and crave wealth and opportunity, but the very newness of these possibilities presupposes an inexperience which is not individual but endemic in society. Social mores and cultural expectations have not had time to adapt to new economic opportunities, and so a young woman who might see herself as taking her life into her own hands is in fact placing herself in the hands of others, perilously. The Church, family and tradition have been removed as a combined framework of social and moral reference – as the novels convey starkly – and have been replaced by a culture of economic gain, which appears to have no ethical dimension. Italy, Scerbanenco suggests, has been invaded by a modernity that nobody is quite prepared for, producing a younger generation devoid of any moral frame of reference, and thus oddly innocent even whilst touched everywhere by sin.[16]

In stressing the critique Scerbanenco progressively mounts in his Duca Lamberti novels of contemporary Italian society, there is a risk of overstating the negative impact of his representations. There are in these novels plentiful indicators of more positive aspects of modernity and of the economic boom. The young, endangered women described above are themselves an aspect: Scerbanenco offers an attractive parade of vignettes of 1960s fashion, the detail of hairstyles, make-up, accessories and clothes facilitated perhaps by his background in women's magazines. Powerful cars, richly stocked shops, technological instruments and gadgets, national and international travel, and an array of leisure opportunities similarly convey a sense of buoyant optimism and of the possibility of freely accessible pleasure, particularly meaningful perhaps to a reader in the 1960s who would himself/herself probably have experienced the austerity of the war-time years and their immediate aftermath. Scerbanenco's description in *Venere privata* of Davide Auseri's journey, accompanied by Alberta Radelli, to Florence and back on the A1 motorway serves as an extended tribute to the motor car and the new transport culture associated with it. What may strike the reader today as the most banal of experiences – a long journey on a motorway with a stop at a motorway services – stands in the novel as a parenthesis of intimate, pleasurable freedom from the concerns of everyday life, during which both blighted characters enjoy some genuine contact with another human being. Furthermore, this sense of well-being is not entirely a function of character and plot development: Scerbanenco's description of the service station is simply a celebration of the facility, a 'cheerful little shack', in its own right.[17] Similarly, the author's apparently coincidental references to pop music or to television programmes which serve as background noise to the events of the narrative have the composite function of evoking immediately the jaunty popular culture of the period.[18]

Women, gender and sexuality

Nowhere is the complexity and ineluctability of Scerbanenco's four 'Italian' *gialli* more powerfully expressed than in his treatment of women, gender roles and sexuality. Undoubtedly, the problematic and occasionally contradictory ways in which he represents these issues are part of his very immediate representation of the period, as discussed above. These novels are set and written in a period in which conventional gender roles have been challenged by both war-time conditions and experiences and subsequent economic changes, and in which attitudes to sexual activity and to sexuality have similarly been shaken up. It is the period when a broad discussion – even movement – concerning women's rights is beginning to take shape, but it still pre-dates the era of the more explicit and organized feminist discourse in Italy.[19] Similarly, the sexual revolution that hit Anglo-American culture in the 1960s is still poised to have its impact on Italy. The novels take place in something of a limbo between the rigid and entrenched codes of the past and the freedoms and tolerance of the future: hence, perhaps, the troublesome ambiguity (and sometimes deep prejudice) with which Scerbanenco represents matters of gender and sexuality.

Women are invariably victims in Scerbanenco's *gialli*, though sometimes indirectly. They are most often simply the victim as constructed by the generic norms of crime fiction. In *Venere privata*, *I ragazzi del massacro* and *I milanesi ammazzano al sabato*, the victims of the crimes that are investigated are all women. *Traditori di tutti* is again different, in that victims and perpetrators are plural and of mixed gender. It is by no means the case that women are invariably the victims of male predators in Scerbanenco's novels: women are very often complicit or even instrumental in the crimes. However, the modalities of male-perpetrated and female-perpetrated crime are different. In some cases of male-perpetrated crime, such as that of the gang of young men in *I ragazzi del massacro* and of the father in *I milanesi ammazzano al sabato*, there appears to be an imperative to offer some rationale behind the crime: these are fundamentally redeemable (the *ragazzi*) or good (the father) men who are precipitated into committing crime by external agency or, one might argue, by endemic criminality itself. As Paoli comments, a violent society begs a violent response.[] In most cases, however, male criminality is presented as a given: no further explanation is required than men will commit crime in order to remove obstacles to their own ambition.

Female-perpetrated crime, however, is always presented with fairly extensive justification in Scerbanenco's *gialli*. Marisella Domenici in *I ragazzi del massacro* is the mother of the crime, the hideous progenitor who conceives the crime, harbours and nourishes it over time, and then delivers it spectacularly and successfully, eliminating rather than creating a life. Her crime is particularly hideous because it not only destroys its single victim but also has a secondary impact in that it results in the death of one of the *ragazzi*, the near-fatal wounding of another and, more insidiously, the definitive initiation into serious criminality of the remainder of the group: it is a crime that spawns crime.[21] Marisella's is a femininity made monstrous by its perversion to negative, destructive ends, but whilst this lends her a certain mythical status, the nature of her monstrousness is mundane: she is a drug user, alcoholic, etc. Furthermore, she is presented as a victim herself. The motive for the crime, as outlined at the start of this chapter, is the death of her partner owed, in her monstrously skewed logic, to the actions of her victim, Matilde Crescenzaghi. That this loss was caused, as she sees it, by the actions of a young, virtuous, gentle woman, means that base jealousy fuels her resolve. Scerbanenco explicitly presents the crime as a hysterical one, and also a histrionic one (given its highly theatrical execution), and Duca Lamberti's expertise in psychology permits him to discuss at some length in the text the origin of both of these terms in female biology, that is, the etymological root of both words in the Greek term for the uterus.[22] In other words, Marisella is a perpetrator but is also the victim of her own biological identity.

Where women are not the victims of crime, then, they are represented as the victims either of their biology or of their society, or indeed of both in combination.[23] When they acquire power, it is by dint of their relationship with a man. This

extremely ficked up

points towards another cliché of gender representation which Scerbanenco freely deploys: that the only instrument of power which women possess and can wield with some effect is their sexuality, which is seen also to prove, of course, their undoing. Where along this spectrum of female subjugation does Livia rest? Just as Duca Lamberti is in many ways the nexus of the representation of masculinity in these novels, so Livia Ussaro is the nexus of the deeply ambiguous representation of femininity. She is a woman empowered by her intelligence, independence, education, professional commitment, single-mindedness and by her looks that are, significantly, identified as quite masculine.[24] As indicated in my synopsis of *Venere privata*, she enters the narrative because of her intellectual involvement in the world of female prostitution in Milan, through which she established a friendship with Alberta Radelli. She appears to be a woman who has avoided the victim/object position within the sex trade and placed herself instead in a position of power, as an observing subject and analyst of the trade, and someone who can thus claim to play the system to her own, non-commercial ends (she has dabbled in prostitution for research purposes). Her direct entry into the plot of the novel is entirely under her control: she agrees to go undercover and pose for nude photographs in order to entrap Alberta Radelli's killers. Her control is imperfect, however. She takes to the appointment at the photographer's studio a bag containing an address book in which Alberta Radelli's name appears, and when the suspicious associate of the photographer decides to search her bag, her cover is blown. At this point, she becomes a victim of violent crime.

Livia is a victim simply of her own oversight, and therefore, one might argue, a 'neutral' victim, whose gender and sexuality have played no role in her victimhood. However, the way in which this episode is contextualized in the narrative of *Venere privata* constructs Livia quite clearly as a kind of victim. In this and subsequent novels, Duca Lamberti repeatedly notes the scars on Livia's face which signal her victimhood and which, the reader is asked to recognize, signal his culpability. Though he never explicitly expresses guilt, it is made absolutely clear that Livia was his responsibility during the slashing incident – despite her having insisted on playing this role – and that it was his failure to protect her that propelled her into the position of victim. The implications are more complex, however, than simply that women, however independent and self-determining they appear, are ultimately men's responsibility, with all the concomitant rights that that position presumes. The complexity lies largely in the fact that the scars borne by Livia are an object of fascination for Lamberti and seem to constitute a significant part of the attraction she holds for him. In a sense, they mark her as his: she is branded with the sign of his responsibility for her.[25] The emphasis placed on this responsibility and the pleasure Lamberti takes in regarding her (through her scars) as 'his' imply that he is complicit in the sadistic crime which bound her to him. In effect, then, Livia is the victim of Lamberti.

Livia's complexity lies in the fact that she functions in many ways as a model of modern femininity – independent, resourceful, confident – and yet she is a damaged model: these equalities have not prevented her from becoming a victim of male-generated criminality and from domestic subjugation, in the form of her ultra-conventional ancillary role in her relationship with Lamberti. In other contexts in the Duca Lamberti novels we see powerful women systematically undone. Female criminals, of whom Marisella Domenici in *I ragazzi del massacro* is a good example, provide one illustration, but there are also further examples of 'good' women who are independent and relatively powerful: Susanna Paganica in *Traditori di tutti*, Alberta Romani, the lead social worker in *I ragazzi del massacro*, and also her sister, Ernesta Romani, an obstetrician, and a Yugoslavian (Bosnian) translator in the same novel. Interestingly, some of these women are foreign and only one, Susanna Paganica, is in a stable heterosexual relationship. Furthermore, the obstetrician is a lesbian and the translator prefers non-penetrative sex with male minors. Incidentally, in the initial presentation to the reader of Livia Ussaro, her academic expertise is seen to be facilitated by the fact that she is 'frigid'.[26] The overwhelming message from these novels, with regard to female gender roles and sexuality, is that it is absolutely not 'normal' for a woman to be independent of a man and to have any autonomous identity or power; indeed, powerful women are coded as abnormal or strange, their positive capacities undermined by some 'flaw' or difference which results in their ultimate subjugation.

Male sexuality is carefully codified in these novels as well. Male heterosexuality is the norm by which all other expressions of sexuality are measured. Interestingly, Lamberti appears to remain sexually abstinent: despite being powerfully attracted, physically, to Livia, their relationship is not explicitly consummated, and indeed, the narrative tends to focus on interruptions to the progression of their physical relationship, as if there simply is no place for human love and pleasure in the environment which they inhabit.[27] Male homosexuality, on the other hand, is regarded as an outrage against nature and against humanity, an absolute perversion that reduces those who practise it to nothing. For example, when Livia meets the photographer of nudes in *Venere privata*, she understands from the way he pronounces a swear word, we are told, that he is 'a queer, a real, wretched member of the third sex', and the narrative goes on to compare him to a mutant in a science fiction novel.[28] The denigration could not be more explicit or more absolute. Though it is of course necessary to recognize that attitudes to homosexuality in the 1960s in Italy and elsewhere were characterized by anxiety, eloquently expressed in the defamatory language used to describe homosexual men in particular, the immoderate way in which adult male homosexuals are described and characterized in Scerbanenco's novels is shocking to today's reader. Female homosexuality is regarded as predatory, somehow sick (as in fact is any manifestation of assertive female sexuality in these novels), but it is treated with a degree of nuance, and indeed with the compassion which I have identified as central to these novels, the implication being that female homosexuals are to be pitied for their affliction.[29] Male homosexuality in the case of Fiorello Grassi, one of the young perpetrators in *I ragazzi del massacro*, is similarly treated generously (in the terms of the novel) by Lamberti, who shows him extraordinary tenderness.[30] His suicide is regarded accordingly as an inevitable outcome. Adult male homosexuality, however, is associated powerfully with criminality and moral abjectness.

The sexuality-criminality nexus is a suggestive one in Scerbanenco's novels. The uncovering of the sexual tastes and activities of large swathes of contemporary society is not simply a by-product of the criminal investigations that Duca Lamberti carries out. Rather, sexuality is seen as some sort of measure and also as a vivid illustration of the transgressive qualities and capacities of modern society. Scerbanenco suggests that one way of exposing the moral portrait of society is to expose its sexual behaviour. This allows him to delve into sexual pursuits that are coded in the novels as marginal or 'perverted' in such a way as to reveal to his reader a catalogue of sexual proclivities clearly arrayed as such for the reader's enjoyment.

Apart from the case of male homosexuality, which is rejected as unspeakable, references to illicit sexual activity shelter under a veneer of gentle disapproval, in as much as they are illicit, but beneath this veneer hint at exotic sexual practices the veiled presence of which in the narrative clearly has the purpose simply of titillation. It is a mouth-watering menu of what are considered sexual irregularities that Scerbanenco invites his reader to peep at: sex with minors is something of a standard (almost always older *signori* with schoolgirls), with dwarves, with exceptionally large women, black women, nymphomaniacs, women with women, and so on. The reader is invited to imagine an apparently limitless scope of idiosyncratic sexual preferences, and to enjoy these under the cover of moral rejection that their association with the criminal world in these novels lends them. There is clearly an element of voyeurism here, as is made apparent by the emphatically periphrastic descriptions of female bodies in a number of scenes: the catalogue of pornographic photographs in *Venere privata*, for example, or the lingering observation of the sexually violated dead body of Matilde Crescenzaghi at the beginning of *I ragazzi del massacro*. The anxiety – partly prurient, partly disapproving, partly permissive – with which Scerbanenco represents the role and impact of sexuality in his contemporary society is perhaps the area where his writing encapsulates most immediately and intensely its times.

Style

As illustrated above with regard to Scerbanenco's representation of male homosexuality, it is in large part the language used to describe and label sexual preferences and identities that conveys the way these are viewed in contemporary society. Terms such as 'invertito' ('queer'), 'negra' ('Negress'), 'pappa'/'pappone' (pimp), 'minorenne' (under-aged boy/girl) indicate the degree to which these individuals and/or sexual activity involving them is negatively marked as different. Language in this area gives an indication of the way in which Scerbanenco skilfully reproduces the idiom of the time (and of the place) in order to enhance the immediacy of his representation of contemporary society. This is also, of course, one of the ways in which he makes his *giallo* specifically Italian. Not only does he drop words and phrases of Milanese dialect into his narratives but, more strikingly, he uses terms and turns of phrase that anchor his characters and scenes precisely to a historical moment.[31] There is no explanation in *Venere privata*, for example, of what sort of car exactly an Alfa Romeo Giulietta is: the vehicle is simply referred to as 'the Giulietta', and the reader is expected to interpret from this term not only the shape, size and performance of the vehicle but also the connotations of wealth and power that it carries. Also, it is an Italian car, a product of Milan and of the 'miracle'.

Scerbanenco's use of metaphor and simile is evocative in similar ways. The referents he selects often strike the reader as incongruous, even banal, but familiarity with his narrative style brings recognition that these odd analogies are part of an orchestrated attempt to align the strange or transgressive with the familiar. For example, at a moment of acute narrative tension in *Venere privata*, when Davide Auseri has finally divulged to Lamberti the story of his encounter with Alberta Radelli, we are told that 'the boy's face, completely broken down by anguish, like mayonnaise which has suddenly separated, evoked his [Lamberti's] pity'.[32] The quotidian, domestic simile seems inapt to describe a condition of psychological trauma, and yet one can recognize its efficacy in almost literally bringing home to the middlebrow reader the rupture in the young man's sense of self.

Examples such as this abound in all four of these novels, and clearly serve to locate the most unimaginable emotions and actions firmly within the imaginary of the Italian reader of popular fiction in the 1960s. Scerbanenco does not, however, eschew the glamour that crime fiction often carries, generated precisely by that which is perhaps dangerous and certainly beyond the experience of the 'ordinary' reader. Brand names and detailed product descriptions of, for example, guns, pharmaceutical products or a high-tech spy camera are intended to *épater les bourgeois*, to dazzle the reader with the sophistication of items s/he will never have encountered. This feature extends also into the stylistic fabric of the narrative itself, in that the author deploys the forms and cadence of American hard-boiled crime fiction in order to give his prose an unfamiliar, exotic edge. The curt, direct language of Duca Lamberti is perhaps the most immediate example of this. A more unusual and striking instance is a phrase that opens the second chapter of part three of *Venere privata*, responding to a phone call in which Livia has announced that she has located the ringleader of the pornography network. The chapter opens: 'You didn't need to be the king of intuition to work out who she'd found: Mister A.'[33] This phrase is perfectly correct and readable in Italian, and yet it echoes American English, its construction and cadence mimicking the indolent irony of a voice-over from an American crime movie of the 1950s. Similarly, whilst Lamberti is a common Italian name, Duca is not (as highlighted on occasion in the narratives), and the name might well be regarded as a direct translation of the name of a notional American counterpart, Duke Lambert.[34]

The style of Scerbanenco's crime fiction in this series is certainly idiosyncratic, but also in many ways typical of the genre. Descriptions and dialogue tend to be sparse, direct, unembellished. The present tense is used relatively extensively to replicate the accelerations in a criminal investigation and to inculcate in the reader an illusion of participation in the crime and/or the investigation. The third person narrative voice is laconic, slightly cynical, as expressed well by the quotation analysed above. Duca Lamberti is characterized by means of his speech and actions, but also of extensive use of free indirect speech, with the effect that the reader is invited to share his narrative point of view and to identify with him and with the interpretations that he makes. Scerbanenco thus performs a sort of balancing act with some mastery, treading a line between familiarization in Italian of a fundamentally foreign form and creative deployment of the narrative opportunities inherent precisely in that foreign-ness.

Conclusions

This chapter has set out the key evidence in support of identifying Giorgio Scerbanenco as a, or even the, 'founding father' of Italian crime fiction. In his still remarkably vital representations of Italian society in the 1960s, of Milan in particular in this period, of the culture and even of the linguistic idiom of the time, he creates in the four Duca Lamberti novels a form of crime fiction that is absolutely at home in Italy. The identification of crime fiction as a form of social commentary, as a way of probing, on the reader's behalf, the dysfunctions of contemporary society, is by now standard, and it is clear that Scerbanenco is a highly informed and astute critic of the society he inhabits, which is, interestingly, one he has adopted rather than been born into. What makes Scerbanenco's *gialli* more than social commentaries, and what I think explains the enthusiastic homage paid to him by Italian crime writers later in the twentieth and twenty-first centuries, is the way he makes crime fascinating for his reader.[35] The crimes he tells are all, in the tradition of good crime fiction, ones that have their origins within the normal and everyday (the *cronaca nera* (crime reports) of the newspapers), and yet the base criminality of these acts has been extrapolated beyond the bounds of 'normal' law-breaking to produce a crime which is extraordinary, awe-inspiring, almost sublime. In Scerbanenco's work, as Paoli has argued compellingly, the violence of these crimes is extreme, but it is also brutally enchanting in the minute, expert precision with which it is described – for example, the careful processing of a barely conscious victim's body using the efficient instruments of a butcher's freezer and electric saw.[36] The readiness with which he marries quotidian banality with extreme violence in his novels is at once seductive and unsettling, and also, I believe, represents something radically new in Italian fiction of this period. Crovi is probably not hyperbolic in describing the publication of *Venere privata* as a moment in which 'The home-grown Italian crime novel experiences a real and genuine earthquake.'[37] As I indicated in my introduction, the title of '*founding* father' is perhaps inappropriate to describe someone whose effect was to shake rather than to lay foundations, but in so doing Scerbanenco clearly opened up a new pathway for crime fiction in Italian that subsequent writers have gone on to explore.

* * *

Extract from Giorgio Scerbanenco's *Venere privata*

Duca Lamberti and Davide Auseri are observing a modern apartment and office block (the 'Ulysses' condominium) on the outskirts of Milan, where Livia Ussaro has attended an appointment to pose for nude photographs as part of a plan to entrap the exploiters and killers of Alberta Radelli. The reader knows at this point that Livia's cover has been blown, and that she has had her face systematically slashed by one of the gang. Duca and Davide do not know this, but do know that Livia is in danger, especially since they have seen a second man – the slasher or 'sadico' (sadist), as he is identified in the narrative – arrive at the building, joining the photographer. An extremely slow-paced section of the narrative, as Duca and Davide recognize the immediate danger Livia is in and the impossibility of acting to protect her, is interrupted by the following passage, where Duca and Davide chase and apprehend the criminals.

And then it happened: they saw the two men leave the Ulysses condominium, and one of the two was the man from the [Mercedes] 230, who seemed to be in a hurry now, he was anything but laid-back as he had been earlier and, for no more than a thousandth of a second, they expected to see Livia come out of that Aztec temple of a building as well, but the two men were alone and they were approaching the 230 and definitely looked like two people running away from something.

'Try to block them,' he said to Davide. They had a disadvantage of about three hundred metres to cover to reach the building, but they had the advantage that the car was ready, doors open, and they only needed to start the engine. The others, however, were only just opening the door of theirs.

And in the time it took them, Davide set off, gobbled up the track, swallowed the two hundred metres of main road that separated them from the others and drove the car straight at the 230, as if determined to ram it.

The 230 skidded violently, the road to Milan where it might lose itself in the traffic was blocked off, it lurched onto the main road towards Melzo, whilst Davide lost a few seconds reversing to get back on course. The man driving the Mercedes was driving with alarming confidence on the almost empty road, he was still three hundred metres or more in front, shooting straight ahead like an aircraft and then he [Duca] said something stupid to Davide: 'If we don't catch them, never mind, we'll get them later.'

'I've already got them,' said Davide. He was something more than alarmingly confident in his driving, he was blind with fury. As if the car in front were just a motor scooter, he was suddenly right on top of it, one second more and he would be past it.

'Watch out in case they turn,' he said to Davide. He ought also to have told him to watch out in case they fired, but he didn't: if they fired there was nothing they could do.

They did indeed turn, to avoid being blocked on the main road, they must have been planning to get off the road suddenly and head across the fields, if that's what they had in mind they weren't armed, and if they weren't armed they were done for, because the road they had had to turn into was a track of only a hundred metres or so which petered out in front of a large farmhouse.

Hens fluttered up into the air, a dog tied to a long chain howled and shot into the air himself, a farm-girl in shorts, bra and straw hat stood with a sort of pitchfork in one hand, astonished to see the two cars explode in front of her, and it was more of an explosion than a screech of brakes. The four doors of the two cars burst open simultaneously, but he and Davide were faster, he grabbed the man, the sadist, before he had taken three steps and before he had time to realize he had been caught, he got him with a kick in the stomach which floored him in front of him, in the dust in the farmyard, abject and howling.

Giorgio Scerbanenco, *Venere privata* (Milan: Garzanti, 1998), pp. 202–3.
Translated by Jennifer Burns.

Notes

[1] Mondadori's series of yellow-covered paperbacks which gave the genre its Italian name was launched in 1929.

[2] The editions referred to hereafter are as follows: Giorgio Scerbanenco, *Venere privata* (Milan: Garzanti, 1998), *Traditori di tutti* (Milan: Garzanti, 1998), *I ragazzi del massacro* (Milan: Garzanti, 1999), *I milanesi ammazzano al sabato* (Milan: Garzanti, 1999). All translations in this chapter are my own.

[3] The fact that the novel was awarded a specialist prize in France is some measure of the scarcity of any tradition of crime writing in Italy.

[4] Giorgio Scerbanenco, *Duca and the Milan Murders*, trans. Eileen Ellenbogen (London: Cassell, 1970). Scerbanenco's novels and stories have been widely translated into French and German.

[5] Arthur Jelling is an investigator based in Boston, USA, who features in five novels published between 1940 and 1942, and published in 1995 in a single volume. See bibliography for details of this and of Scerbanenco's short story collections.

[6] He takes a post in the police force at the end of *Venere privata*.

[7] Examples of other kinds of expertise that have significant status (positive and negative) in these novels are expertise in driving (Davide Auseri in *Venere privata*), in facial disfiguration (the 'sadico' or sadist in *Venere privata*), in crime histories (Susanna Paganica in *Traditori di tutti*), in chess (Alberta Radelli, Livia Ussaro, the photographer in *Venere privata*) and in butchery (one of the killers in *Traditori di tutti*).

[8] The title of *I milanesi ammazzano al sabato* (*The Milanese Kill on a Saturday*) is a good example of the author's attention to characterizations of local culture. The implication is that the Milanese work ethic is such that an individual would not take time off to kill on a working day.

[9] 'Parla di piazza Cavour, e noi non la vediamo. Parla di via Manzoni, e noi non la vediamo': Luca Doninelli, 'Prefazione', in *Venere privata*, pp. i–viii (p. i).

[10] Giuliana Pieri, 'Crime and the city in the detective fiction of Giorgio Scerbanenco', in Robert Lumley and John Foot (eds), *Italian Cityscapes. Culture and Urban Change in Contemporary Italy* (Exeter: University of Exeter Press, 2004), pp. 144–55 (p. 150).

[11] See Marco Paoli's discussion of Scerbanenco's representation of those possessing wealth and those excluded from economic advancement or, as he puts it, the '*miracolati*' (miracled) and the '*non miracolati*' (non-miracled): M. Paoli, 'Duca Lamberti nel contesto della criminalità e del miracolo economico nei gialli di Giorgio Scerbanenco', in Gillian Ania

and John Butcher (eds), *Narrativa italiana degli anni Sessanta e Settanta* (Naples: Libreria Dante & Descartes, 2007), pp. 117–24 (p. 117; italics in text).

[12] On the economic boom of 1958–63 (approximately), see chapter 7 of Paul Ginsborg, *A History of Contemporary Italy: Society and Politics 1943–1988* (London: Penguin, 1990), pp. 210–53.

[13] It is interesting that Turiddu Sompani is revealed to be of French origin and to have a French name, Jean Saintpouan. He acquired Italian citizenship and switched to his Italian name in September 1943, as Mussolini stepped down from power and handed control of the majority of Italy to the Allies. The personal history traced by his official documents catalogues all the major forces at work in Western Europe in that period, and conveys a sense of the transience of national and political allegiances. See *Traditori di tutti*, p. 81.

[14] See, for example, Leonardo Sciascia, *Il giorno della civetta* (1961; Milan: Adelphi, 2002).

[15] There are two cousins, immigrants from southern Italy, who feature in this novel, and both are named Franco Baronia. One is a perpetrator of the crime, whilst the other is an honest hotel proprietor who has been forced into accommodating prostitution by his dishonest namesake, and whose willing confession exposes to Lamberti the truth of the crime.

[16] There is a comparison to be made that may appear incongruous between Scerbanenco's novels and those of Natalia Ginzburg in the 1960s. In *Le voci della sera* (Turin: Einaudi, 1961), for example, Ginzburg portrays a younger generation who are similarly at a loss to understand their 'new' world and thus appear radically disempowered by the new freedoms that they can claim. Ginzburg focuses on the rural upper middle class, and the effects of being caught in this generational trap are therefore different. Nevertheless, it is interesting that two writers from almost opposite ends of the literary spectrum in Italy in the 1960s depict a generation which appears to be sliding into a moral abyss left behind by diverging economic and social models of behaviour.

[17] 'festosa baracchetta': *Venere privata*, pp. 63 and 65.

[18] For example, as Lamberti and his sidekick, Mascaranti, climb the stairs to the apartment of Alberta Radelli's sister in *Venere privata*, they hear the same television programme, featuring the popular personality Milva, emanating from televisions in every apartment at every level (*Venere privata*, p. 99). Doninelli comments on this in his preface (*Venere privata*, p. iv).

[19] On feminism in Italy, see Paola Bono and Sandra Kemp (eds), *Italian Feminist Thought: A Reader* (Oxford: Basil Blackwell, 1991).

[20] Paoli, 'Duca Lamberti nel contesto della criminalità e del miracolo economico nei gialli di Giorgio Scerbanenco', p. 118.

[21] Her own offspring, her son Ettore, is in fact one of the perpetrators.

[22] *I ragazzi del massacro*, pp. 79–80.

[23] Lorenza, Lamberti's sister, is a victim of both, in the sense that she was seduced and impregnated by an older man, who then abandoned her. She has no income and no positive social status as a single mother, and therefore is entirely dependent on her brother.

[24] She is tall with dark hair cut quite short, and tends to wear clothes that are cut simply and unembellished. See for example Lamberti's first meeting with her, *Venere privata*, p. 114.

[25] She is referred to frequently in Lamberti's free indirect speech as '*his* Livia' ('*la sua* Livia'; italics added).

26 Interestingly, once her relationship with Lamberti is established (but not consummated), her 'frigidity' plays no further role. She is portrayed on one occasion as suffering from almost overwhelming physical desire for him, and he tells himself not to touch her even casually, in order not to torment her (*I ragazzi del massacro*, p. 179).

27 A key episode is *I ragazzi del massacro*, pp. 193–8, when they share a hotel room and the scene appears to be set for them to consummate their relationship, but both remain preoccupied with the ongoing investigation.

28 'un invertito, un vero, squallido terzo sesso': *Venere privata*, p. 185.

29 An example is Ernesta Romani, sister of the social worker Alberta Romani in *I ragazzi del massacro*, whom Lamberti meets in her consulting rooms along with her young lover whom she employs as a nurse, and whom she met when she aborted her foetus illegally. This couple is represented with curiosity, some distaste, but with respect. See *I ragazzi del massacro*, pp. 136–41.

30 Lamberti caresses his cheek and hair three times in the course of a short interview, and expresses a deeply reflective concern for the boy, in stark contrast with the psychological violence he inflicts on the other young male suspects. See ibid., pp. 75–7.

31 See Pieri, 'Crime and the city in the detective fiction of Giorgio Scerbanenco', pp. 148 and 152, for interesting comments on the polyphonic texture of Scerbanenco's crime novels.

32 'il viso completamente ammollito dall'angoscia del ragazzo, come una maionese che d'un tratto si è "slegata", lo impietosì': *Venere privata*, p. 77.

33 'Non occorreva essere dei campioni di intuizione per capire chi aveva trovato: il signor A': ibid., p. 171.

34 An inverse example is offered in *Traditori di tutti*, where it is stated that Americans found it too difficult to pronounce the surname of Anthony Paganica, so named him Tony Paany. The surname is an implausible rendition of the name in English, but nevertheless demonstrates recognition of the extended open vowel sound in American English. See *Traditori di tutti*, p. 192.

35 For example, Carlo Lucarelli's introduction to a recently published collection of Scerbanenco's short stories is a detailed tribute to his skills as a crime writer. See 'Presentazione', in Giorgio Scerbanenco, *Racconti neri* (Milan: Garzanti, 2005), pp. 5–7.

36 See *Traditori di tutti*, pp. 148–55.

37 'Il giallo made in Italy subisce . . . un vero e proprio terremoto': Luca Crovi, *Tutti i colori del giallo. Il giallo italiano da De Marchi a Scerbanenco a Camilleri* (Venice: Marsilio, 2002), p. 21.

Bibliography

Works by Giorgio Scerbanenco

Al servizio di chi mi vuole/Lupa in convento (Milan: Garzanti, 1999).
Cinque casi per l'investigatore Jelling (Milan: Frassinelli, 1995).
I milanesi ammazzano al sabato (Milan: Garzanti, 1999).
I ragazzi del massacro (Milan: Garzanti, 1999).
Il Cinquecentodelitti (Milan: Frassinelli, 1994).
Racconti neri (Milan: Garzanti, 2005).
Traditori di tutti (Milan: Garzanti, 1998).

Uccidere per amore. Racconti 1948–1952 (Palermo: Sellerio, 2002).
Venere privata (Milan: Garzanti, 1998).
Duca and the Milan Murders, trans. Eileen Ellenbogen (London: Cassell, 1970).

Works by other authors

Bono, Paola, and Sandra Kemp (eds), *Italian Feminist Thought: A Reader* (Oxford: Basil Blackwell, 1991).
Crovi, Luca, *Tutti i colori del giallo. Il giallo italiano da De Marchi a Scerbanenco a Camilleri* (Venice: Marsilio, 2002).
Doninelli, Luca, 'Prefazione', in Giorgio Scerbanenco, *Venere privata* (Milan: Garzanti, 1998), pp. i–viii.
Ginsborg, Paul, *A History of Contemporary Italy: Society and Politics 1943–1988* (London: Penguin, 1990).
Ginzburg, Natalia, *Le voci della sera* (Turin: Einaudi, 1961).
Lucarelli, Carlo, 'Presentazione', in Giorgio Scerbanenco, *Racconti neri* (Milan: Garzanti, 2005), pp. 5–7.
Paoli, Marco, 'Duca Lamberti nel contesto della criminalità e del miracolo economico nei gialli di Giorgio Scerbanenco', in Gillian Ania and John Butcher (eds), *Narrativa italiana degli anni Sessanta e Settanta* (Naples: Libreria Dante & Descartes, 2007), pp. 117–24.
Pieri, Giuliana, 'Crime and the city in the detective fiction of Giorgio Scerbanenco', in Robert Lumley and John Foot (eds), *Italian Cityscapes. Culture and Urban Change in Contemporary Italy* (Exeter: University of Exeter Press, 2004), pp. 144–55.
Sciascia, Leonardo, *Il giorno della civetta* (1961; Milan: Adelphi, 2002).

4

Literature and the Giallo*: Gadda, Eco, Tabucchi and Sciascia*

JOSEPH FARRELL

The history and analysis of the *giallo* written by Leonardo Sciascia in his much debated *Brief History of the Detective Novel* seem now dated and even perverse in the light of Sciascia's own output and even more so in the light of recent developments in the crime story in Italy.[1] Early forms of the essay had appeared in 1953,[2] and while it was always intended as a historical survey and not as a manifesto for his own idiosyncratic *gialli*, the essay now reads like an epitaph for a form of the genre which was exhausted and near to extinction. His discussion does not presage the radical change of direction in what could approximately be called the 'postmodern' crime story in Italy, a change of direction apparent in his own novels. Indeed, Sciascia excludes the Italian detective novel almost entirely from his consideration and gives no inkling of the characteristics that distinguish it from British, American or other European models. It is significant that he considers Mario Soldati and Carlo Emilio Gadda the only Italians worthy of mention, and even to them he devotes only a cursory, if respectful, closing comment. Italian precursors of the genre are neglected. For instance, he writes that psychological considerations play no part in the process of detection, except in the case of 'that great detective novel',[3] which is Dostoevsky's *Crime and Punishment,* but on the same grounds he could have referred to Emilio De Marchi's dark masterpiece, *The Priest's Hat*, an acute psychological study of a guilty mind reaching the point of breakdown under police and judicial scrutiny.[4]

Sciascia's emphasis on foreign works is scarcely surprising since, although the detective story was popular in Italy, for many years the majority of the works available were translations. His analysis of the historical reasons for the worldwide popularity of the genre displays his customary perspicacity of judgement, but is now of value principally as a point of contrast with the crime story as it was to develop in Italy. The detective novel attained its success, in Sciascia's view, on account of the low demands it makes of the reader. He quotes Alain as explaining the pleasure it gives as arising from 'the flight of thought', and adds his own gloss that the detective story is 'in the most precise sense, a pastime'. The ideal reader, making no effort to out-guess or out-think the investigator, should allow his mind to become a *tabula rasa*, and should happily enter a blissful state of dependence where he hands over his intellectual capacities to the detective, convinced that the latter's superior abilities will resolve the conundrum and unmask the guilty party.

> The good reader knows . . . that the enjoyment, the pastime, consists in the condition – one of absolute intellectual rest – of entrusting himself to the investigator, to his exceptional ability for reconstructing a crime and identifying the person responsible.[5]

Excellent though this may be as a description of what it will be convenient to call the 'classical detective story' – although that is at best a portmanteau term, as incapable of precise delimitation as other comprehensive literary classifications, such as romanticism – it differs widely from the detective story as written in Italy in recent decades. Sciascia himself never permits his own reader to reach that state of 'intellectual rest', but instead requires him to track the detective, to think ahead of him, to scrutinize the workings of society as a whole and to identify the obstacles that, while they may not prevent him from penetrating the motivations and nature of the crime, will prevent him from reaching the perpetrator of it. Few Italian *giallisti*, and none of the four writers considered here – Carlo Emilio. Gadda, Sciascia himself, Umberto Eco and Antonio Tabucchi – will ever create the superior-minded detective capable of inspiring in the reader the awe or trust which Sciascia sees as a defining characteristic of the *genre*.

Sciascia considers the genre essentially a moral tract, in which the white knight invariably triumphs, the villain is vanquished and just order is restored. In his own words:

> In its most original and autonomous form, the detective story assumes a metaphysic, a world 'beyond the physical', of God, of grace, and of that grace which theologians call enlightening. The investigator may even be considered the bearer of that grace, like St Lucy in the *Divine Comedy*.[6]

Sciascia was not the first to make this point, and the exponents of the classical crime story were well aware of upholding a social ethic. In her autobiography, Agatha Christie wrote that her novels dramatized 'the hunting down of Evil and the triumph of Good', while later P. D. James was quite uncompromising in her statement that 'I like the form the detective novel takes: the restoration of order.' G. K. Chesterton, whom Sciascia admired and whose detective, Father Brown, was for Sciascia dedicated to the defence of ethical standards, himself rose to heights of rhetorical brilliance in defence of the morality of the detective story.

> The romance of the police activity keeps in some sense before the mind the fact that civilisation itself is the most sensational of departures and the most romantic of rebellions. By dealing with the unsleeping sentinels who guard the outposts of society, it tends to remind us that we live in an armed camp, making war with a chaotic world, and that the criminals, the children of chaos, are nothing but the traitors within our

gates . . . The romance of the police force is thus the whole romance of man. It is based on the fact that morality itself is the most dark and daring of conspiracies.[7]

Crime fiction, or 'postmodern' crime fiction, now operates on different premises, making the moral, or tidy, ending rare, while altered concepts of justice or of what makes for the just society render such solutions difficult to reconcile with the world as seen by contemporary writers. Many detectives in recent crime fiction operate on the fringes of legality, and writers such as Sciascia himself are motivated by a distaste for a society that they view as conniving with organized criminality. Readers of Gadda are called on to shift preconceptions, and justice is not given within the parameters of the fiction. Eco will provide the traditional ending, but his approach is playful, while Tabucchi inhabits an ontologically disordered cosmos. The structure of the traditional crime story – the shattering of order by crime, its restoration following investigation and the elimination of the source of the disorder – is no longer respected by contemporary writers, even if the question of order retains its central place among the issues confronted at a deep level by the detective story of whatever stamp, with the crucial difference that the previous instinctive belief that 'whatever is, is right' has been jettisoned. The *idée fixe* behind all four writers discussed here is that a new narrative form, separate from both the novel as it emerged from the eighteenth century and from the classical detective story, was necessary as a tool for the dissection of contemporary 'reality' (the inverted commas are de rigueur), which is conceived of as shifting, decentred and fragmented. The metaphysical or postmodern detective crime novel is the genre deemed fit to describe and probe the *comédie humaine* of our days. This changed vision has implications for the role of the detective and for the structure of the crime novel itself but, more unexpectedly, has consequences outside the confines of the genre for what Arnold Bennett called the 'art novel'. The barriers which separated literature from lesser forms such as the crime novel no longer hold.

The assumption of such barriers lies behind Sciascia's dissection of the crime story. The issue of primary and secondary forms of writing had previously intrigued Antonio Gramsci in his examination of popular culture. Gramsci found it hard to establish an acceptable relationship between 'art' and the 'crime story', a distinction that carries the unstated but unavoidable assumption that these were incompatible categories. He identified two currents inside the genre, the 'mechanical' and the 'artistic', and drew a further distinction between the detective as 'scientist' and as 'psychologist', differing on this point from Sciascia. Both characteristics are for Gramsci present in Sherlock Holmes, while Father Brown incarnates the ideal of the 'psychological' approach to detection. Certain crime stories, those which make use of psychological probing, possess for Gramsci that greater depth and seriousness which allow them to be viewed as 'art', but these subtleties do not help him resolve the question fundamental to his probes: why has non-artistic literature gained such popularity?[8] The question is integral to Gramsci's own thinking on the intellectually formative power of popular and hegemonic cultures, but the formulation of the question betrays the unconscious *parti pris* that the humble detective story is a secondary form which must be excluded from the upper reaches of art or literature. Even establishing an adequate terminology for what he called 'this kind of literature' was a problem, so Gramsci had to resort to such terms as 'popular literature', 'non-artistic literature' and 'mechanical literature – of intrigue'.[9] Years later, Umberto Eco would wonder whether 'we can still identify the pleasing with the non-artistic',[10] but he would, as a valiant postmodernist, answer in the affirmative. Gramsci, like Sciascia, is of course well aware that there are 'art' writers who have written crime fiction: Sciascia referred to Dostoevsky in this respect, and Gramsci to Balzac. In his creation of Vautrin, Gramsci writes, Balzac confronted the criminal but, he adds, Balzac 'is not "technically" a writer of detective novels'. The inverted commas around the word 'technically' are a decisive sign in underwriting the 'art' versus 'popular culture' divide. Balzac is not included among members of the lower species.

The paucity of native Italian detective stories puzzled Gramsci, who worried over why the Italian intelligentsia and hegemonic forces in society were so prepared to allow the national-popular culture to be formed by elements outside their control. That is a separate question, but it is interesting that when, with the four writers under discussion here, Italian detective fiction became acceptable, it was when the prestige and talent of the writers themselves meant that their work, and hence the genre, could be regarded as art and not as 'mechanics' or craftsmanship. Agatha Christie, Dorothy Sayers, as well as the Americans S. S. Van Dine and Erle Stanley Gardner and others on whom Sciascia lavished such attention, were happy to view themselves as artisans rather than artists, and did not view themselves as lesser beings for that. To all appearances, Sciascia was in agreement with this assessment of crime writers, even in regard to such masters of the trade as Conan Doyle, since he refers to Conan Doyle's 'undoubtedly mediocre mind'.[11] Perhaps it is time not only to question the standard patrician judgement that separates literature from genre fiction but also to overturn the canons, and judge what is by common consent 'literature' by the standards of the detective story, on the assumption that this categorization in no way demeans or diminishes Gadda, Sciascia, Eco or Tabucchi as men of letters.

The detective story is today an arena in which issues of order and chaos, and not merely law and order, can be disputed. For a generation whose faith in the tragic was reasserted by Schopenhauer and Heidegger but which lacks other means for debating the tragic sense of life in a godless cosmos, the literary detective story provides one of the few viable options. Umberto Eco was not being totally ironic when, in explaining his choice of genre for *The Name of the Rose*, he declared that 'it only remained to me to choose (among plot models) the one that was most metaphysical and philosophical: the detective novel'.[12] Modernism has swept away the conviction unquestioned by writers of the classical detective story that there is some given cosmic order, some fixed standard of good and evil, to be asserted and defended, but the question of order – metaphysical, cosmic, ethical, political – remains at the heart of the quest that is the crime novel. While the quest may take on forms which may include the playful, ironic or ludic it is by no means limited to them. The quest may end in the recognition that the belief in order is an illusion. The genre deals not only with crime and society, but can provide a forum for discussing death and meaning. The detective novel is a quest, one of the oldest and most frequent motifs in storytelling,[13] and whether the detection is at the metaphysical or social level, the probing for order is primary. There will not necessarily be an unmasking at the end of the quest, as there was in Conan Doyle, but in their various ways and at various levels, Carlo Emilio Gadda, Leonardo Sciascia, Umberto Eco and Antonio Tabucchi all provide a dénouement that reveals a philosophical stance on the issue of order. These writers do not represent a new canon, and certainly do not follow one common template. They were not involved in some common act of transgressing the established rules of the detective story, and in fact Eco adheres to the central conventions fairly closely, but his is a consciously knowing book, composed in an imaginary mental library.

Sciascia judged Carlo Emilio Gadda's tantalizing *That Awful Mess on Via Merulana* 'the most absolute detective story ever written: a detective story without a solution'.[14] The reasons for the absence of a solution are more than technical and transcend even the social-political conditions of the Italian Fascist society in the 1920s in which Gadda's novel was set. The absence of a traditional solution was, it was to become clear, the first harbinger of the overturning of the conventions of the genre.

Carlo Emilio Gadda: the politics and metaphysics of disorder

The final version of Carlo Emilio Gadda's *That Awful Mess on Via Merulana*, published in book form in 1957, consists of ten chapters, but the work itself had a long, tormented gestation period, and much attention has, paradoxically, been concentrated on the chapter Gadda chose to omit from the final form of the work. The earliest version, appearing in a literary review, contained only five episodes, and the reasons for the excision of one of these are hotly debated among Gadda's numerous exegetes.[15] The writer himself seemingly concluded that the chapter contained a precocious revelation of the identity of the guilty party, leading to a lessening of the 'suspense' indispensable to the crime story format. In the final version, the identity of the perpetrator remains unclear, or at least unstated, and this too has given rise to endless debates. Is the novel finished or unfinished, as were several of Gadda's works, was Sciascia right in thinking that no solution was given or even conceivable, or is the identity in fact clear to readers willing to act as surrogate investigators? If the last hypothesis is correct, which of several possible murderers is the one who actually wielded the knife? There are as many theories as there are hypotheses on the identity of Jack the Ripper.

The novel begins with the abruptness of *Moby Dick*: 'Everybody called him Don Ciccio by now.'[16] He was in fact Francesco Ingravallo, a serving officer with the police force in Rome, first seen as a dinner guest in the house of the wealthy Liliana Balducci on Via Merulana, where he is distracted by the pretty niece at the table and by the allure of Liliana herself. Ingravallo never attains any emotional detachment in the investigations, which begin when he is summoned back to the same apartment block on professional business, first to investigate the violent robbery of jewellery belonging to a neighbour, Countess Menegazzi, and a few days later to lead enquiries into the brutal murder of Liliana herself. Were these two crimes related? Ingravallo follows the procedures of Sherlock Holmes, moving from the single event into the tangled financial and sexual morass of the family circumstances. There are here sufficient false leads to satisfy any aficionado of the genre. Is Liliana's handsome cousin, Giuliano Valdarena, a suspect, since he is found in possession of cash and precious stones allegedly gifted by the dead woman, and what about the neighbour Angeloni, whose unexplained reticence lands him in prison? While interrogating the family, Ingravallo focuses on the victim's over-whelming, but frustrated, desire to have children, a longing which causes her to invite into her house a series of four 'nieces' who will receive generous dowries when they leave to marry. The most recent, Assunta, had been there when Ingravallo was a guest, while the previous one, Virginia, is the subject of anxious whispers by the parish priest over her lesbian tendencies.

If the enquiry into the murder concerned prosperous bourgeois Roman society, leads relating to the theft of the countess's jewels take other detectives into the impoverished peasant communities in the villages surrounding Rome. This enquiry has a more successful outcome, with two female cousins found in possession of some topazes and unwillingly revealing the name of the boyfriend who has com-promised both of them. Ingravallo's separate enquiry into the murder leads him to the home of Assunta, but the novel closes with her anguished cry – 'Nun so' stata io' ('It was not me') – which leaves the policeman in a state of repentance over suspecting her and the reader in a state of confusion.

The names of the characters – Aeneas, Diomedes, Ascanio, Virginia – have classical echoes and underline Gadda's ambition to write some kind of modern *epos*, but he was equally unambiguous about his wish to use the modern genre of the crime story. As early as 1928, in preparatory notes for the work which was later entitled *Second Novella* and was published only in 1971, Gadda had expressed his admiration for Conan Doyle.[17] He was fascinated at the time by the real life case of a young man who had killed his mother and concealed her body in a trunk. The theme of matricide engrossed him, and may, at a more metaphorical level, have provided a motive for one of the possible killers in *That Awful Mess*. In his private notes on how to reconstruct the original matricide case as fiction, he writes that his ambition is to be 'novel-ish, interesting, Conan-Doylian', but not straightforwardly so since readers now 'know him by heart and there is no longer any enjoyment in it'. He added: 'It is not the case that life is always simple, even flat. Sometimes it is highly complex and novel-like.'[18] No one could accuse Gadda of entertaining philosophical or aesthetic notions on the simplicity of life. In his introduction to *That Awful Mess*, Italo Calvino points out that Gadda planned to write 'not only a murder novel, but a philo-sophical novel as well'.[19]

Probably no other crime novel in any European language is based on such deep intellectual sophistication. While irony acts to provide some distancing from seriousness in the work of Umberto Eco, Gadda has no fear of *gravitas*. His fiction presupposes a previous philosophical discourse that draws on the thought of Leibnitz, the subject of his undergraduate thesis, with an admixture of Spinoza. Broadly, if superficially, the philosophy could be defined as addressing epistemology and even metaphysics. Contemporary readers will see in it a foretaste of contemporary chaos theory. The distance between Gadda and his protagonists is always small, so this philosophical stance is attributed by the author to Ciccio Ingravallo, and is stated in the early pages of the novel, before the action gets underway. Stripped of the cosmic optimism that caused Voltaire to satirize Leibnitz in *Candide*, the outlook (philosophy may be too grand a term) tends to be expressed in defensive formulations. Ingravallo seemed to those who knew him to live in 'silence and sleep', occasionally awakening to enunciate 'some theoretical idea (a general idea, that is) on the affairs of men, and of women. At first sight, or rather on first hearing, these seemed banalities. They weren't banalities.'[20] Ingravallo's mind inhabits a world of complexity ruled by a chain of causality whose nature escapes even the attentive observer. The notion of the 'mess' indicated by the title is more than a metaphor. The Italian word *pasticcio* is strengthened by the addition of the pejorative suffix, so that while Ingravallo is investigating a nasty tangle of brutal or squalid events, underlying that contingent inquiry lies Gadda's core conviction that, even if the great names of Aristotle or Immanuel Kant can be produced to uphold the contrary viewpoint, all actions, events, catastrophes, crimes, happenings, however unforeseen and seemingly random, are 'never the consequence or the effect, if you prefer, of a single motive, of *a* cause singular'. Reality is a complex phenomenon described by words 'like knot or tangle, or muddle, or *gnommero*, which in Roman dialect means skein'.[21] He viewed the crimes he investigated in that light, as the outcome of a bedlam of causes and not of one cause or motive. This is a world from which all harmony, design, order has been banished. It is not a functioning piece of clockwork but a tissue of odds and ends on to which some form of rationality may be appended.

The brief list of words, 'knot, tangle, etc.' just quoted – and there are many longer lists throughout the book – is in the original a dizzy mixture of dialect and standard Italian terminology. Gadda's chief impact on the world of Italian letters was not through the complexity of his plotting or psychological probing, deft and subtle though they were, but through his invention of a wholly original, idiosyncratic, multi-layered linguistic style forged from a mixture of poetic rhythms, dialect usages, idiolects, new coinages, eccentric word-plays, proper names forged into caricature generic terms and submerged intertextual quotations. This style has been described variously as baroque, mannered, macaronic, Joycean, polyphonic, Rabelaisian and there are more. Discussion of that topic lies beyond the scope of this essay, save to say that the result is a work which delves into the matter of tragedy but maintains the feel of comedy, even at times grotesque farce. If another epithet could be added to those employed to categorize Gadda, it would be the non-Italian adjective Chekhovian, with its connotations of bitter-sweet observation of the burlesque but brutal spectacle of humanity, all of whose members are guilty in some way.

The question of order and disorder lay at the heart of the philosophy of Ingravallo, and of Gadda. 'Why investigate, if entanglement is an integral part of both nature and history?' is the trenchant question posed by the late Robert Dombroski.[22] Some critics persist in seeing in Gadda the same quest for order that is the spine of the classical detective tale, so Gian Carlo Ferretti views *That Awful Mess* as a return to the *giallo* understood as 'an enquiry inside disorder, as a process for re-establishing an order'.[23] For Gadda, on the other hand, order is an aspiration rather than a reality in a cosmos in which disorder is sovereign unless overthrown momentarily by chance. There are two separate levels of disorder depicted in the novel: the action unfolds in 1927 when, even if Mussolini had only recently come to power, his grip on society was unyielding. Gadda, like many other Italian intellectuals, had flirted briefly with Fascism, but grew quickly scornful and embittered, so that the references to the *Duce* and the regime have the polemical, inventive biliousness of the prophetic books in the Old Testament denouncing the corruption of Jerusalem. According to the edicts of Mussolini, mocked later by Sciascia in *Open Doors*, crime could not by definition exist in the glorious new order ushered in by the *fasci*, and could certainly not be reported in public.[24] However, while it is true that in *That Awful Mess*, Fascism appears to have reduced Rome to the status of a Sophoclean Thebes, it is an exaggeration to see Mussolini as 'the absolute emblem of the senselessness of the world and of the stupidity of men',[25] because the realization that the times are out of joint is separate from, even if accompanied by, an ontological awareness of cosmic disorder, of an imbroglio inherent in the very nature of things, of the *pasticcio* that is life itself.

So who did commit the crime, does it matter and is the reader supposed to know?[26] Sophisticated critics of Gadda now affect a weariness over such questions as whether the novel was finished or not, why the identity of the murderer is not given and whether that identity is, or should be, clear, but in a Conan-Doylian novel curiosity would be satisfied. Virginia is indicated by several, since Gadda seemed to point towards her in the excised chapter, but in an interview with the novelist Dacia Maraini, Gadda remained gnomic:

> I deliberately cut off *That Awful Mess* half-way because the *giallo* should not be dragged out, as happens with certain artificial crime stories which go on ad nauseam, and end up wearying the mind of the reader. I consider it finished . . . concluded in a literary sense. The detective knows who the murderer is and that is sufficient.[27]

Sherlock Holmes would not have stopped there, but Gadda both imitated and subverted the form. The detective may know who the murderer is, but the reader is left in a labyrinth, without any clearly signed exit.

Umberto Eco: finesse and focus

The primary requirement of critics, if not of readers, of Umberto Eco's *The Name of the Rose* is to distinguish between the novel's finesse and focus.[28] The finesse involves the detailed, erudite discussions of such medieval themes as the nature of Franciscan poverty, the symbolism of precious stones in medieval iconography, the theological differences between Waldensians and Cathars, the impact of Fra Dolcino on religious life, the role of the Inquisition, as well as the wider, possible, allegory which may depict the divided Europe of the Cold War in the portrait of an Italy torn between papacy and empire. These matters could, on the other hand, be viewed as intrinsic to a novel which is also a historical novel, since in that genre authors are expected to sketch the culture and history of the historical age and embed the characters in it so deeply that the actions that constitute the plot emerge naturally from that setting. Eco's knowledge of scholastic thought was deep: his first book was a study of the aesthetics of St Thomas Aquinas, and these conversations between monks could be seen as equivalent to the explanation of the clan system in Walter Scott's *Rob Roy*. They can, in other words, be viewed as helpful to the plot and indispensable to the cultural climate and historical background.

For a pure detective novel, on the other hand, these matters could be regarded as part of the decorative finesse, but this is a very impure detective novel, so the question of the writer's intended focus comes to the fore. The very mention of the writer takes us into the heart of Umberto Eco's literary theories and requires that attention be paid to such contemporary philosophical-critical themes as the *intentio auctoris* as distinct from the *intentio operis*, interpretation and over-interpretation, the model and the ingenuous reader, as well as to the kind of prior learning that readers would require to appreciate the book and to experience the jouissance Eco was offering. When writing on *Foucault's Pendulum*, one of Eco's more sensitive critics suggested that 'a successful reading of the novel requires Eco's brand of model reader', that is, one who has 'at least a passing knowledge of Eco's other theoretical works on narrative theory, semiotics and popular culture'.[29] Rocco Capozzi unhesitatingly writes that in order to 'grasp more than one level of meaning in these intricate and rhizomatic intertextual pastiches', the reader must decide whether to 'dialogue only with the voices in the written text' or whether he should allow himself to 'automatically converse also with the ironic voices of the implied narrator/author'.[30] Others go further, and in certain quarters the notion has gained currency that the novel was an illustration of Eco's philosophical beliefs, or else an elaboration of them.[31] Eco was already very well established as a literary theorist before turning to fiction and in much of the voluminous criticism he has attracted, his novels are often treated as an exemplum of his theories on reception aesthetics, on semiotics and semiology, on the open text, and on modernism and postmodernism. Eco leaves clues which invite that approach. 'When we consider a book, we mustn't ask ourselves what it says but what it means', the protagonist reminds his young companion while the two are waiting to gain entrance to the library.[32] A little further on he informs him that 'the idea is sign of things, and the image is sign of the idea, sign of sign', and the deliberately anachronistic vocabulary and philosophy could be taken as a statement of the semiotic strategies he had himself expounded in treatises published at about the same time.[33]

However else it is categorized, *The Name of the Rose* undoubtedly rests on a high measure of erudition. Like *Foucault's Pendulum*, it could be likened to a brass-rubbing of a tombstone in a medieval chapel, consciously imitating existing work but elaborated with new materials and recycled for different purposes. The philosophy discussed *passim* is medieval, but the frame is the traditional convention of the detective story as conceived by Conan Doyle, inherited, inhabited and imitated by Eco without parody. Pastiche is playfulness and is not synonymous with satire or parody, while irony, as Ariosto demonstrated, is a device that allows the ironist to have it both ways, simultaneously paying homage and delivering gentle, not corrosive, mockery. Eco is an Ariosto to Conan Doyle's Tasso. The story of the murders in the monastery is narrated by a Dr Watson figure, the naive postulant Adso, who drafts his account in his old age. Although the detective may initially seem gifted with the piercing insight of Sherlock Holmes, as in the early scene when, without being asked and using pure a priori reasoning, he tells Remigio where the horse he has been seeking is to be found, and even gives its correct name. However, at the conclusion of the murder investigation, William shows himself to be a frail, fallible modern detective, not the superman that the sleuth of Baker Street had been, but even his final failure in detection is an expression of the medieval mindset with which Eco endows him. The investigative reasoning which led him astray derived from his excessive zeal to detect a pattern and order in the murders in the monastery, and was based on an assumption founded on medieval theology that order was inherent in a numinous cosmos. The third of Aquinas's five proofs of the existence of God relied on the observation of design in the created world, a design which could emanate only from the omnipotent Divinity. Granted that the cosmos is based on an intelligent design, Brother William convinces himself that there must be a pattern even to the series of murders. He admits he is mistaken. As a modernist or postmodernist, Eco could never assent to that belief.

The novel has the classical three-stage structure of crime, investigation and un-masking. William sifts evidence, interviews suspects, weighs hypotheses, examines the *loci* of crimes exactly as Holmes had done. The mission that brought Brother William, a Franciscan friar, to the Benedictine monastery was to seek for some means of reconciling the Pope and his critics, but the monastery chosen as venue for the encounter between the papal and imperial delegations is in turmoil following the discovery of the dead, perhaps murdered, body of one of the monks. His investigations are unsuccessful in putting an end to the spate of killings, or suicides, but William comes to focus his attention on 'a book and a man'.[34] He believes that the crimes mimic the prophecies concerning the Seven Angels of the Apocalypse, but as he comes to understand the mind of the librarian, the blind Jorge of Burgos, he realizes that he had been mistaken and had arrived at the right solution for the wrong reasons. Not all the deaths were linked, since the first victim had killed himself in a fit of jealousy over the loss of his homosexual partner. Before discovering he is on the wrong track, William tells Adso of his delight in finding 'a series of connections in small areas of the world's affairs', at a time when 'as a philosopher I doubt the world has an order' (p. 394). His task is to 'imagine all possible orders, and all disorders' (p. 418), not to be impressed by the grand architecture of the monastery which, as the abbot outlines, is an expression of a biblical order (p. 444), and to face the fact that his own hypothesis represented a false pattern, even if it did put him onto the trail of the guilty party (p. 470).

The obsession with unveiling patterns of semiotic thought in the novel has caused critics to lose sight of the sheer originality and bravura of the workings of the detective story. The motivations attributed to Jorge show Eco's imagination operating on a plane of high creativity. His motives could hardly be construed as plausible in the humdrum world of contemporary society, but they represent a fascinating weaving of inventive erudition into a deviant, medieval, theological mind. Jorge is revealed as the holder of the only remaining copy of the second part of Aristotle's *Poetics*, the one dealing with comedy, but he viewed laughter as incompatible with the reverence due to God, so anyone who penetrated the secret deserved death. The structure of the detective plot, independently of the scholastic debates or semiotic underpinnings, is imbued with deep implications for the order that the investigator was seeking. In the final confrontation between William, the fallible representative of Good, and Jorge, the *Übermensch* representative of the Antichrist, it emerges that Jorge had been driven to murder on account of his own notion of order and his conviction that comedy and laughter are a rebellion 'against God's established order' (p. 474). Aristotle's treatise ennobled laughter, and for that reason required to be obliterated from the world's memory. The ending of the novel is as unambiguous as any in Conan Doyle.

Antonio Tabucchi: confronting chaos

Indian Nocturne (1984) scarcely deserves the title of a detective novel, nor could its author Antonio Tabucchi be described as a crime writer any more than Jane Austen could usefully be viewed as a romantic author, and yet there is sufficient truth in the assertion as regards both novelists to give the descriptions some value. Tabucchi's novel is remarkable not only for its haunting encounters and probing dialogues on matters beyond Western notions of rationality but for the intriguing insight it offers into how the structures and techniques of the detective story – the mystery, the quest, the enquiry, the assessment of clues and above all the suspense – have become mainstream in the literary novel.[35] Tabucchi was self-conscious over his adoption of such techniques and went so far as to state that the later *Declares Pereira* (1994), a novel set in Portugal in the days of the Salazar dictatorship and chronicling the reluctant movement towards political dissidence of a man who had previously sought only a quiet life,[36] was fundamentally a *giallo* since it involved 'reference to an authority' and took as its model the 'search and interrogation which are characteristic of detective literature'.[37]

Discussion of Tabucchi requires the reversal of the usual critical stance that evaluates crimes stories as a secondary genre. Crime writers still complain of their exclusion from the canon and of the consequent unwillingness of critics to assess their work by the normal literary standards, but in the case of Tabucchi, a writer of unquestioned seriousness who displays a deft merging of narrative and philosophy, it will enhance his work if his use of the techniques of crime fictions is brought to light. On more than one occasion, he has expressed his admiration for Simenon and French detective novels: 'The "polar" too takes on great importance and I have read a lot of Simenon, whom I consider a great novelist.'[38] Some of his more insightful critics have hinted at the same point, even if they then decline to pursue the implications of their aperçus. Claudio Pezzin, for instance, writing of *Indian Nocturne*, opines that:

> The twelve chapters are presented as varying draft-fragments of a novel in the making, in which each one successively synthesizes an interrupted experiment with a literary genre adopted and then rejected: from the detective to the spy genre, from the philosophical-moral to the picaresque genre, modelling itself in turn on Hess's *Siddharta*, on Conrad's *Lord Jim*, on Conan Doyle's Sherlock Holmes or on Jack Kerouac's *On The Road*, in every case focusing on the instability of the game of fiction inside that genre, on mechanisms of de- or re-composition.[39]

Plainly, far from being an innovation introduced by the crime story, the quest is one of the most ancient motifs in storytelling, but although Tabucchi is anxious to make the connection between his novels and detective fiction, the differences are not secondary. The quest undertaken by the narrator in such works as *Indian Nocturne* may be likened to that undertaken in Wilkie Collins's *The Moonstone*, but the vision of reality to which he adheres means that for Tabucchi there can be no final unveiling or dénouement. As a crafter of tales, Tabucchi has an affinity to J. L. Borges, whom he admires, but his irreverence towards tradition is deeper and sufficiently all-embracing to include scepticism over the validity of the very literary enterprise that the writer is engaged on. Tabucchi takes apart the conventional structures of several genres, including that of the crime novel, as has been the case with many other Italian writers in the same field. At best, Tabucchi hovers on the fringes of the crime novel, re-moulding aspects of the genre according to his own needs. In *Indian Nocturne*, no crime has been committed and there is no detective, neither as public official nor private operator, but there is an investigator and the spine of the plot is a mystery story, involving inquiry, pursuit and search for a person inexplicably missing in India. The investigator-pursuer follows a trail of clues, undertakes a series of interviews with people who knew the vanished man and who are more or less honest and privy to information which is more or less re-liable. The investigator and the reader have each to make their own assessment of the facts unearthed and reported, as is the case in the game which is the detective story.

The choice of India is in itself intriguing for, among other things, the philosophical and cultural encounters the country offers the Western mind. At one narrative level, the journey through India is banal, being made with the assistance of a real guide book, *India: a Travel Survival Kit*, published in English as part of the Lonely Planet series. The introduction to the novel lists the hotels in which Rouxignol, the traveller-investigator, stays in his search for the missing Xavier. The people Rouxignol encounters are an idiosyncratic lot, who include the prostitute Vimala Sar who had first invited him to seek out Xavier, the female thief on the run in the Taj Coromandel Hotel, the crippled seer at a bus stop between Madras and Mandalore, the madman who appears in a dream in the library in Goa, and the theosophist in Madras. Tabucchi is customarily heedless of boundaries between life and imagination, having his protagonists converse indifferently with the living and dead, with products of observation and of fantasy. This India is both the Orient of the fiction of Rudyard Kipling, Somerset Maugham and Joseph Conrad, who are all mentioned by name as creators of an India of the mind,[40] and also the home of mystical oriental religions that have long been an enriching enigma to the Western mind. Rouxignol's, or Tabucchi's, encounter with the shaman-seer at the bus stop or with the thinker in the archive are oddly reminiscent of comparable encounters made in fiction and philosophy by the Romanian Mircea Eliade, novelist and historian of religion.[41] Curiously, years after the publication of the novel, Tabucchi resumed a debate on the deep sense of the novel with a story-cum-essay consisting of letters exchanged between Tabucchi himself in the first person and the imaginary theosophist, who is then unambiguously revealed to have been Xavier, the object of the novel's quest.[42] The two correspondents debate the validity of interpretations of the novel offered by Western reviewers and the possibility that those viewpoints reveal a chasm between occidental and oriental mindsets. The twin cultures of East and West are intertwined in the novel, and the quest itself reaches its intellectual climax in Goa, once a Portuguese colony, in an archive tended by a Portuguese religious order and containing works written by seventeenth-century missionaries from Europe. It is scarcely worth labouring the associations between the name Xavier with the name of the early Jesuit who went to India as missionary apostle and who is still buried in Goa.

The twelve chapters are almost distinct stories assembled by a process of cinematic montage, and while the dialogue in the final chapter contains the stark warning, 'méfiez-vous des morceaux choisis', the dilemma for the reader is to know what can be trusted.[43] The final episode has, *mutatis mutandis*, the function given to the closing section of such classic crime novels as *Murder on the Orient Express*, that of revelation and the conveyance of meaning. However, while in the mainstream novels meaning coincides with clarity and restored order, in Tabucchi meaning involves the recognition that univocal clarity is impossible and order cannot be asserted, much less restored. There are three characters involved in the final meeting that occurs in a hotel restaurant, but perhaps all three are aspects of the one being. The object of the quest has been located but in a bewildering *coup de scène*, the first person narrator is now Xavier, not Rouxignol, and he gives a flirtatious account of a pseudo-seductive conversation over dinner with Christine, a woman with whom he had, perhaps, shared a taxi that morning. They become aware of the presence in the far corner of the same room of a third diner, who pays their bill and who may well be the pursuer, Rouxignol. No definitive interpretation that makes unequivocal sense is possible, a situation that has left critics free to indulge the notions that the novel was a series of quests for identity or that it illustrated the imprecision of the postmodern intellectual cosmos. Tabucchi's own intellectual mindset was designed principally by Fernando Pessoa, with the heteronyms behind which he concealed his writing self, and by Luigi Pirandello, with his belief in masks that conceal an unknowable face. Having identified the impact of these two writers, Dolfi adds that 'Tabucchi sets himself up in the first person as a multiple figure'.[44] Tabucchi himself is of little assistance in the search for the meaning of his works as was Samuel Beckett. Adopting the perspective of a crime writer, he once told an interviewer:

> Perhaps I am not a good detective. You see, I have always been attracted by stories that present themselves as charades, by incongruous stories which are hard to connect in a logical framework, but my investigative capability stops at a certain point. Perhaps deep down I have a distrust in reason . . .[45]

The incompetent detective is a feature of much contemporary crime writing, but the statement represents a separation point between Tabucchi and the world of writers of such transgressive detective stories as Leonardo Sciascia. Sciascia's investigations too will falter before justice is done, but his trust in reason never wavers. In Tabucchi, it is difficult, as Christine in *Indian Nocturne* avers, to know what occurs inside the framework of fiction and what occurs outside. What depth of emotional and intellectual investment does the writer expect of the reader? The matter seems clearer initially in *Vanishing Point* (1986), which opens with a murder and proceeds as a mystery story, although one which concerns the identity of the victim rather than that of the murderer.[46]

> For the first time, at that moment, I dealt with an interrogative literature, the literature of the *giallo*, which I love deeply both in its more popular form – the crime stories that come out week by week – and in the high literary form, as is the case with the 'crime stories' written by Sciascia or Dürrenmatt.[47]

In *Vanishing Point*, Spino is an attendant in the mortuary to which the body is brought, and he even has the idiosyncratic, unsatisfactory relationship with Sara which is the lot of many fictional detectives, right up to Camilleri's Montalbano. He could be the dilettante investigator common enough in fiction, but it is Tabucchi himself who, in the postface, alerts the reader to the connection between his name and that of Spinoza.[48] Spino's interest in establishing the identity of the victim is in line with the tendency of many Italian writers to place the focus away from the standard whodunnit interest and to play with or parody its normal central concerns. In *Vanishing Point*, the real focus is not on the investigation but on the investigator and his motivations. The object of the quest is given only his own alias of Carlo Nobodi, and it becomes clear that Spino is not moved by human compassion for an anonymous statistic in lists of the urban disappeared, nor is he engaged with a quest for truth, for the restoration of a fractured order or for justice for a victim of gang violence, but by something more subtle relating to his own psyche and identity. 'The dissonance of ambiguity pursues even Tabucchi's investigators,' writes Monica Jansen, and clarity is not forthcoming.[49] Spino is asked continually why he should care about the fate of this man who was unknown to him, and after looking at a photograph, Sara suggests that the victim looks like Spino when he was twenty years younger.[50] If the victim is nobody – or Nobodi – is the investigator investigating himself? The city may be Genoa, but there hangs over it an unfocused sense of sin or guilt, but a guilt that can be neither expunged nor expiated, only dramatized.[51] There is no water that can cleanse the offence, which is ultimately that of being human. In an age in which logic and coherence have been dispersed, one of the enriching aspects of the crime story is that it can perform a multitude of functions once covered by reputedly higher genres of literature.

Requiem (Portuguese version 1991, Italian publication 1992), where the mystery to be solved concerns why Isabella killed herself, places readers of detective fiction on seemingly familiar ground.[52] The enigma is discussed by two men who had been close friends and her lovers, and although they discuss the matter amicably, one of them, Tadeus Waclaw, is dead and buried. Death is no obstacle to conversation, or even to enjoying wholesome Portuguese cuisine, but if Tadeus cannot satisfy the narrator's curiosity, he has a suggestion: ask her yourself. In his enquiry, the narrator visits a lighthouse to which he had come previously to write a novel years ago, but he is now afflicted by a doubt over why he had bothered to write at all: 'I wondered why I was writing, my story was an odd one, a story with no solution, how had the idea of writing a story like that come into my mind'.[53] The writer deciphers rather than investigates, as is expressed emblematically by the reflections aroused in the narrator by Hieronymus Bosch's painting of *The Temptations of St Antony*. No single scene in Tabucchi is so rich with multiple layers of metaphorical significance as this contemplation of Bosch's canvas as a repository of meaning. The narrator comes across a man copying not the whole painting but the detail of a plump man and an elderly woman seated astride a flying fish: the detail was a 'monstrosity which underlined the monstrosity of the scene' (p. 74). The man engaged in producing the copy explains: 'Life is strange and in life strange things occur, in addition this painting is strange and in itself produces strange things.'[54] The vocabulary is simple, but the implications of the words for life and for fictions which seek to meditate on human life are profound. The strangeness of life means that there can be no final unravelling, no revelation of order.

Leonardo Sciascia: justice denied

In an interview, Leonardo Sciascia offered critics an assessment of his own *oeuvre* by recalling that André Malraux had once described William Faulkner's writing as representing the 'intrusion of Greek tragedy into the detective story': he went on to express regret that no one had noted that he himself had 'introduced Pirandellian drama into the detective story'.[55] The Pirandellian drama and the detective story are seemingly incompatible categories, based on differing philosophies, but these are part of a series of clashing dialectical principles that underwrite Sciascia's idiosyncratic mindset and hence his *giallo*. Pirandellian drama, most notably *Right You Are (If You Think So!)*, advances the notion that truth is personal or unknowable, that relativism is all and that inquiries to establish a truth behind appearances are futile.[56] The detective story, most obviously in its classic form, dramatizes the process by which an investigator sweeps aside lies, deceit and subterfuge to establish not a truth but the truth. At the same time, while Sciascia's admiration for Pirandello was unbounded, it was balanced by his regard for the French Enlightenment and for Voltaire in particular. That Voltaire's thought was itself imbued with scepticism is beyond debate, but it was not that aspect but rather his ethical passion which aroused Sciascia's respect. It is no accident that the corrupt judge, Riches, in *To Each His Own*, was composing a refutation of Voltaire's *Traité sur la tolérance à l'occasion de la mort de Jean Calas* when the detective Rogas went to interrogate him about a possible miscarriage of justice, a possibility which the judge dismissed a priori as incompatible with the very idea of administrative justice.[57] In Sciascia, the (Voltairean) ethical passion sits uncomfortably alongside the (Pirandellian) scepticism, but the force of both is undeniable. Nowhere is this clash more apparent than in the conflict between his overriding belief in justice and his distrust, deeply embedded in the Sicilian tradition, of the figure of the judge, seen in other European cultures as the embodiment of justice. 'I believe in human reason, and in liberty and justice which flow from reason', he wrote in the introduction to his first book, *The Parishes of Regalpetra*, a statement of the intellectual and moral credo underpinning all his work,[58] but his books are also filled with expressions of an antipathy, deeper than dismay at incidental episodes of corruption, for the judicial figure. In *One Way or Another*, the detective-narrator engages the highly cultured priest, don Gaetano, in conversation on the impact of the evangelical precept, 'do not judge that you may not be judged', as a seeming rejection by Christian doctrine of the function of the judge. Elsewhere he calls on the great name of Cervantes to strengthen the incomprehension of the judge common, Sciascia writes, in Sicily, where understanding a judge who imprisons another out of self-interest is easier than understanding a judge who punishes another towards whom he nurtures no animosity. Such passages revealing a scornful attitude towards judges could be multiplied.[59]

Sciascia's *oeuvre* could be divided into two categories, fiction and a more individual genre which can only be referred to as the *inchiesta*, literally 'inquiry'.[60] The *inchiesta* normally takes as its starting point some disputed, controversial or scandalous event from history, and on the basis of documentary evidence and reflection on them, the author deconstructs the official version and reconstructs a more plausible, if heterodox, view of the facts. The majority of Sciascia's fictional works are *gialli*, so it can be said that the inquiry is the dominant form in both categories of his writing. The central paradox is that Sciascia was engaged in a search for truth and for justice, even if an innate pessimism and an attachment to Pirandello had convinced him that such virtues did not exist or could not be realized. No conciliation of these positions is possible, but Sciascia lived happily with an awareness of his own contradictions and never ceased denouncing, both in fiction and in more factual writing, the abuses of power he saw in society. By his own account, what differentiated him from Pirandello was that he (Sciascia) did not have a 'great creative imagination', so that for him 'between real life and the sheet of paper the distance was small and break was extremely slight'.[61] The novel and the *inchiesta* had common traits and comparable themes, but in fiction the 'discourse of the detective novel, this form of account that tends towards the factual truth and to the denunciation of the guilty', always attracted him, but he added significantly that 'it is not always possible to find the guilty party'.[62]

In Sciascia's detective story, the guilty party is normally, but not invariably, identified but is never handed over to justice. The typical detective is the policeman who had hoped to be a lawyer and who retains a passionate belief in law, but who sees his efforts and his aspirations frustrated by the machinations of the apparatus of power. It is helpful to divide Sciascia's *gialli* into two periods. There are common themes in the first four: *The Day of the Owl* (1961), *To Each his Own* (1966), *Equal Danger* (1971), *One Way or Another* (1974). Sciascia returned to the detective story with *1912 +1* (1986), followed by *Open Doors* (1987), *The Knight and Death* (1988) and finally *A Straightforward Tale* (1989). Claude Ambroise, Sciascia's favourite critic, was convinced that there was a metaphysical dimension in all his *gialli*, in the sense that Sciascia transformed the crime writer's question – who did it? – into the metaphysician's question: why death?[63] In my view, while Sciascia's *gialli* show a marked move towards the metaphysical and his policemen do increasingly become 'God's policemen', this metaphysical dimension develops over time, and is not a constant of his fiction. Sciascia's *gialli* are an amalgam of the Voltairean *conte philosophique* and the moral tract that the crime story was in its origin, but the early novels focus on the social and the political, as is clear in Sciascia's own elucidation of his first novel. He was not an arrogant man, but he did boast that *The Day of the Owl* merited the title of the first 'non apologetic novel on the mafia in the history of Italian literature'.[64] The mafia is an invariable presence in his *gialli*, originally in its literal form but latterly in a metaphorical guise.

Part of the impulse to re-form the detective story, apparent from the outset, derived from his need to find a means of depicting the corruption introduced into social and political life mores by mafia power. *The Day of the Owl* opens, in the classical style, with a murder committed in a small Sicilian village, but the investigation sees the honest policeman, Captain Bellodi, pitted not only against a criminal organization but also against the *omertà* (code of silent noncompliance) of the community and against the hostility of holders of power in the Church and state. Of itself, that reality necessitates a change in the structure of the detective story. Whereas the classical detective novel has a unilinear structure of crime-investigation-unmasking, with society ranged alongside the investigator, the conditions of Sicilian society meant that society stood alongside the criminal, leaving the detective isolated. *The Day of the Owl* has a bilinear structure in which the efforts of the policeman are frustrated by the unnamed authorities whose conversations and phone calls are aimed at ensuring that Bellodi's investigations are frustrated. The novel reaches its climax with the interrogation of the local mafia boss, Don Mariano Arena, by Bellodi, a dialogue which later aroused polemics when the novelist Sebastiano Vassalli wrote that the tones of the encounter revealed Sciascia's equivocation towards, or even covert admiration for, the mafia.[65] While that view is difficult to support, it is true that Arena has a flesh-and-blood energy that the idealized Bellodi lacks. The machinations of the powerful ensure that Arena is freed, but the nature of his responsibility will be clear to the reader, who will never be permitted to fall into that state of passivity which in his *Brief History of the Detective Novel* Sciascia had identified as the ideal state of mind for the reader of such fiction.

To Each his Own, perhaps Sciascia's finest novel and one with overtones not only of Pirandello but also of Vitaliano Brancati, still deals with the mafia in a local setting. The investigator, Laurana, is a dilettante, a teacher brought into the case by accident and displaying that bumbledom and proneness to error which are characteristics of many postmodern crime stories. There are in this novel elements of Brancatian eroticism uncommon in Sciascia, who was not at ease in the depiction of female characters. Laurana falls for the snares of the female suspect, and it is he who is eliminated, leaving the guilty couple, with the full approval of the Church and state, in possession of goods and reputation. The closing judgement on Laurana – he was a cretin – is tantalizingly ambiguous.[66] Is it a dismissal of the deficiencies of the unfortunate Laurana, or a judgement of a cynical society which sneers at honesty and fawns on unscrupulous hierarchies of the powerful?

Sciascia became increasingly concerned with questions of power, whether in politics, in the Church, in industry or in justice and the courts, and his subsequent detective novels represent an inquiry into a metaphorical mafia that has occupied the upper echelons of seemingly democratic societies. *Equal Danger* appeared during Italy's terrorist emergency and features the murder of a succession of judges, presumably by a victim of a miscarriage of justice, but the waters are muddied by the anxious political authorities who, in an attempt to shore up their own position, use dissident groups as scapegoats. Once again, it is the investigator, Rogas, who is slain, presumably after killing the leader of the opposition party, a lightly disguised form of Italy's communist party. In the following novel, *One Way or Another*, as in Gadda, it is not possible to identify with certainty the murderer. This rich, enigmatic novel sees the learned, charismatic priest Don Gaetano gather together in a retreat house the wealthy and influential members of society. The artist-narrator engages Don Gaetano in conversation on recondite theological points and erudite artistic matters while members of the group are gunned down by an assassin whose motives are unclear. If justice is done in these novels, it is not executed through the orthodox judicial institutions, but by the actions of a figure similar to the *giustiziere*, common in popular fiction from *The Count of Monte Cristo* onwards, the dedicated individual who acts on his own but in the interests of ethical justice to right wrongs perpetrated by those who see themselves as above the law.

Sciascia abandoned the *giallo* for some years, only returning to it in 1986 with *1912 +1* and *Open Doors*, works that rely on investigation but which occupy some uncertain place on the fact-fiction spectrum. *The Knight and Death* takes the detective story into a new dimension. The title refers to a mysterious etching by Dürer showing a knight on horseback with a demonic figure at his side and a castle on a hill in the middle distance. A copy of this work is in the possession of the detective, known only as the Deputy, and inspires his thinking as he conducts his investigations into a spate of killings claimed by the *Boys of '89*. But which '89? The year in the twentieth-century or the year of the French Revolution? The Deputy is himself, like Sciascia at the time of writing, suffering from cancer which he knows to be terminal, so discussions on the likely identity and motivations of the terrorist group and their role as useful idiots for the authorities are interspersed with ontological reflections on the imminence of death. Justice is a fading dream in a world ruled by cynical puppet-masters. Sciascia's fiction closed with the denial of justice in the posthumous *A Straightforward Tale*, a deftly structured tale of drug dealing by a gang including a priest and a senior police officer, uncovered futilely by a junior officer who knows that the gang will enjoy immunity.

None of these writers has founded a school, but their works have ensured that the *giallo* has a respected place in the canon of Italian writing.

Extract from Leonardo Sciascia's *The Knight and Death*

'For what it is worth, and personally I believe it to be worth very little, I may be able to give you one.' He remained silent for some time, leaving the Chief in a state of anxiety which to the Deputy appeared too clearly expressed to be true: just as the president's face also turned too excessively expressive: with the promise of what he was about to reveal and, simultaneously, with regret for the puny content of the revelation itself. And indeed: 'It is not that it seems to me a line of enquiry with any real foundation; in fact it seems to me more of a joke: poor Sandoz too spoke of it as a joke . . .' (Another joke, thought the Deputy, these people spend their lives making jokes.) 'No later than yesterday evening, as we were making our way out of the restaurant, he told me he had received a threatening telephone call – perhaps one, perhaps more than one, I can't recall – from a . . . let me try to remember from whom, because it couldn't be . . . the words coming into my head right this moment are . . . *the Boys of Ninety-nine* . . . That can't be right: *the Boys of Ninety-nine* were the ones who were called up after Caporetto in 1917: "the Piave was murmuring", and all that . . . Anyone of those boys still alive would be nearly ninety today: and in any case, it would be a reference to an indecently patriotic event . . . No, no, it couldn't be . . . Let me think . . .' They let him think, until they saw his face light up with the relocated memory. 'That's it: *the Boys of Eighty-nine*, I think . . . yes, eighty-nine . . . But not the boys, now that I think of it: the children, perhaps . . .'

'The Children of Eighty-nine,' the Chief savoured the words, but found there the bitterness of incomprehension. 'Eighty-nine, then. The children of the present year – 1989.'

The Deputy, who, observing the outcome of the President's efforts of memory, had thought that it would have been much easier to remember the year Eighty-nine, since only a very few days had passed since the New Year festivities, than the year Ninety-nine for all its associations with the Piave, found himself saying: '1789, more likely. A wonderful idea, that.'

Neither the President nor the Chief found this intrusion to their liking. 'You are always obsessed with history,' said the Chief. And the President said, 'What idea?'

'That notion of Eighty-nine. Where else does the idea of revolution spring from if not from that year? It does not take much now to admit that, as they used to say of a certain drink – it was the first and remains the best . . . yes, quite wonderful.'

'Wonderful is hardly the word I would use.' The President gestured as though swatting a troublesome fly.

Leonardo Sciascia, *The Knight and Death*, trans. Joseph Farrell
(Manchester: Carcanet, 1991), pp. 8–9.

Notes

1. Leonardo Sciascia, 'Breve storia del romanzo poliziesco', now in Claude Ambroise (ed.) *Opere*, 11 (Milan: Bompiani, 1989), pp. 1181–96. All references to Sciascia will be by volume and page to that edition. This essay has not been published in English.

2. Sciascia, 'Letteratura del giallo', *Letteratura*, 1/3 (1953), 2–11, and 'Appunti sul giallo', *Nuova Corrente*, 1/1, (1954), 19–28.

3. My translation. 'Quel grande romanzo poliziesco': *Opere*, 2, p. 1187.

4. Emilio De Marchi, *Il cappello del prete* (Milan: Gammarò, 2006).

5. My translation. 'La fuga dei pensieri. Nel senso più proprio della parola, passatempo; Il buon lettore sa . . . che il divertimento, il passatempo consiste nella condizione – di assoluto riposo intellettuale – di affidarsi all'investigatore, alla sua eccezionale capacità di ricostruire un crimine e di raggiungerne l'autore': Sciascia, *Opere*, 2, p. 1182.

6. My translation. 'Nella sua forma più originale e autonoma, il romanzo poliziesco presuppone una metafisica: l'esistenza di un mondo "al di là del fisico", di Dio, della Grazia, di quella Grazia che i teologi chiamano illuminante. Della Grazia illuminante l'investigatore si può anzi considerare il portatore, così come santa Lucia nella *Divina Commedia*': Sciascia, *Opere*, 11, p. 1183.

7. G. K. Chesterton, *The Defendant* (London: Methuen, 1901), pp. 161–2.

8. Antonio Gramsci, *Selections from Cultural Writings*, ed. David Forgacs and Geoffrey Nowell-Smith (London: Lawrence and Wishart, 1985), pp. 369–74. The original sections are to be found in Antonio Gramsci, *Quaderni dal carcere*, ed. Vittorio Gerretana (Turin: Einaudi, 1975), pp. 697–9, chapter 21, sections 12 and 13.

9. Gramsci, *Quaderni*, pp. 697 and 699. See also Giuseppe Petronio, 'Sulle tracce del giallo', *Delitti di carta*, 1 (October 1997), 56–7.

10. My translation. 'Possiamo ancora identificare il piacevole con il non artistico?' Umberto Eco, 'Il testo, il piacere, il consumo', in *Sugli specchi e altri saggi* (Milan: Bompiani, 1985), p. 108.

11. My translation. 'Mente indubbiamente mediocre': Sciascia, *Opere*, 2, p. 1188.

12. My translation. 'Non mi restava che scegliere (tra i modelli di trama) quella più metafisica e filosofica, il romanzo poliziesco': Umberto Eco, *Postille a Il nome della rosa*, p. 524.

[13] Christopher Booker, *The Seven Basic Plots* (London: Continuum, 2004), pp. 69–87.

[14] Carlo Emilio Gadda, *Quer pasticciaccio brutto de Via Merulana* (Milan: Garzanti, 1957); *That Awful Mess on Via Merulana*, trans. William Weaver (London: Quartet Books, 1985); 'Il piú assoluto "giallo" che sia mai stato scritto: un "giallo" senza soluzione': Sciascia, *Opere*, 2, p. 1196.

[15] The five episodes appeared in *Letteratura*, vols 26–31 (1946–7).

[16] 'Tutti ormai lo chiamavano don Ciccio': *Quer pasticciaccio*, p. 5

[17] Carlo Emilio Gadda, *Novella seconda* (Milan: Garzanti, 1971), p. 163.

[18] 'Romanzesco, interessante, conandoyliano: il pubblico lo sa a memoria e non ci si diverte piú. Non è detto che la vita sia sempre semplice, piana, piatta. Talora è complicatissima e romanzesca': the note is quoted in full in Elisabetta Bolla, *Come leggere Quer pasticciaccio brutto de Via Merulana di Carlo Emilio Gadda* (Milan: Mursia, 1976).

[19] Italo Calvino, introduction to *That Awful Mess*, p. v.

[20] 'Per enunciare qualche teorica idea (idea generale, s'intende) sui casi degli uomini: e delle donne. A prima vista, cioè al primo udirle, sembravano banalità. Non erano banalità': *That Awful Mess*, p. 4; *Quer pasticciaccio brutto*, p. 6.

[21] 'Diceva anche nodo o groviglio, o garbuglio, o gnommero, che alla Romana vuol dire gomitolo': *That Awful Mess*, p. 5; *Quer pasticciaccio brutto*, p. 7.

[22] Robert S. Dombroski, *Properties of Writing* (Baltimore: John Hopkins University Press, 1994), p. 125.

[23] 'Indagine dentro il *disordine*, come processo di ristabilimento di un *ordine*': Gian Carlo Ferretti, *Ritratto di Gadda* (Bari-Rome: Laterza, 1987), p. 118.

[24] Sciascia, *Porte aperte*, now in *Opere*, 3.

[25] 'L'emblema assoluto dell'insensatezza del mondo e della stupidità degli uomini': Ferretti, *Ritratto*, p. 118.

[26] See Giuseppe Papponetti, '"Fusse quisse l'assassine?" Per il finale del "Pasticciaccio" gaddiano', *The Edinburgh Journal of Gadda Studies* (2004), 1–12.

[27] Il *Pasticciaccio*, 'ho troncato apposta a metà perché il "giallo" non deve essere trascinato come certi gialli artificiali che vengono poratati avanti fino alla nausea e finiscono per stancare la mente del lettore. Ma io lo considero finito . . . letterariamente concluso. Il poliziotto sa chi è l'assassino e questo basta': Dacia Maraini, interview now in *E tu chi eri?* (Milan: Bompiani, 1973), p. 45.

[28] Umberto Eco, *Il nome della rosa* (Milan: Bompiani, 1980); English version, *The Name of the Rose*, trans. William Weaver (London: Secker and Warburg, 1983).

[29] Peter Bondanella, *Umberto Eco and the Open Text* (Cambridge: Cambridge University Press, 1997), p. 126.

[30] Rocco Capozzi, 'Interpretation and overinterpretation: the rights of texts, readers and implied authors', in Rocco Capozzi (ed.) *Reading Eco: An Anthology* (Bloomington and Indianapolis: Indiana University Press, 1997), p. 226.

[31] See Margherita Ganeri, *'Il nome della rosa': una strategia di successo* (Marina di Belvedere: Grisolia editore, 1990).

[32] Eco, *The Name of the Rose*, p. 316; 'Di fronte ad un libro non dobbiamo chiederci cosa dice, ma cosa vuole dire': *Il nome della rosa*, p. 319.

[33] Ibid., p. 317; 'L'idea è segno delle cose, e l'immagine è segno dell'idea, segno di un segno': *Il nome della rosa*, p. 319.

[34] Ibid., p. 392. All references are to this edition and are included in parentheses in the text.

[35] Antonio Tabucchi, *Notturno indiano* (Palermo: Sellerio, 1984). All references are to this edition and are included in parentheses in the text. *Indian Nocturne*, trans. Tim Parks (London: Chatto and Windus, 1988). All translations from Tabucchi are mine.

[36] Antonio Tabucchi, *Sostiene Pereira* (Milan: Feltrinelli, 1994). *Declares Pereira*, trans. Patrick Creagh (London: Harvill, 1995).

[37] 'Ho poi utilizzato questo modello (quello del romanzo poliziesco) anche in *Pereira*, che in fondo è un romanzo giallo, con la struttura di una storia poliziesca, modellata secondo un riferimento a un'autorità, secondo quel motivo di ricerca e di interrogazione che è caratteristica della letteratura poliziesca': quoted in Giuliana Pieri, 'Il nuovo giallo italiano: tra tradizione e postmodernità', *Delitti di carta*, 6 (June 2000), 56. Original quote taken from *Conversazione con Antonio Tabucchi. Dove va il il romanzo?* (Rome: Omicron, 1995).

[38] 'Le polar aussi prend beaucoup d'importance et j'ai beaucoup lu Simenon, que je considère comme un grand romancier': interview, 'Antonio Tabucchi, la quête d'un détective métaphysique', *Le matricule des anges*, 7 (April–June 1994), 4–7.

[39] 'I dodici capitoli si presentano come frammenti-abbozzo divergenti di un romanzo da fare, in una successione in cui ognuno sintetizza un percorso interrotto di scrittura di un genere letterario adottato e poi dimesso: dal genere poliziesco al genere spionistico, dal genere filosofico-morale a quello picaresco, modellandosi a turno su un *Siddharta* di Hesse, su un *Lord Jim* di Conrad, su uno Sherlock Holmes di Conan Doyle o su un *On The Road* di Jack Kerouac, in ogni caso mettendo in evidenza l'instabilità dello stesso gioco della finzione al proprio interno, nei propri meccanismi di scomposizione o ricomposizione': Claudio Pezzin, *Antonio Tabucchi* (Verona: Cierre edizioni, 2000), p. 43.

[40] *Notturno indiano*, p. 80.

[41] Mircea Eliade, *Le sacré et le profane* (Paris: Gallimard, 1965), especially chapter four.

[42] Antonio Tabucchi, *I volatili del Beato Angelico* (Palermo: Sellerio, 1987), pp. 42–53.

[43] *Notturno indiano*, p. 102.

[44] 'Tabucchi si pone anche in prima persona come figura plurima': Anna Dolfi, *Tabucchi: la specularità, il rimorso* (Rome: Bulzoni, 2006), p. 17.

[45] 'Forse non sono un buon detective. Vede sono sempre stato attratto da storie che si presentanto come sciarade, da storie incongrue, difficili da collegare in un nesso logico, ma la mia capacità di indagine si arresta ad un certo punto. Forse la mia è una sotteranea sfiducia nella ragione': Antonio Tabucchi, in *Gazzetta di Pesaro*, 12 July 1992, quoted by Dolfi, *Tabucchi*, p. 125.

[46] Antonio Tabucchi, *Il filo dell'orizzonte* (Milan: Feltrinelli, 1986); *Vanishing Point*, trans. Tim Parks (London: Chatto and Windus, 1989).

[47] 'Per la prima volta, in quel momento, mi sono confrontato con una letteratura interrogativa, quella gialla, che io amo molto sia nella sua forma più popolare – i gialli che escono settimanalmente – che in quella di alto livello letterario come potrebbere essere i "gialli" scritti da Sciascia o Dürrenmatt': Pieri, 'Il nuovo giallo italiano', p. 56.

[48] *Vanishing Point*, p. 107.

[49] 'La dissonanza dell'equivoco insegue anche i personaggi investigatori di Tabucchi': Monica Jansen, 'Tabucchi: molteplicità e rovescio', in Nathalie Roelens and Inge Lanslots (eds), *Piccole finzioni con importanza: valori della narrativa italiana contemporanea* (Ravenna: Longo, 1993), p. 138. See also Tiziana Arvigo, 'From *Notturno indiano* to *Il filo dell'orizzonte*: "Landscape of Absence" and "Landscape of Disappearance"', in Bruno Ferraro and Nicole Prunster (eds), *Antonio Tabucchi: A Collection of Essays* (Melbourne: Spunti e Ricerche, 1996–7), pp. 99–109.

[50] *Vanishing Point*, p. 32.

[51] See Dolfi, Tabucchi, p. 239–42.

[52] Antonio Tabucchi, *Requiem*, trans. from Portuguese Sergio Vecchio (Milan: Feltrinelli, 1992); *Requiem*, trans. Margaret Jull Costa (London: Chatto and Windus, 1994).

[53] 'Mi chiedevo perché stessi scrivendo, la mia storia era una storia balorda, una storia senza soluzione, come mi era venuto in mente di scrivere una storia del genere': *Requiem*, p. 90. All references are to this edition and are included in parentheses in the text.

[54] 'Una mostruosità che sottolineava la mostruosità della scena. La vita è strana e nella vita capitano strane cose, inoltre questo quadro è strano e di per sé produce cose strane': ibid., pp. 74 and 75.

[55] 'L'intrusione della tragedia greca nel romanzo poliziesco. Si potrebbe dire di me che ho introdotto il dramma pirandelliano nel romanzo poliziesco': Leonardo Sciascia, *La Sicilia come metafora: intervista di Marcelle Padovani* (Milan: Mondadori, 1979), p. 88.

[56] Sciascia wrote many books, pamphlets and articles on Pirandello, while references to him are to be found in many of his works. See, in particular, *Pirandello e il Pirandellismo* (1953), *Pirandello e la Sicilia* (1961), both now in *Opere*, 3. See also the posthumous 'Pirandello, mio padre', in *MicroMega*, 1 (1989), 31–51.

[57] Leonardo Sciascia, *Il contesto*, now in *Opere*, 2, pp. 66–79.

[58] 'Credo nella ragione umana e nella libertà e nella giustizia che dalla ragione scaturiscono': Sciascia, *Le parrocchie di Regalpetra*, in *Opere*, 1, p. 9.

[59] See for instance *Opere*, 3, pp. 847–8.

[60] See Anne Mullen, *Inquisition and Inquiry: Sciascia's* Inchiesta (Market Harborough: Troubador, 2000).

[61] 'Non ho una grande fantasia creatrice. I miei eroi sono il contrario di quelli di Pirandello: tra la vita reale e il foglio di carta la distanza è minima, lo scarto lievissimo': Sciascia, *La Sicilia come metafora*, p. 63.

[62] 'Utilizzo spesso il "discorso" del romanzo poliziesco, questa forma di resoconto che tende alla verità dei fatti e alla denuncia del colpevole, anche se non sempre il colpevole si riesce a trovarlo': ibid., p. 88.

[63] 'Le romancier traduit en un 'qui l'a tué', l'interogation du métaphysicien: pourquoi la mort?': Claude Ambroise, 'Les traces de vie', *L'arc*, 77 (n.d.), 20.

[64] 'Io, che, primo nella storia della letteratura italiana, avevo dato rappresentazione non apologetica del fenomeno mafioso': Leonardo Sciascia, *A futura memoria*, now in *Opere*, 3, p. 769.

[65] Sebastiano Vassalli, 'Signora Mafia con gli occhi della Medusa', *La Repubblica*, 7 August 1992. See also Massimo Onofri, *Storia di Sciascia* (Bari-Rome: Laterza, 1994), p. 108.

[66] 'Era un cretino': *Opere*, 1, p. 887.

Bibliography

Works by Eco

Eco, Umberto, *Il nome della rosa* (Milan: Bompani, 1980); *The Name of the Rose*, trans. William Weaver (London: Secker and Warburg, 1992).

——, *Sugli specchi e altri saggi* (Milan: Bompiani, 1985).

——, *Il pendolo di Foucault* (Milan: Bompiani, 1988); *Foucault's Pendulum*, trans. William Weaver (London: Secker and Warburg, 1989).

Works by Gadda

Gadda, Carlo Emilio, *Quer pasticciaccio brutto de Via Merulana* (Milan: Garzanti, 1957);
 That Awful Mess on Via Merulana, trans. William Weaver (London: Quartet Books, 1985).
——, *Novella seconda* (Milan: Garzanti, 1971).

Works by Sciascia

Sciascia's works are now collected in Claude Ambroise (ed.), *Opere*, vols 1–11 (Milan:
 Bompiani, 1987–91).
Sciascia, Leonardo, 'Letteratura del giallo', *Letteratura*, 1/3 (1953), 2–11.
——, 'Appunti sul giallo', *Nuova Corrente*, 1/1 (1954), 19–28.
——, 'Pirandello, mio padre', in *MicroMega*, 1 (1989).
Colquhoun, Archibald and Arthur Oliver, trans., *The Day of the Owl* (London: Jonathan
 Cape, 1963).
Farrell, Joseph, trans., *The Knight and Death* (Manchester: Carcanet, 1991).
——, trans., *A Straightforward Tale* (Manchester: Carcanet, 1991).
Foulke, Adrienne, trans., *To Each His Own* (London: Jonathan Cape, 1968).
——, trans., *Equal Danger* (London: Jonathan Cape, 1973).
Jones, Marie, trans., *Open Doors* (Manchester: Carcanet, 1991).
Rabinovich, Sacha, trans., *One Way or Another* (Manchester: Carcanet, 1987).
——, *1912+1* (Manchester: Carcanet, 1989).

Works by Tabucchi

Tabucchi, Antonio, *Notturno indiano* (Palermo: Sellerio, 1984); *Indian Nocturne*, trans.
 Tim Parks (London: Chatto and Windus, 1988).
——, *Il filo dell'orizzonte* (Milan: Feltrinelli, 1986); *Vanishing Point*, trans. Tim Parks
 (London: Chatto and Windus, 1989).
——, *I volatili del Beato Angelico* (Palermo: Sellerio, 1987).
——, *Requiem*, trans. from Portuguese Sergio Vecchio (Milan: Feltrinelli, 1992); *Requiem*,
 trans. Margaret Jull Costa (London: Chatto and Windus, 1994).
——, *Sostiene Pereira* (Milan: Feltrinelli, 1994); *Declares Pereira*, trans. Patrick Creagh
 (London: Harvill, 1995).

Works by other authors

Ambroise, Claude, *Invito alla lettura di Sciascia* (Milan: Mursia, 1974).
——, 'Les traces de vie', *L'arc*, 77, 20.
Bolla, Elisabetta, *Come leggere Quer pasticciaccio brutto de Via Merulana di Carlo Emilio
 Gadda* (Milan: Mursia, 1976).
Bondanella, Peter, *Umberto Eco and the Open Text* (Cambridge: Cambridge University
 Press, 1997).
Booker, Christopher, *The Seven Basic Plots* (London: Continuum, 2004).
Capozzi, Rocco (ed.), *Reading Eco: An Anthology* (Bloomington and Indianapolis: Indiana
 University Press, 1997).
Cattanei, Luigi, *Carlo Emilio Gadda* (Florence: Le Monnier, 1975).
Chesterton, G. K., *The Defendant* (London: Methuen, 1901).

De Marchi, Emilio, *Il cappello del prete* (Milan: Gammarò, 2006).

Dolfi, Anna, *Tabucchi: la specularità, il rimorso* (Rome: Bulzoni, 2006).

Farrell, Joseph, *Leonardo Sciascia* (Edinburgh: Edinburgh University Press, 1995).

Ferraro, Bruno and Nicole Prunster (eds), *Antonio Tabucchi: A Collection of Essays* (Melbourne: Spunti e Ricereche, 1996–7).

Ferrero, Ernesto, *Invito alla lettura di Carlo Emilio Gadda* (Milan: Mursia, 1972).

Ganeri, Margherita, *Il nome della rosa* (Marina di Belvedere: Grisolia Editore, 1990).

Gramsci, Antonio, *Quaderni dal carcere*, ed. Vittorio Gerretana (Turin: Einaudi, 1975).

——, *Selections from Cultural Writings*, ed. David Forgacs and Geoffrey Nowell-Smith (London: Lawrence and Wishart, 1985).

Jansen, Monica, 'Tabucchi: molteplicità e rovescio', in Nathalie Roelens and Inge Lanslots (eds), *Piccole finzioni con importanza: valori della narrativa italiana contemporanea* (Ravenna: Longo, 1993).

Maraini, Dacia, interview in *E tu chi eri?* (Milan: Bompiani, 1973).

Mullen, Anne, *Inquisition and Inquiry: Sciascia's Inchiesta* (Market Harborough: Troubador, 2000).

Onofri, Massimo, *Storia di Sciascia* (Bari-Rome: Laterza, 1994).

Pezzin, Claudio, *Antonio Tabucchi* (Verona: Cierre edizioni, 2000).

Petronio, Giuseppe, 'Sulle tracce del giallo', *Delitti di carta*, 1 (October 1997), 56–7.

Seroni, Adriano, *Carlo E Gadda* (Florence: La Nuova Italia, 1973).

Vassalli, Sebastiano, 'Signora Mafia con gli occhi della Medusa', *La Repubblica*, 7 August 1992.

5

The Mysteries of <u>Bologna</u>*: On Some Trends of the Contemporary* Giallo

LUCA SOMIGLI

The extraordinary popularity of detective fiction 'made in Italy' is one of the most striking and to a great extent puzzling characteristics of the landscape of Italian literature at the turn of the millennium. Rather suddenly, and for reasons that have not yet been fully historicized, by the mid-1990s the critical and popular attitude toward a genre that had heretofore been considered as pure entertainment that could properly be practised only by foreign writers was turned on its head as *gialli* by Italian authors began to crowd the bookstore and to sell in great numbers.[1] The 'caso Camilleri' was perhaps the most glaring example of the changed status of the genre: what distinguished the success of the Sicilian writer from that of previous authors who had enjoyed a brief moment of glory as the standard bearers of an Italian way to detective fiction – Scerbanenco in the late 1960s, Fruttero and Lucentini with *La donna della domenica* (1972; The Sunday Woman), Umberto Eco with *Il nome della rosa* (1980; The Name of the Rose) – was that in fact Camilleri's was not an isolated case. By the turn of the decade, other writers working within one of the many permutations of the genre came close to matching (and in some cases even surpassed) him in terms of sales and critical acclaim: Carlo Lucarelli, Massimo Carlotto, Marcello Fois, Gianrico Carofiglio, to name only a few. In a recent article, Bruno Pischedda has traced the origins of this decisive victory of the genre to the period between the late 1950s and the late 1970s.[2] Prima facie, Pischedda's claim may appear counter-intuitive, given the overall marginality of Italian detective fiction in that period (Scerbanenco is of course the exception that proves the rule), but it is ultimately valid: it was precisely in this twenty-year span that detective fiction became a serious object of critical enquiry and that an increasing number of already consecrated writers (notably, Mario Soldati, Leonardo Sciascia and Piero Chiara) turned to its structures and narrative strategies. Genre historian Roberto Pirani has likewise remarked on the importance of this transitional period and of the 1970s in particular: 'With Scerbanenco and starting from Scerbanenco the Italian *giallo* partially closed the gap between "high" and "low" literature, it offered new options to an often colourless literature now incapable of expressing in some way the problems of society.'[3] While critics debated the existence of an Italian tradition of detective fiction, a conspicuous number of writers (Pirani counts over 300 just in the 1970s) turned to the genre to tell stories that dealt increasingly with the social reality of the nation.

The seeds of the *giallo* as a 'new social novel' (to quote the title of a recent collection of essays)[4] which would bloom fully in the 1990s were sown in this period of relative obscurity.

The production of the 1960s and 1970s also brought to the foreground one of the salient characteristics of Italian detective fiction: its lack of an obvious centre. To be sure, over the years a good number of writers have turned to Milan, the industrial, economic and self-styled 'moral' capital of the nation, and to Rome, its political capital, to find the Italian equivalents of the *noir* cities of Anglo-American detective fiction or of the French *polar*.[5] However, an equally great number of writers have preferred to root their stories in other environments, including other large urban centres such as Turin, Florence or Naples, provincial towns such as Siena or Padua, or rural areas such as the Emilian countryside of Erasmo Baldini's fiction, carving out for their heroes a particular section of the peninsula, of which they explore, at times with almost anthropological precision, the various social milieus, traditions, cuisine, and so on. It has been suggested, and with good reason, that the constitutive cipher of Italian detective fiction might be precisely its 'poly-centric nature', which in fact mirrors that of the literary tradition *tout court*. In any case, this vocation to the local was recognized quite early on by critics of the genre, in particular by Massimo Carloni, who in 1994 gave to his *L'Italia in giallo*, an overview of the previous twenty-five years of detective fiction, the subtitle *Geografia e storia del giallo italiano* (Geography and History of the Italian *Giallo*).[6] In this context, the city that has emerged as the de facto 'capital' of the Italian *giallo* is an apparently unlikely candidate: Bologna, best known for its gastronomy, its ancient university and, until recently, its efficient left-wing administrations. In this essay, I will consider the works of some of the authors who have managed to consolidate the status of Bologna as the premier *noir* city in the country, and in the process I will also discuss some of the main trends of the contemporary *giallo*.[7]

The rise to murder mystery fame of Bologna began in 1974, when an unknown *giallista*, Loriano Macchiavelli (1934–) won second place in the first edition of the 'Premio Cattolica', an award for detective fiction, with a novel entitled *Le piste dell'attentato* (The Tracks of the Terrorist Attack), then published by the Milanese publisher Campironi in its short-lived, if forward-looking, series 'Gialli Italiani Calibro '90'. Macchiavelli, a master contractor for the Bologna city council, was well known in the fringe theatre circles of the region as a playwright and director with the Gruppo Teatrale Viaggiante, an amateur company that he had co-founded in 1960 and that specialized in political drama. In fact, the originality of his approach to the genre may result from the occasional nature of his turn to fiction. As Macchiavelli has declared on several occasions, he had previously been quite indifferent to detective fiction, and his first novel came about by accident: during a vacation in 1972 his wife Franca, a voracious consumer of mysteries, ran out of reading material and Macchiavelli decided to try his hand at writing one for her private entertainment.[8] Thus, not being particularly beholden to any of the established traditions of the genre, he was free of the influence of the great foreign masters and able to articulate his own vision. Indeed, what set apart the series begun with *Le piste dell'attentato* was precisely the utter disregard for most rules of the genre. Even in this early work, a number of elements stood out and marked the author as the most original voice in the landscape of the Italian *giallo* of the 1970s.

The first striking aspect of the novel, evident in its very title, was its close proximity to the political and social conflicts of the time. Following Scerbanenco, in the early 1970s other mystery writers – for instance, Massimo Felisatti, Fabio Pittorru, Franco Enna, Antonio Perria –had sought to renew the genre by injecting it with the hard-boiled realism and violence of the American *noir* and of Hollywood crime films, such as the paradigmatic *Dirty Harry* (1971), starring Clint Eastwood as Inspector Harry Callahan (in fact, the 1970s also saw the rise of the *poliziottesco*, or *poliziesco all'italiana*, a crime film genre characterized by a high degree of violence and by plots often inspired by current events). Bringing into their novels 'social crimes' such as organized crime, prostitution, drug-trafficking and 'sexual perversion', these writers attempted to show the dark side of the economic miracle, with its growing economic disparities and its marginalization of the poor and the underprivileged. The book that beat Macchiavelli's first novel in the 'Premio Cattolica' competition, Felisatti and Pittorru's *Violenza a Roma* (1974; Violence in Rome), is a good example of this trend. Based on the authors' successful television serial *Qui squadra mobile*, an attempt to transpose into an Italian context the procedural à la Ed McBain, the book portrayed Rome as a haven of dishonesty and crime, often hidden behind the façade of respectability of the arrogant professional and entrepreneurial bourgeoisie. The thin blue line is represented by the team of policemen led by the chief of the *squadra mobile* Antonio Carraro, who has the distinction of having achieved his position not through political connections and protection, but through his own merit as an investigator. Profoundly apolitical, or rather anti-political in the best tradition of the *poliziottesco*, in which tough but fair policemen are the only genuine and trustworthy components of an otherwise corrupt system (the politicians are in the pocket of big business, the judges are only concerned with their career and the form of the law, etc.), this narrative certainly had a kind of coarse, naive and even liberating unruliness. And yet, for all the references to well-known Italian landmarks and familiar sights the urban reality represented by Felisatti, Pittorru and their contemporaries remained profoundly indebted to its literary models, a sort of generic urban background for stories which, *mutatis mutandis*, could be set in McBain's fictional city Isola or in Simenon's Paris. From the beginning, Macchiavelli went much further. *Le piste dell'attentato* is not about some non-specific urban crime but rather deals with the issue that would emerge as perhaps the defining phenomenon of the 1970s: political terrorism (its year of publication, it is worth recalling, was 1974, so it might well be the first work of fiction on the subject).

The novel follows the investigation of the terrorist bombing of an army radio station on the hills overlooking Bologna, the prime suspect of which is Rosas, a young university student and far left-wing militant. The protagonist – Macchiavelli's best-known character and one of the most popular detectives in Italian fiction – is Sergeant Antonio Sarti, or rather, as he is usually called, Sarti Antonio, of the Questura of Bologna. The almost constant inversion of first and last name is of course meant to evoke the rituals of the bureaucracy that pervades all Italian institutions. Perhaps more importantly, the military rank of sergeant, which does not exist in the Italian police,[9] has no other function than to underline the subordinate position of our hero, constantly subjected to the mutable temper of his superior, Chief Inspector Raimondi Cesare. Unlike the tough cops of his contemporaries, Macchiavelli's humble *questurino* never rebels openly against the arrogance, stupidity and authoritarianism of his superior officer. Rather, he confines his objections to snide comments muttered under his breath or well out of Raimondi Cesare's earshot, and somatizes his frustration as a colitis that often forces him to repair to the nearest toilet in the middle of an investigation. Sarti's is literally a 'mestiere di merda' ('shitty job') – one of his favorite interjections – chosen not out of any sense of duty to society or desire for justice, but rather because, as he often repeats, it is 'a job like any other'.[10] Neither the thinking machine of classical detective fiction nor the cynical, tough-talking P.I. of the contemporary *noir*, Sarti is a hero by accident rather than inclination; first and foremost, he is intended to mirror the author's own lived experience, the real policemen that, Macchiavelli has said, 'I had met in the various police stations where I was often summoned because of the "political" theatre I used to do.'[11]

However, unlike much of the *giallo* of the 1970s, realism is not the constitutive element upon which the fiction is built. Rather, it is only the starting point for a strategy of deformation and estrangement that gives greater efficacy to the critical thrust of the fiction. In an interview, Macchiavelli said: 'I don't particularly like realism. Real facts are always my point of departure, but then I am for the grotesque, for a reversal, for what isn't there.'[12] Thus, his characters are often stylized figures, bundles of mannerisms through which the author portrays both the ideals and the limitations of the different sides of the social conflicts of his times (for instance Rosas, who becomes Sarti's regular sidekick, represents the aspirations of the student movement of the 1970s but is also a lucid critic of the political errors of the violence to which some turned in the so-called 'anni di piombo'). The most original instrument in Macchiavelli's strategy of grotesque 'reversal' is probably the narrator, a diegetically ambiguous figure whose personal history is closely patterned after that of the author and who is both actor and spectator of the events. He lacks the omniscience of the traditional third-person narrator (his point of view is emphatically subjective, and he often confesses his bafflement regarding the twists and turns of the investigation), but he also lacks the diegetic status of the typical first-person narrator, the Watson-like companion (he speaks to Sarti, who often answers back, but for the most is otherwise absent from the action, a ghost-like figure hovering above the story). Thus, the narrator does not perform any directorial function, organizing the narrative for the reader, but rather acts a sort of chorus, commenting on the action and even going off on polemical tangents in which he remarks, often sarcastically, on everything from his own misadventures to the decadence of political and social mores in modern-day Bologna. Most likely the product of Macchiavelli's own engagement with Brechtian pedagogical theatre, the narrator has the task of breaking the fourth wall of the narrative, of reminding readers of the constructed nature of a highly formalized genre such as the *giallo*, and of the larger socio-political implications of the apparently simple stories that unfold before them. Indeed, for Macchiavelli, the defining characteristic of the genre lies in its potential for social criticism. In an interview with Maria Agostinelli he has said: 'Detective fiction has always been a possible source of disturbance, a virus within the healthy body of literature, authorized to speak ill of the society within which it developed.'[13] Thus, nothing escapes the withering irony of the narrator, not even – indeed, especially – his protagonist.

In this context, the city of Bologna becomes an indispensable component of the narrative. Macchiavelli himself has remarked that one of his intentions was to trace the recent history of his hometown, then the crown jewel among the cities governed by the Communist party, and to cast a critical light on the self-complacency of its administrators and its inhabitants. The iconoclasm of the Sarti series was quickly recognized by the critics. In his introduction to a 1979 collection of Macchiavelli's early novels, Oreste Del Buono wrote:

> When he chose it, Bologna still affected the rhetoric of the red city where everything worked and everything went well . . . Bologna could manage to be red and fat at the same time. A sort of miracle, and an example for the whole of Italy . . . On the contrary, Macchiavelli sniffed out something else in Bologna, and threw his unusual character into the fray.[14]

What distinguishes Macchiavelli's approach to the setting is the fact that in his narrative Bologna is always and simultaneously generic and specific: in other words, while it may well serve as a synecdoche for Italian society, it is also and most importantly itself, rooted in a well-defined historical and geographical context which is often crucially linked to the investigation. Bologna extends vertically in time, a palimpsest of different historical moments reflected in the tangle of its streets, porticos or underground canals and in the patchwork of its neighborhoods, but it also expands horizontally, in space, in a complex relationship with the out-lying countryside, the mountains of the Tosco-Emilian Apennines, and the ambiguous in-between spaces of the newer working class or lower middle-class suburbs. Bologna is not a city, but rather a multiplicity of urban realities layered, often in a conflictual way, over the same physical space. The struggle at the core of much of Macchiavelli's narrative is between two conceptions of the city: on the one hand, a sometimes chaotic but vital space of diverse and multiple experiences; on the other, a cold and sterile urban environment regulated only by the imperatives of profit and efficiency that puts at risk the viability of any other form of social interaction. Indeed, if there are heroes in his fiction, they are not his various detectives, but rather those figures who represent dying ways of life, almost endangered species that no one seems interested in protecting. For instance, in *Cos'è accaduto alla signora perbene?* (1979; Whatever Happened to the Respectable Lady?) – where 'signora perbene' alludes not so much to any specific female figure but to the city itself – the old carter Treasse, whose very livelihood is threatened by a new by-law outlawing horse-drawn carts from entering the city centre, rises above all the other characters as the only morally righteous figure. In a scene that sees him pitted against the police, he is given an invective to match his actions:

> Do you know who built these buildings? Do you know? The cement, the sand for these buildings were brought here, from the bottom of the Reno river, by horses like my Bigio. And by my Bigio himself. Did you know? We built this city and now you can't stand us anymore? You can't stand the stink of horses.[15]

Macchiavelli's fondness for figures such as Treasse or for the places of old Bologna – the *osterie* (taverns), the old-fashioned artisan shops, the neighborhood markets – is not simply nostalgia for a simpler, more innocent way of life. Rather, such people and places are the physical embodiment of the history of the city, and their disappearance carries with it the danger of an almost wilful repression of that history – and indeed, of historical depth *tout court*.

For the same reason, in Macchiavelli's fiction crime must usually be understood in relation to the history of the people whose lives become enmeshed in it. The criminal act that shatters the apparently peaceful surface of present-day Bolognese life is frequently only the visible epiphenomenon of a more complex and repressed trauma which erupts suddenly and violently. In particular, the author returns insistently to the Fascist past as a source of these social neuroses. In *Le pista dell'attentato*, for example, the responsibility for the bombing lies not with left-wing anarchists but with a former militant of the Fascist Salò Republic and neo-Fascist sympathizer, in a manual example of what would become known as 'strategia della tensione' (strategy of tension), that is, the use of political terrorism by right-wing groups to foment a repressive reaction of the State against leftist movements. In his next work, *Fiori alla memoria* (1975; Flowers to the Memory), Macchiavelli delves even more deeply into the troubled legacy of Fascism and the Resistance, starting with a series of acts of vandalism against a monument to a group of fallen partisans and ending with the discovery of the identity of the traitor who caused their death. In *Sequenze di memoria* (1976; Fragments of Memory), his first non-Sarti novel, and perhaps his most ambitious early work, the author provocatively connects the cruelty of the Fascist past and the destructiveness of capitalist economy with the forced transformations of the way of life of entire communities during the 'economic miracle' of the 1950s and 1960s. In general, then, in Macchiavelli's fiction violence and death are the result of the refusal to come to terms with history, to understand and deal with the wounds left by it upon the social body. In more recent years, his exploration of modern Italian history through detective fiction has found new life in the extremely popular series featuring the Marshall of the Carabinieri Benedetto Santovito, written in collaboration with the singer and songwriter Francesco Guccini (1940–), with whom he shares a profound love for the local traditions of Emilia-Romagna. Begun in 1997 with *Macaronì*, the series, while set in the past, has dealt with topics that very much resonate with the present, such as the economic boom and its social repercussions or anti-immigrant sentiments.

In the 1980s, current events continued to provide fodder for Macchiavelli's imagination. From the famous murder of the art critic and university professor Francesca Alinovi in 1983 to the ferocious crimes of the gang of the 'Uno bianca', committed between 1987 and 1994 by a group of policemen[16] to, most famously and tragically, the terrorist bombing that destroyed the city train station on 2 August 1980, killing eighty-five people, Bologna becomes a veritable crossroad of Italian crime, belying the image of well-administered, comfortable and self-satisfied provincial city that Macchiavelli had been dismantling for years.[17] Indeed, in this period his fiction begins to lose some of its playfulness. The tone of the narrative becomes increasingly sombre, and Bologna more threatening and alien even – or perhaps especially – for those such as Sarti and the narrator (and Macchiavelli himself) who have lived through its transformation and have been changed by it. The protagonist's increasing sense of solitude and disillusionment positions some of the novels of this period close to the territory of the *noir*. The process culminates with *Stop per Sarti Antonio* (1987; Sarti Antonio is Stopped), in which the policeman is killed by an agent of the American secret services, John Smith, while investigating the connections of the services with the train station massacre. Free of his best-known character, the writer turned to the genre of the socio-political thriller with the trilogy *Funerale dopo Ustica* (1989; A Funeral after Ustica), *Strage* (1990; Massacre) – both published under the pseudonym of Jules Quicher – and *Un triangolo a quattro lati* (1992; A Four-sided Triangle), in which he tackled the two great civilian tragedies of the period, the station bombing (an obsessive topos in Italian detective fiction, and not only for Macchiavelli) and the explosion of an Itavia airplane off the coast of the island of Ustica on 27 June 1980, as well as the crisis of Italian communism after the fall of the Soviet Union. Even when he 'resurrected' Sarti, bowing, like Arthur Conan Doyle a century before him, to popular demand, Macchiavelli continued to probe into the social afflictions of the country and to derive his inspiration from the newspaper headlines, as in *Coscienza sporca* (1995; Dirty Conscience), in which, among other things, his humble cop has to come to terms with the corruption within the police revealed by the recent discovery of the identity of the 'Uno bianca' killers.

Almost from the beginning of his career as a *giallista*, Macchiavelli has also played an important role as a cultural organizer. As early as 1980, he was one of the founders as well as the author of the programmatic document of the group SIGMA (Scrittori italiani del giallo e del mistero associati), the first of a series of usually short-lived professional associations for the promotion and legitimization of the genre. The most successful of these initiatives was the formation, in the summer of 1990, of the 'Gruppo 13', a group of writers and illustrators based in Bologna and its environs which produced an important anthology, *I delitti del Gruppo 13* (The Crimes of the Gruppo 13) in 1991, and a collection of chapbooks in 1992.[18] While this experience also lasted a relatively short period of time, being effectively over by 1993, it constituted an important turning point for the genre, first of all because it influenced similar initiatives in other parts of Italy, such as Milan's 'Scuola dei Duri' founded by Andrea G. Pinketts in 1993, but also and perhaps most importantly because it provided a space of practice and experimentation for some of the most interesting genre writers of the new wave of the 1990s – figures like Carlo Lucarelli, Marcello Fois, Pino Cacucci, or Lorenzo Marzaduri. However, Macchiavelli's role was not merely that of organizer and promoter: rather, the increasingly cynical and sinister vision of Italian society and of Bologna in particular in his fiction of the 1980s set the stage for the more violent and disturbing urban reality of the authors of the Gruppo 13.

Among them, the versatile Carlo Lucarelli (1960–), who made his debut with the novel *Carta bianca* (Carte Blanche) in 1990, is perhaps best known to the general public for his very successful television programme *Blu Notte-Misteri italiani* (begun in 1998 with the title *Mistero in Blu*) in which he reconstructs through a skilful blend of narrative and documentary evidence the many mysteries of contemporary Italian society, from unsolved crimes such as the murder of writer and film-maker Pier Paolo Pasolini to more complex criminal phenomena such as the mafia or political violence in the 1970s. From the beginning, Lucarelli realized and vindicated the effectiveness of detective fiction as a tool for the exploration of the problems and dysfunctions of contemporary Italian society and he is, with Fois, Carlotto and a few others, the *caposcuola* of the new vision of the genre as a form of socially engaged fiction that, as we have mentioned, has contributed to its unprecedented success in the 1990s. Lucarelli's narrative has moved along two trajectories. The first is that of historical detective fiction or, to be precise, of detective fiction set during the Fascist period and its immediate aftermath. From *Carta bianca* to the more ambitious and less satisfying *L'isola dell'angelo caduto* (1999; The Island of the Fallen Angel), Lucarelli has turned the Fascist regime into the testing ground for a wide-ranging inquiry into 'the ethical question of the problematic relationship between truth and justice on the one hand and the logic of power on the other', as Elisabetta Bacchereti has written in her monograph on the author.[19] Set during the waning days of Mussolini's Repubblica Sociale Italiana, *Carta bianca* introduces one of Lucarelli's recurrent characters, police inspector De Luca, an intelligent and dedicated detective who is called upon to investigate the murder of Vittorio Rehinard, an ambiguous figure with powerful connections in the regime. Driven by his sense of professional responsibility, De Luca appears oblivious to his own entanglement with the society around him, believing – out of naivety more than bad faith – that his social role places him above the corruption of the times, protects him from the need to make clear moral choices and, in general, endows him with a sort of political neutrality. As the focus of the narrative shifts from the investigation of the crime to the detective and the ethical implications of his actions, he is forced to realize, with increasing genuine surprise, that his ambiguous position is in fact an untenable one. Thus, the solution of the mystery turns into a hollow victory, as De Luca finds himself caught between on the one hand the machinations of his Fascist superiors (which, among other things, result in the death of one of his men), and on the other the encroaching forces of the anti-Fascist Resistance, who see him merely as a Fascist collaborator. The chaos of the civil war does not offer any easy solutions or alibis. In the other two volumes of the De Luca trilogy, *L'estate torbida* (1991; The Damned Season) and *Via delle Oche* (1996), Lucarelli's project becomes more ambitious, as he paints an unflinching portrait of the moral disorder of the nation as it emerged from the war. Like the Macchiavelli of novels such as *Fiori alla memoria*, Lucarelli denounces the failure of the republic to deal with the legacy of its Fascist past. The issue is not only that no one seems to have paid for the crimes of Fascism – no Nuremberg trial forced Italians to work through their own involvement with the regime and, if anything, what prevailed was the self-absolving attitude epitomized by Benedetto Croce's explanation of Fascism as a 'parenthesis' in the course of history – but also and perhaps most importantly that the new nation inherited the regime's corrupt view of politics as a means of social control and accumulation of power rather than service to citizens.

Lucarelli's second narrative trend consists of novels and short stories set in contemporary Bologna and its environs.[20] Unlike his historical novels, which are characterized for the most part by a suffocating atmosphere of corruption and hopelessness, those set in the present run the gamut from the broad comedy of 'Nikita', Lucarelli's contribution to the Gruppo 13 anthology, featuring the unlikely sleuthing duo of Coliandro, a politically incorrect would-be tough cop in the mould of Clint Eastwood's Dirty Harry, and smart punk 'grrl' Simona, aka Nikita, to the claustrophobic and disturbing game of cat and mouse between a neurotic policeman and a serial killer in *Lupo mannaro* (1994; Werewolf). His themes expand to include, among others, anti-immigrant racism, neo-fascist terrorism, organized crime, gender politics and police corruption – one of the plot elements of the second Coliandro story, *Falange armata* (1993; Armed Squad), is that recurrent theme of Bolognese detective fiction, the 'Uno bianca' crimes – to represent contemporary Italian society in all its complexity. Like the creator of Sarti Antonio, Lucarelli skilfully plays off the received ideas regarding Bologna with his own portrayal of a mysterious, nocturnal city in which nothing is quite like what it seems on the surface. In *Almost Blue* (1997), possibly his best novel to date, Lucarelli intertwines these themes in a structurally complex narrative of alienation and loneliness.

Almost Blue tells the story of the hunt for a serial killer nicknamed the 'Iguana' for his uncanny ability of metaphorically shedding his own skin and impersonating his victims after killing them. The main detective is Grazia Negro, a member of a police agency known as UASC, Unit for the Analysis of Serial Crimes. In the course of the investigation, she enlists the help of Simone, a blind young man whose interaction with the world is mostly limited to listening to the conversations he can pick up on his electronic scanner and who can recognize the elusive killer because he has overheard his voice. The narrative weaves together three converging strands focusing on Simone, the Iguana and Grazia, and moves from the first-person point of view of the first two characters to the third-person narration of the chapters centred on the detective. The shifts in narrative perspective provide the rhythm for the narrative, slowing it down when the investigation is in its earlier stages and quickening it as the climax approaches: indeed, the cadence of the scenes, the tempo of the narrative blocks owe much to cinematic technique, as in the remarkable climactic sequence in which the lives of the three characters collide, where the increasingly rapid shifts in point of view produce a sort of narrative version of parallel montage.

Lucarelli's use of the theme of the serial killer is an example of his originality as a writer. Instead of relying on the usual treatments of this worn-out cliché of the contemporary thriller – the suave artist of murder of the Hannibal Lecter series, the deranged criminal mastermind of works such as Giorgio Faletti's best-selling *Io uccido* (2002; *I Kill*), the metaphor for the greed of Western capitalism of Bret Easton Ellis's *American Psycho* (1991) – he delves into the psyche of his character who is, more simply and terrifyingly, a victim of mental illness and of a traumatic childhood. However, the Iguana's schizophrenic disconnection from others is a radical and deranged version of the solitude and isolation experienced by all the characters. Grazia, who comes from the south, finds herself working in an unknown and hostile city, constantly marginalized by her status as a 'foreigner' and as a woman in a traditionally masculine profession. Likewise, Simone lives in a personal and incommunicable world of sounds which obeys its own internal and alien logic. For him, the city is a soundscape defined by the range of his scanner, 'a well-defined perimeter . . . bordered by silence'.[21] Thus, the thematic core of the novel is an exploration of a kind of existential loneliness characterizing the modern subject, who appears all the more alone as his or her means of remote communication increase (significantly, the killer preys upon the longing for companionship of the frequenters of electronic chat rooms). Hence, the note of melancholy that pervades the narrative, starting from the title of the book which is also the title of a blues song.

While Macchiavelli and Lucarelli are probably the best known *giallisti* of their respective generation, they are only the tip of the iceberg of the practitioners of the genre working in and around Bologna. One of the most influential is undoubtedly Danila Comastri Montanari (1948–), who won the prestigious 'Premio Tedeschi' with her debut novel *Mors tua* (1990), published in the series 'I Gialli Mondadori'. Set in Rome in first century AD, *Mors tua* introduced her long-running investigator, the Roman nobleman Publius Aurelius Statius, who investigates crime with the help of his servant, the freedman Castor. In spite of the remarkable success of Eco's historical detective novel *Il nome della rosa*, Comastri Montanari was the first, in Italy, to realize fully the potential of the sub-genre, of which she is the undisputed master and, more recently, theorist with the publication of *Giallo Antico. Come si scrive un poliziesco storico* (2007; Ancient Mystery. How to Write a Historical Detective Novel). The 'Aurelius Statius' series has many of the qualities and the problems of historical detective fiction, including a tendency to reinterpret the past according to social practices and codes of behaviour more appropriate to the present. As Gianni Turchetta has remarked, 'the concern for historical precision intertwines with blatant anachronisms, within a framework of absolute anti-realism':[22] witness, for instance, the protagonist's democratic sentiments more appropriate to a man of the twentieth-century than to a Roman aristocrat. Thus, Comastri Montanari's best works may be those in which she has shifted the time and place of the narrative to the more recent past and to her own region of Emilia Romagna, such as *La campana dell'arciprete* (1996; The Archpriest's Bell), which takes place in the aftermath of the papal restoration after the fall of Napoleon, or *Una strada giallo sangue* (1999; A Road Coloured by Murder), in which twelve short stories set along the Via Emilia trace, through the topos of murder, the history and traditions of the region from prehistory to the nineteenth century. Her success contributed greatly to the proliferation of the historical *giallo*, now one of the most popular sub-genres. More recently, the trend has been towards novels where more-or-less famous figures from Italian history are called upon to solve the umpteenth mysterious murder, such as the best-selling and widely translated series by Giulio Leoni begun in 2000 with *I delitti della Medusa* (The Medusa Crimes), the protagonist of which is Dante Alighieri.

At the other end of the spectrum, we find the gritty realism of the authors who are 'insiders' within the world of crime investigation, in different capacities and on both sides of the law: lawyers, policemen, judges – one of the most successful novels of the beginning of the century was court of assizes judge Giancarlo De Cataldo's *Romanzo criminale* (2002; Crime Novel), a portrait of Italian society in the late 1970s and 1980s through the deeds of a group of criminals in Rome – but also figures such as Pietro Valpreda, the anarchist unjustly sentenced to prison for the 1969 Piazza Fontana bombing, who shortly before his death in 2002 wrote a series of moody and melancholic *gialli* in collaboration with Piero Colaprico (see chapter 8). The privileged perspective of these authors on the various institutions charged with the administration of justice often results in stories that eschew the more formulaic aspects of the genre and rather focus on the individual dramas of those who are caught in the aftermath of a criminal act. An example of this subgenre is the work of Maurizio Matrone (1966–), a policeman at the Questura of Bologna who is also the author of essays on police work and minors. In his second novel, *Erba alta* (2003; Tall Grass), set against the investigation of the crimes of the 'Uno bianca' gang, he provides an unflinching portrait (made all-the-more cogent by the use of alternating first-person narrators) of the contradictions of the police force, in which honest and hard-working defenders of the law rub shoulders with officers who do not hesitate to abuse their power for personal gain or to advance more-or-less secret political projects.

Another popular variation on the crime novel, which also often discards the traditional whodunnit plot in favour of character study, is the narrative centred on figures on the margin of the law (and often of society) or downright criminals. The results may vary greatly, ranging from complacent aestheticizations of crime, as in certain serial killer novels, to complex meditations on crime and violence as social symptoms. The latter perspective is adopted by Pino Cacucci (1955–), a talented and versatile writer whose diverse narrative production frequently draws upon the genre of the thriller with original results. A native of Liguria, Cacucci first moved to Bologna in 1975 to attend the DAMS, a university programme in arts, music and performance which has played an important role in re-vitalizing the cultural life of the city since its inception in 1971. He then travelled extensively, especially in Mexico and South America (he is also a prolific translator from Spanish, and has translated the work of the great Spanish-Mexican genre writer Ignacio Paco Taibo II). A good example of his approach to the thriller is the short novel *Punti di fuga* (2000; Vanishing Points), the story of Andrea Durante, a middle-aged Italian living under a false identity in Paris where he works 'out of necessity'[23] as an assassin for hire and who finds himself accidentally dragged into a crime war (while his background is never told explicitly, it seems likely that he was implicated in the political violence of the 1970s, hence his self-imposed exile). As Cacucci explains in his afterword to the novel, Durante, in constant flight from his past but also from his present, represents the disillusionment of the generation of the 1970s, which had sought to change the world through political action and was utterly defeated by the consumerism and political cynicism of the following decade. In this context, 'escape is the only respectable choice when you cannot change anything, and yet you do not want to be implicated, or to become an accomplice'.[24] In less capable hands than Cacucci's, this can lead to a veritable romanticization of crime, to a rhetoric of the criminal as the marginal or the outsider that in the end trivializes the real suffering of the victims. In his fiction, however, the skilful subversion of genre tropes, the irony that often undercuts the events and the genuine ability to portray complex and well-rounded characters usually keep the narrative from falling into sentimentality and endow it with a robust, if at times quixotic, sense of moral indignation. And indeed, if there is a unifying element characterizing the majority of the literary production that we have reviewed in these pages, it is precisely this belief that genre fiction, with its closeness to its readers and their problems, can be a form of 'engaged' literature for the twenty-first century, capable of carrying out that social critique that high literature seems to have abdicated. Naturally, this ambitious project may overstate both the effectiveness of genre fiction and the lack of commitment of 'traditional' literature:[25] be that as it may, some eighty years after its birth, the Italian *giallo* has now reached a level of maturity that makes it one of the most vibrant and significant phenomena in the cultural life of the country.

* * *

Extract from Carlo Lucarelli's *Almost Blue*

Inspector Grazia Negro is a member of a police unit that specializes in the investigation of serial crimes. A southerner who has most recently been living and working in Rome, she is deployed to Bologna to investigate a string of brutal murders that seem to point to the presence of a serial killer in the city, and has to struggle not only with the case but with her own status as an outsider in an unfamiliar environment. In this passage, which occurs about halfway through the novel, Grazia is wandering through Bologna and her perception of its sounds and colours mixes with her recollections of a conversation with one of her assistants, Matera, regarding the contradictory and complex nature of the city.

Earlier, driving through the city in search of the murdered girl's roommate, Matera had told her that Bologna wasn't like other cities. It isn't what it seems, he said, tapping at the windshield with his knuckles and indicating 'out there' with a toss of his head. You think it's small, he said to her, because you're looking at what lies within the city walls, which isn't much bigger than a big town. But that's not the way it really is, Ispettore. Not at all. The city called Bologna actually extends all the way from Parma, in the north, to Cattolica, on the Adriatic coast. The city grew up out of the old Via Emilia. There are people here who live in Modena, work in Bologna, and go dancing at night in Rimini. It's an odd metropolis – two million inhabitants in two thousand square kilometers. It spreads like an oil spill between the sea and the Apennine Mountains. And it has no real center, only marginal cities: Ferrara, Imola, Ravenna, the Adriatic coastal towns.
. . .

When the sun goes behind the rooftops and the light becomes more opaque, darkened by the violet filter of the lowering clouds, then the shadows under the porticoes turn light gray. Then the color of steel. Then a deep, rich, ferrous, chrome-tinted color – almost blue. The entire piazza goes through a complete transformation. At a quarter past seven it's an entirely different place than it was fifteen minutes earlier.

Grazia noticed this as she was walking by the university library, where she stopped to bend down and tie her shoe. The custodian was at the door, locking up for the night. When Grazia straightened up, the custodian of the library was glaring at her but Grazia didn't take any notice. What struck Grazia, instead, were the brightly colored concert posters pasted on the passage-way walls, the graffiti scrawled on the columns, the spray-painted words in Arabic, the piles of flyers that had collected in the dark corners. The students had all disappeared. Even the junkie that usually stood in front of the Teatro Comunale begging for change had gone to sit down on the steps, his hands in his pockets.

This city isn't like others, Matera had said. It's not only big, it's complicated. It's contradictory. If you look at it from a pedestrian perspective, it seems like there are a lot of piazzas and porticoes. But if you fly over it in a helicopter, because of the courtyards and gardens between the buildings, it looks like there's a forest below. And if you go beneath its surface, you'll find that it's a city built on water and canals, like Venezia. It's freezing cold in the winter and tropical in the summer. It has Communist ideals and millionaire cooperative organizations. It's run by four different mafia groups that, rather than shoot each other, help each other recycle Italy's drug money. Tortellini and satanic cults. This city isn't what it seems, Ispettore; it's always hiding something.

Carlo Lucarelli, *Almost Blue*, trans. by Oonagh Stransky
(San Francisco: City Lights Books, 2001), pp. 103–5.

Notes

1. For statistical data on the rise of the *giallo* as a publishing phenomenon, see Elisabetta Mondello, 'Il *noir* "*made in Italy*"'. Oltre il genere', in Elisabetta Mondello (ed.), *Roma noir 2006. Modelli a confronto: L'Italia, l'Europa, l'America* (Rome: Robin Edizioni, 2006), pp. 17–41.

2. Bruno Pischedda, 'Maturità del giallo classico', in Vittorio Spinazzola (ed.), *Tirature '07. Le avventure del giallo* (Milan: il Saggiatore, 2007), pp. 10–19.

3. 'Con Scerbanenco e a partire da Scerbanenco il "giallo" italiano colmava in parte il fossato tra letteratura "alta" e letteratura "bassa", dimostrava nuove possibilità ad una narrativa spesso esangue ed ormai incapace di interpretare in qualche modo il disagio sociale': Roberto Pirani, 'Loriano Macchiavelli e la "Critica". Avventure di uno scrittore di "indagini" (1972–2003)', in Massimo Carloni and Roberto Pirani, *Loriano Macchiavelli un romanziere una città* (Molino del Piano (FI): Pirani Bibliografica Editrice, 2004), p. 140. Unless otherwise stated, all translations are mine.

4. Cf. Marco Sangiorgi and Luca Telò (eds), *Il giallo italiano come nuovo romanzo sociale* (Ravenna: Longo, 2004).

5. On Milan, see Giuliana Pieri, '*Milano nera*: representing and imaging Milan in Italian *noir* and crime fiction', *Romance Studies*, 25/2 (2007), 123–35. On Rome, Nicoletta Di Ciolla, 'Roma in *noir* – the eternal city as dystopia. Or perfect imperfection', *Romance Studies*, 25/4 (2007), 297–307, and the section 'Il noir a Roma: autori, testi, riviste, editori', in Elisabetta Mondello (ed.), *Roma noir 2005. Tendenze di un nuovo genere metropolitano* (Rome: Robin Edizioni, 2005).

6. *L'Italia in giallo: Geografia e storia del giallo italiano contemporaneo* (Reggio Emilia: Diabasis, 1994). The expression 'natura policentrica' is used by Roberto Barbolini in his preface to Carloni's volume, where he also points out that, in his well-known essay, 'Geografia e storia della letteratura italiana' (*Italian Studies*, 4 (1951), 70–93), Carlo Dionisotti had argued that the Italian literary tradition is best understood in terms of local traditions rather than of a unitary identity.

7. Here and elsewhere I follow the established practice of using the term '*giallo*' in the broadest possible sense of fiction about crime. The terminological debate on the boundaries of this and other terms (*noir*, thriller, crime novel, etc.) remains open, as, indeed, do the boundaries of the genre itself. For a basic taxonomy, see Yves Reuter, *Il romanzo poliziesco*, trans. Flavio Sorrentino (Rome: Armando Editore, 1998).

8. On Macchiavelli's theatrical career and his debut as a *giallista*, see Massimo Carloni and Roberto Pirani, *Loriano Macchiavelli un romanziere una città* (Molino del Piano (FI): Pirani Bibliografica Editrice, 2004).

9. Significantly, it was changed to 'Ispettore' in the two television series based on Macchiavelli's fiction (1988–9 and 1993–4).

10. 'Un mestiere come un altro': Loriano Macchiavelli, *Cos'è accaduto alla signora perbene*, in *Sarti Antonio, un questurino una città* (Milan: Garzanti-Vallardi, 1979), p. 431.

11. 'che avevo conosciuto nelle varie Questure dove ero stato più volte convocato per via di quel teatro "politico" che facevo': Carloni and Pirani, *Loriano Macchiavelli*, p. 15.

12. 'Non amo il realismo. Ho sempre dei dati di partenza reali, ma poi cerco il grottesco, il ribaltamento, quello che non c'è': ibid., p. 148.

13. 'il giallo è sempre stato un possibile motivo di squilibrio, un virus nel corpo sano della letteratura, autorizzato a parlar male della società in cui si sviluppava': Maria Agostinelli, 'Loriano Macchiavelli e il destino del giallo. La sconfitta del vittorioso', interview with Loriano Macchiavelli, *RaiLibro. Settimanale di letture e scritture, www.railibro.rai.it/interviste.asp?id=15* (accessed 21 October 2010).

[14] 'Quando l'ha scelta lui, Bologna era ancora ammantata della retorica della città rossa dove tutto funzionava e tutto andava bene . . . Bologna poteva essere rossa e grassa allo stesso tempo. Una specie di miracolo e d'esempio per l'Italia intera . . . E, invece, Loriano Macchiavelli ha fiutato altro in Bologna, e ha buttato nella mischia il suo personaggio insolito': Oreste del Buono, introduction to Macchiavelli, *Sarti Antonio*, p. v.

[15] 'Sapete chi ha costruito questi palazzi? Lo sapete voi? Il cemento, i mattoni, la sabbia per questi palazzi l'hanno portata qui, dal fondo del Reno, i cavalli come il mio Bigio. E il mio Bigio pure. Lo sapete? Questa città l'abbiamo costruita noi e adesso non ci sopportate più? Non sopportate più l'odore del cavallo': Macchiavelli, *Cos'è accaduto alla signora perbene*, p. 445.

[16] The name of the gang derives from their preferred means of transportation, a white Fiat 'Uno' model.

[17] On the influence of real life crimes on detective fiction set in Bologna, see Michele Righini, 'Come si costruisce un luogo letterario; Bologna nera', *Delitti di carta*, 8/4 (2005), 79–100.

[18] On SIGMA, Gruppo 13 and other similar initiatives, see Loriano Macchiavelli, 'Associazioni a delinquere', *Narrativa*, 26 (2004), 5–14. Specifically on the Gruppo, see also Danila Comastri Montanari, 'La Bologna gialla del "Gruppo 13"', *Achab. Il corriere dell'avventura*, 5/3 (1994), 50–2.

[19] 'sulla questione etica del rapporto tra verità e giustizia, da un lato, e dall'altro, le logiche del potere': Elisabetta Bacchereti, *Carlo Lucarelli* (Fiesole: Cadmo, 2004), p. 57.

[20] On Lucarelli's representation of the city, see Lucia Rinaldi, 'Bologna's *noir* identity: narrating the city in Carlo Lucarelli's crime fiction', *Italian Studies*, 64/1 (2009), 120–33.

[21] Carlo Lucarelli, *Almost Blue*, trans. Oonagh Stransky (San Francisco: City Lights Books, 2001), p. 8.

[22] 'la preoccupazione dell'esattezza storica s'intreccia con anacronismi flagranti, in un quadro di assoluto antirealismo': Gianni Turchetta, 'Tante storie per i gialli storici', in Vittorio Spinazzola (ed.), *Tirature '07. Le avventure del giallo* (Milan: Mondadori, 2007), p. 30.

[23] 'per "bisogno"': Pino Cacucci, *Punti di fuga* (Milan: Feltrinelli, 2000), p. 153.

[24] 'La fuga invece è l'unica scelta dignitosa quando non puoi cambiare più nulla, e non vuoi neppure lasciarti coinvolgere, diventare complice': ibid., p. 151.

[25] For a cogent critique of the genre, see Filippo La Porta, 'Contro il Nuovo Giallo Italiano (e se avessimo trovato il genere a noi congeniale?)', in Giulio Ferroni et al., *Sul banco dei cattivi. A proposito di Baricco e di altri scrittori alla moda* (Rome: Donzelli, 2006), pp. 55–75.

Select bibliography

Cacucci, Pino, *Punti di fuga* (Milan: Feltrinelli, 2000).

Eco, Umberto, *Il nome della rosa* (Milan: Bompani, 1980).

Felisatti, Massimo and Fabio Pittorru, *Violenza a Roma* (Milan: Garzanti, 1973).

Fruttero, Carlo and Franco Lucentini, *La donna della domenica* (Milan: Mondadori, 1972); *The Sunday Woman*, trans. William Weaver (New York: Harcourt Brace Jovanovich, 1973).

Lucarelli, Carlo, *Carta bianca* (Palermo: Sellerio, 1990); *Carte Blanche*, trans. Michael Reynolds (New York: Europa Editions, 2006).

——, *L'estate torbida* (Palermo: Sellerio, 1991); *The Damned Summer*, trans. Michael Reynolds (New York: Europa Editions, 2007).

——, *Falange armata* (Bologna: Metrolibri, 1993).

——, *Lupo mannaro* (Rome: Theoria, 1994).

——, *Via delle oche* (Palermo: Sellerio, 1996); *Via delle oche*, trans. Michael Reynolds (New York: Europa Editions, 2008).

——, *L'isola dell'angelo caduto* (Turin: Einaudi, 1999).

——, *Almost Blue* (Turin: Einaudi, 1997); *Almost Blue*, trans. Oonagh Stransky (San Francisco: City Lights Books, 2001).

Macchiavelli, Loriano, *Le piste dell'attentato* (Milan: Campironi, 1974; 2nd rev. edn, Milan: Garzanti, 1978).

——, *Fiori alla memoria* (Milan: Garzanti, 1975).

——, *Sequenze di memoria* (Milan: Garzanti, 1976).

——, *Cos'è accaduto alla signora perbene?* in *Sarti Antonio, un questurino una città* (Milan: Garzanti-Vallardi, 1979).

——, *Stop per Sarti Antonio* (Bologna: Cappelli, 1987).

—— [as Jules Quicher], *Funerale dopo Ustica* (Milan: Rizzoli, 1989).

—— [as Jules Quicher], *Strage* (Milan: Rizzoli, 1990).

——, *Un triangolo a quattro lati* (Milan: Rizzoli, 1992).

——, *Coscienza sporca* (Milan: Mondadori, 1995).

——, and Francesco Guccini, *Macaronì* (Milan: Mondadori, 1997).

——, 'Associazioni a delinquere', *Narrativa*, 26 (2004), 5–14.

Matrone, Maurizio, *Erba alta* (Milan: Frassinelli, 2003).

Montanari, Danila Comastri, *Mors tua* (Milan: Mondadori, 1990).

——, *La campana dell'arciprete* (Milan: Garzanti, 1996).

——, *Una strada giallo sangue* (Reggio Emilia: Diabasis, 1999).

——, *Giallo Antico. Come si scrive un poliziesco storico* (Bresso, Milan: Hobby & Work, 2007).

Selected secondary readings

Bacchereti, Elisabetta, *Carlo Lucarelli* (Fiesole: Cadmo, 2004).

Carloni, Massimo, *L'Italia in giallo. Geografia e storia del giallo italiano contemporaneo* (Reggio Emilia: Diabasis, 1994).

Carloni, Massimo and Roberto Pirani, *Loriano Macchiavelli un romanziere una città* (Molino del Piano (FI): Pirani Bibliografica Editrice, 2004).

Crovi, Luca, *Tutti i colori del giallo. Il giallo italiano da De Marchi a Scerbanenco a Camilleri* (Venice: Marsilio, 2002).

Di Ciolla, Nicoletta, 'Roma in *noir* – the eternal city as dystopia. Or perfect imperfection', *Romance Studies*, 25/4 (2007), 297–307.

Mondello, Elisabetta (ed.), *Roma noir 2006. Modelli a confronto: L'Italia, l'Europa, l'America* (Rome: Robin Edizioni, 2006).

Pieri, Giuliana, '*Milano nera*: representing and imaging Milan in Italian *noir* and crime fiction', *Romance Studies*, 25/2 (2007), 123–35.

Righini, Michele, 'Come si costruisce un luogo letterario; Bologna nera', *Delitti di carta*, 8/4 (2005), 79–100.

Rinaldi, Lucia, 'Bologna's *noir* identity: narrating the city in Carlo Lucarelli's crime fiction', *Italian Studies*, 64/1 (2009), 120–33.

Sangiorgi, Marco, and Luca Telò (eds), *Il giallo italiano come nuovo romanzo sociale* (Ravenna: Longo, 2004).

Spinazzola, Vittorio (ed), *Tirature '07. Le avventure del giallo* (Milan: Mondadori, 2007).

Trent'anni di giallo italiano, special issue of *Narrativa*, 26 (2004).

6

Crime and the South

MARK CHU

In contrast to the largely non-specific setting of early English detective fiction, such as the archetypical but generic 'country house', and more in common with the hard-boiled novels of the American tradition, of which the representation of a geographically specific, usually urban, environment is characteristic, Italian crime fiction has had a strong tendency to emphasize locale. This is probably due at least as much to localist forces within Italian society and culture – such as strong regional and provincial institutions and identities – as to any literary lineage. The Milan of Scerbanenco, Sciascia's Sicily, and Bologna as represented by Macchiavelli and Lucarelli – all analysed in earlier chapters – as well as the Turin of the writing pair of Carlo Fruttero and Franco Lucentini are examples of the way in which Italian writers of crime fiction have made the depiction and exposition of regional realities a key part of their works. Regional publishers have also capitalized on the growing popularity of the genre, as is the case of Fratelli Frilli Editori of Genoa with their recent Ligurian crime series featuring local writers such as Maria Masella and Bruno Morchio. While, on occasion, the setting appears to be used merely to provide colour and to differentiate one product from another, frequently the representation of a regional reality serves as a medium for the critique – originating from a variety of ethical or moral stances – of a particular social (dis)order, which may subsequently be extended to a more general commentary on Italian society, as is the case of Sciascia's notion of 'Sicily as a metaphor'.[1]

As a prelude to the examination in this chapter of the works of three contemporary southern Italian crime writers – Andrea Camilleri (Porto Empedocle, 1925), Marcello Fois (Nuoro, 1960) and Gianrico Carofiglio (Bari, 1961) – it is necessary to consider very briefly the notion of the Italian South. While apparently a natural geographical category, rather than simply referring to a part of the peninsula to the south of 'northern' and 'central' Italy, the *Mezzogiorno*, which also includes the islands of Sardinia and Sicily, is a political and ideological construct which has become naturalized through policy and discourse. As an internalized 'Other' within the Italian body politic, the south has come to be associated monolithically with social and economic backwardness, political corruption, violence and criminality, in a way which has tended to disregard or minimize the differences in the multiple realities pertaining to the area.[2] It is, of course, not intended here to deny the existence and exacerbation of certain social problems in parts of the southern regions of Italy, but neither, as its title might instead suggest, does this chapter seek to represent 'the south' as a homogeneous entity. Indeed, the examination of three markedly different representations of southern regions – Sicily, Sardinia and Puglia – may serve as a useful exemplification of the futility and artificiality of treating the whole area as a single block.

This essay will not attempt to deal with the entire production of the three authors, not least because of the scale of that production, especially in the case of Andrea Camilleri, who, since the early 1990s and up to the time of writing, has published around fifty novels and collections of short stories, although not all of these would fall strictly into the category of crime fiction.[3] It will not address Camilleri's historical novels, even those containing elements of the mystery, but will examine instead the phenomenal success of the – to date – seventeen detective novels and some of the short stories set in and around the fictional Sicilian town of Vigàta and featuring Commissario Salvo Montalbano.[4] Despite this attempt to confine observations to just a selection of this part of Camilleri's output, the number and success of his books, and the high profile this success has brought, necessitate his being given greater space in the chapter and comments on the other two authors' works being restricted to a smaller sample of their novels. Marcello Fois, a member of the Bologna School examined in the previous chapter, is, like Camilleri, also the author of historical novels, but the focus here will be on his trilogy of crime novels set in contemporary Sardinia.[5] The third author considered, Gianrico Carofiglio, is a public prosecutor in Bari, and particular consideration will be paid to the first of his three legal thrillers set in his native city, *Testimone inconsapevole*.[6] As well as providing an introduction to some of the issues central to the works considered, including the authors' references to local, national and global concerns, the chapter will discuss the different narrative functions of the regional settings used.

Camilleri and the Montalbano phenomenon

After a career in various roles in the world of theatre, cinema and television, in 1978 Camilleri published his first novel, *Il corso delle cose*, written ten years earlier, with the small Tuscan publisher Lalli. The language of the novel is a mixture of Sicilian dialect and standard Italian which the author would further develop in his later works and which would become a distinguishing feature of them.[7] His second novel, *Un filo di fumo* – according to the author, based, like many of the historical novels to follow, on a document referring to an episode in the history of Porto Empedocle – was published by the mainstream publishing house, Garzanti. From this point on, Camilleri's novels are set in the fictional Vigàta, based on the town of Porto Empedocle. *Un filo di fumo* drew the attention of Leonardo Sciascia, and it was through him that *La strage dimenticata* – a book of the kind Sciascia himself had written, exploring the context of a little-known episode of injustice in local history – was published by Elvira Sellerio in Palermo, with whom Camilleri subsequently published many of his other works, including the novels of the Montalbano series.[8] Indeed, the author's fourth book with Sellerio was *La forma dell'acqua* (1994), in which he introduced the character of Salvo Montalbano, who is in charge of the *commissariato* in Vigàta. In a recent edition collecting the first three Montalbano novels, Camilleri describes how he came to write them:

> It all started with an 'historical' novel . . . *Il birraio di Preston* [1995; The Brewer of Preston]. I had realized, while I was tied up with this novel, that my personal way of putting a story down on paper was, how can I say, rather disorderly . . .
>
> So it was that I asked myself a question: was I capable of writing a novel beginning at the first chapter and proceeding straight on, without temporal or logical leaps, until the final chapter? My answer was that perhaps I would be able to if I were to harness myself within a quite robust narrative structure.
>
> It was at this point that an essay by Leonardo Sciascia on the detective novel came back to me, an essay on the rules that a writer of *gialli* is required to respect. And at the same time I remembered an affirmation by Italo Calvino, according to whom it was impossible to set a detective novel in Sicily. So I decided to take on a double bet: with myself and with the unwitting Calvino.[9]

This statement is revealing of Camilleri's initial choice of the detective genre as purely a stylistic one, and points to his formulaic use of the genre,[10] a fact highlighted all the more by the author's reference to Sciascia, who had instead revitalized the *giallo* by subverting its rules, and who had exploited the narrative appeal of the form to secure the widest readership for his novels which were driven by a desire to denounce the machinations of power, be it mafia, Church or political power. Camilleri goes on to say that, while he had not intended to write more than the one *giallo*, his dissatisfaction at the lack of development of the character of Montalbano led him to write *Il cane di terracotta*, and that the success of the two novels, and the renewed interest in his earlier works which that success brought, resulted in his writing *Il ladro di merendine*, once again with the intention of it being his last *giallo*, but once again resulting in increased public demand for more of the same. At the same time, Camilleri describes how ideas for the character came to be an obsession and to interfere with his other writing, so that, while he acknowledges that Montalbano has contributed to the success of all his writings, that very success and the demands it creates irritate him.[11] The extent of that success, due also to the popularity of the RAI television series, *Il commissario Montalbano*, based on Camilleri's books and featuring the Roman actor Luca Zingaretti in the title role, can be measured by the fact that in the last fifteen years the author has dominated the best-seller list in Italy, with as many as four books in the top ten at once, and with the Montalbano books, as the author acknowledges to some extent, serving to attract customers to his other works. A systematic account of all the Montalbano novels is beyond the scope of this brief essay, which will instead examine some of the characteristics of the series and attempt to explain its fortune with Italian and other readers.

At the same time, it will explore the representation of place in the novels and the ideology that underpins them.

As stated above, Camilleri's Vigàta is based largely on Porto Empedocle in the province of Agrigento, with which it shares numerous toponyms, while the provincial capital, Montelusa, is identifiable with Agrigento. The television series is filmed at numerous locations in the provinces of Agrigento and Ragusa. These facts are significant in that the fictional Sicily represented by Camilleri has, as a result of the media profile of his works, overflowed into reality. In 2003, the town council of Porto Empedocle, with Camilleri's permission, took the decision to add the name Vigàta to the town's welcome signs in an attempt to capitalize on the growing tourist industry connected to the author's success. Sellerio, who, as previously mentioned, is the primary publisher of the Montalbano books, has published a guidebook to *I luoghi di Montalbano* (Montalbano's Locations), which proposes itineraries taking in the settings of the books and television series. This exacerbates the phenomenon of Sicily as a textual reality which I have discussed elsewhere.[12]

The Montalbano novels refer frequently to current affairs and news items. Indeed, in response to the many readers who apparently ask Camilleri how he invents the stories in the novels, in an article first published in the Sicilian edition of *la Repubblica* (18 April 1999), the author proposes an improbable story of corruption which, at the end, he reveals is not his invention, but had appeared in the Sicilian newspapers: 'So don't come and ask me any more how I "invent" the stories I tell. I don't invent them: if anything, I re-elaborate them until they are no longer recognizable as news items.'[13] While this statement is perhaps polemically extreme, in the opening pages of *La forma dell'acqua* – in a pattern that was to be reproduced in the subsequent novels – one finds reference to such aspects of Italian society (and not only) as clientelism, qualified surveyors working as street cleaners, artificial and ineffectual state intervention in an attempt to establish industries in Sicily, and immigration.[14] There is also a scathing comment on the political decision to deploy the army in Sicily to assert state control of the territory, but which, according to the narrative voice, is futile, given that the territory is really controlled by the local mafiosi, who authorize the various illegal activities.[15] While one might agree that the deployment of the military in Sicily in 'Operation Sicilian Vespers' (25 July 1992–8 July 1998) was probably aimed more at reassuring the public than at truly tackling the mafia, the absence of a reference to the reason for the decision – namely, the murders of the anti-mafia prosecutors, Giovanni Falcone and Paolo Borsellino, in May and July 1992 – trivializes the whole issue. The mafia appears incidentally in a number of the Montalbano novels, but is never central to Camilleri's plots, even in *Il cane di terracotta*, in which Tano u grecu, a tired mafioso, allows Montalbano to arrest him and the new generation of bosses kill Tano while he is in custody and attempt to kill the inspector: instead, the events are the pretext for the discovery of the hidden tomb of a young couple murdered fifty years previously for motives unrelated to organized crime. This reticence may be attributable in part to the Van Dine dictum according to which 'secret societies, camorras, mafias, *et al.*, have no place in a detective story'.[16]

There is also, on Camilleri's part, a declared refusal to dignify mafiosi by making them the main focus of a novel.[17] Nevertheless, the refusal to address in a serious manner the issue of the mafia in these Sicilian-set detective novels is in stark contrast to Sciascia's 1961 novel, *Il giorno della civetta* (The Day of the Owl), about mafia intimidation and its social and political context, all the more so because Camilleri claims that it is to Sciascia's works that he turns when he needs 're-charging'.[18]

At the beginning of *Il giro di boa*, the seventh Montalbano novel, the protagonist is on the point of resigning from the police, tired, disillusioned and above all disgusted by the behaviour of some of his colleagues in Genova during the G8 meeting of July 2001, and by the political context that had prepared the ground for that behaviour. In a long passage in italics, which occupies the bulk of the first chapter, we find a description of the reasons for Montalbano's sleepless night, and the most direct and sustained reference to current affairs:[19] to Prime Minister Silvio Berlusconi and his Interior Minister Claudio Scajola's controversial security measures for the G8 meeting, although neither is named directly; to the violent clashes between the police and demonstrators (together with the suggestion that agents provocateurs were used to justify police actions), culminating in the shooting dead by a *Carabiniere* of the protestor Carlo Giuliani; to the violent night raid by police on the Diaz school, where a hundred or so demonstrators and foreign journalists were sleeping (pp. 12–13). The passage also includes reflections by Montalbano on the presence of right-wing politicians in the police operations rooms in Genova as an encouragement and guarantee to the violent elements in the police (p. 16), on the revolt of policemen in Naples in response to the arrest of some of their colleagues for abuses of their position and acts of violence, and on the possibility that the whole event in Genova had been staged to test the waters and see how the public would react to a show of force by the police.[20] However, the indignation of the character at the conduct of his police colleagues in Genova is undermined and trivialized by being put on the same level as the closure of his favourite restaurant a month later:

> The confirmation that the inspector's world was starting to go to the dogs had come barely a month after the G8 meetings, when, after a meal of considerable magnitude, Calogero, the owner-cook-waiter of the Trattoria San Calogero, had announced he was retiring, however reluctantly.[21]

Repeatedly, from the very beginning of the series, Montalbano is accused by his subordinates of being a communist, because of his affinity for the weak and the dispossessed. Nevertheless, his liberal credentials are suspect, as demonstrated, for example, by his attitude towards women, and especially towards his companion Livia: the women in the novels are rarely women as such, but are instead bodies made into the object of Montalbano's gaze, or appreciated by him for the fact that they do not talk. The same ambiguity emerges from the representation of immigrants in the Montalbano series: on the one hand, we find the character's compassion in the face of the plight of individual immigrants (such as François Moussa, the 'snack thief' whom Livia and, with some hesitation, Montalbano would like to adopt)[22] or of that of the poor of the world which forces them to migrate, suffering violence and exploitation along the way (*Il ladro di merendine*, *Il giro di boa, Le ali della sfinge*); on the other, we have the parodic representation of the speech of anonymous immigrants. Notwithstanding his invectives against the 'Fortress Italy' legislation of the centre-right government and his compassion and affection for François, Montalbano's contact with immigrants is repeatedly reduced to his phone conversations with the maids of his Swedish friend Ingrid Sjostrom, marked by an ambiguous and formulaic polyphony, which is, however, manifestly moderated in Stephen Sartarelli's translations – 'Who dat speakin? . . . I go see, you wait';[23] 'You token I lissin' – which is followed by Montalbano's reflections on his dialogue with the generic *extracomunitaria*:

> Ingrid may have changed houses, but she hadn't changed her habit of hiring house-keepers who she went looking for in Tierra del Fuego, on Mount Kilimanjaro, or inside the Arctic Circle.
> 'This is Montalbano.'
> 'Watt say you?'
> She must have been an Australian Aborigine. A conversation between her and Catarella would have been memorable.[24]

This last parallel could be an attempt to mitigate a racist element in the character of Montalbano, but it fails to resolve the problematic aspect, in so far as the police telephonist Catarella, for all his malapropisms and ignorance, is still a character with a name and, as the series develops, human qualities. Indeed, although Catarella and even Montalbano himself are to a great extent comic Sicilians along the lines of the 'stage Irishman', their representation is not comparable to that of the de-humanized *extracomunitari*.[25]

It is obviously not suggested that the opinions and attitudes of Montalbano are those of the author Camilleri. It could be argued, however, that the author exploits the image of the character as a man of the people, with his ambiguous leftist 'impegno' and indignation in the face of injustice and the irrational nature of power, as a formal category which tends to represent the notion of 'italiani brava gente', notwithstanding their faults.

Fois's contemporary Sardinia

Characteristic of the three novels by Fois considered here is the use of multiple points of view, in contrast to the traditional detective novel, which tends on the whole to privilege the perception of the investigator. Even the investigators are more than one, with the Sardinians Judge Salvatore Corona, *carabiniere* Nicola Pili and police inspector Giacomo Curreli appearing and reappearing in different roles in the novels, alongside other, non-Sardinian figures. In particular, the third novel of the trilogy, *Dura madre*, is in part a choral work, with some sections explicitly narrated by individual characters – at times micro-narratives within the novel – and others seemingly voices overheard.

The three novels also share a concern with the representation of their Sardinian setting. In his note to the 1999 Einaudi edition of his first novel, *Ferro Recente* – written, according to the author ten years previously – Fois describes the work and makes direct reference to the importance of place in it:

> I love this novel in particular, even if, almost certainly, now, exactly ten years after it was drafted, I would write it differently. No regrets, let's be clear. The story is what it is, and remains such: the tale of a place; the attempt to establish to what extent a culture which is thousands of years old can resist in the face of the enchantments of modernity. A story of terrorism in Sardinia, in Nuoro. A story of generations confused or, perhaps, too aware of an irreversible crisis. A story of delays and excesses.[26]

In particular, Fois explains his desire as a novice writer to address the theme of what he portrays as Sardinia's problematic relationship with modern society. At the same time, in the dedication of the novel *A Nuoro*, the author refers to the city as 'Entità inventata e inesistente', an invented and non-existent entity, alluding explicitly to the textual nature of this particular location and implicitly to that of any real location represented in fiction. Nevertheless, in *Ferro Recente*, *Meglio morti* and *Dura madre*, Fois juxtaposes conventional elements of the representation of a 'backward' Sardinia – emigration, kidnapping, sheep-rustling, family feuds or *faide*, magic, tradition, *omertà* – and aspects of society not specific or peculiar to the island, and generally associated with modernity, such as terrorism, building speculation and corruption, environmental degradation, the misappropriation of European Union funds, marginalized urban youths and hackers.

Frequently, Sardinian characters come into contact with *continentali*, whose attitudes and expectations provide the occasion to reflect on stereotypes of the island. In *Ferro Recente*, Mauro Piras recalls an argument in Bologna a decade earlier with a fellow student and activist, who had accused him and other Sardinians of wallowing in self-pity:

> 'Sure!' Mauro had replied 'Colonialist and Manichaean. Some people are still surprised if they arrive in Sardinia and don't find what they expect, if they see industry, city life: who knows, even drug addicts, transvestites, et cetera. They prefer that Sardinia which is elsewhere, a somewhat bastardized fake, like the plastic garlands they put around the tourists' necks at Honolulu Airport. I've heard people talking about atrocities, such as kidnaps, killings, vendettas, as though they were an indispensable constituent of the territory, an element of fascination. It's absurd . . .'[27]

Returning to the present, we find Mauro disillusioned with what he considers the 'constitutional farce' (p. 26) which he associates with the Christian democrat exploitation of the spoils system (p. 42) and involved in the attempted resurrection of the 'Ferro Recente' autonomist terrorist group.[28] He reflects on the impact of modernity on Sardinia and sees the island as having failed to find a working compromise between tradition and change: 'What was left was folklore, the exhibition of rites which were no longer rituals and were without meaning; what was left was that subconscious link to extraneous and fatal values. What was left was the violence.'[29] While Mauro is obviously an ambiguous figure, through him Fois rehearses the tensions created in a long-isolated region upon its integration into national society.

Elsewhere, Fois introduces characters who are *continentali*, which allows him to explore stereotypical attitudes to Sardinia in a critical way, although the fact that particular comments made by these characters are true permits the author to acknowledge the existence of certain traits or problems. In *Meglio morti*, Danila Comastri, the magistrate from Lombardy investigating the circumstances surrounding the discovery of a girl's body, [30] deliberately provokes Commissario Curreli with the observation that *omertà*, the question of the 'reticent witness' is the definitive problem of 'you Sardinians':

> Now the *commissario* began to feel truly annoyed. 'Of us Sardinians,' he repeated mechanically, as though repeating the affirmation to himself would make it truer. 'So it's a regional problem?' he snapped at her disapprovingly and without respect. 'My dear lady,' he went on, condescendingly, 'don't you think that we've already had enough of sociologists and anthropologists and that it might be time to stop studying *us Sardinians*?' *Two-bit*, he would have liked to add, *two-bit sociologists and anthropologists.*[31]

Curreli expresses the frustration of the 'orientalized' Sardinian, but ironically Comastri is aware that the policeman himself is hiding information from her and, when she reveals this, he is forced to come clean timidly. Later, however, an involuntary joke has the effect of chilling her relations with Curreli and with Salvatore Corona, who are collaborating with her on the investigation:

> 'Unbelievable stuff: a pregnant twelve-year-old and a sixty-five-year-old virgin. How I love Sardinia,' she suddenly commented without thinking . . .

> However, what was meant to be a joke did not have the desired effect. The *commissario* and the judge didn't seem amused.

> 'Sorry,' hesitated Danila Comastri, feeling on her skin the icy chill that had descended in the room despite the heating. 'I didn't mean it in that sense. It's tiredness making me say stupid things.'[32]

While Fois has Comastri comment on the facts of the case represented, the episode provides a critique of her generalization of the episode to make it 'typical' of the whole region.

In *Dura madre*, Corona works with Commissario Angelo Sanuti, who is from the Rimini area. Early in the novel, Sanuti, after explaining that he is experiencing difficulty sleeping because of the wind, states that his recent posting is not, however, the first time that he has been to Sardinia, but that he has visited the island five or six years previously for a beach holiday. It might be suggested that the introduction of this fact renders Sanuti's perception of Sardinia akin to that of the summer tourist. This, in turn, intensifies the surprise effect on the reader of his following comment ('Che razza di posto') on entering the partially completed but inhabited apartment block near the building site where a body has been discovered, which initially seems almost to be a comment on the island itself:

> 'In any case, it's not the first time I've been to Sardinia: I was here five or six years ago, on a beach holiday . . . What a strange place . . .,' he commented, entering the rough entrance hall of a building, 'is it lived in?' he asked quietly, passing the sign WORK IN PROGRESS NO ENTRY TO UNAUTHORIZED PERSONNEL and noticing that some of the apartments were already occupied.[33]

Sanuti's status as a fresh arrival allows Fois to have Corona explain or provide commentary on various aspects of local culture to him and, at the same time, to the reader. Similarly, Corona at times avails of the more extensive knowledge of retired Maresciallo Pili. One example of Corona providing Sanuti with information, ostensibly to help him understand the local culture, is the story of 'Fronteddu's dog', which he narrates in section 9 (pp. 37–40). The story has legendary status, and it is this fact that leads Sanuti to reflect on what appears to him to be the impenetrable nature of a society whose members share such cultural referents:

> 'Let me get this right: so . . .,' began Sanuti, gathering up his strength with a good, deep breath, 'I'll try to explain to you what I've understood: you people go around with impunity saying things, let's say, like So-and-so's dog . . .'

> 'Fronteddu's'.

> 'That's it, and you understand each other just like that? I mean you cite this guy's dog in any kind of conversation and your interlocutors understand you?'

> 'Those who know the story, but around here everyone knows it.'[34]

Corona, however, seems to be teasing the *continentale* when he warns him against nit-picking with parables, especially if it is a question of parables about dogs (p. 43), and there is also, perhaps, an element of the Sardinian Fois toying with a non-Sardinian readership keen to acquire an understanding of the island's culture through his texts.[35]

To return to the question of voice mentioned at the beginning of this section, *Dura madre* is, despite the final unravelling of the mystery, a kind of anti-detective novel, in that it ends with a section – numbered 62 of the sections or chapters from 0 to 62, and given the title '(what we have always known)' – in which the idea of the need for an investigation in the society described is totally undermined:

> We know that knowledge is not of this world. And that explanations are voices, voices of the place. They are the songs of a choir which modulates to the four winds.
>
> We know that the whole truth is on everyone's lips . . .[36]

In this light, it is interesting to note that Fois's *Piccole storie nere* – published by Einaudi in 2002, a year after the novel – which follow the character of Commissario Curreli as he is transferred around Italy, shift away from the conventions of the *giallo* and include elements of horror and comedy, of the grotesque, the gothic and the fantastic.

Carofiglio, Bari and the Italian legal thriller

Gianrico Carofiglio is an assistant public prosecutor who has worked on anti-mafia cases and, while he does not focus on organized crime in his novels, he exploits his professional expertise to create the character of Guido Guerrieri, a Bari lawyer, around the same age as the author and apparently sharing his literary and musical tastes.[37] Apart from courtroom scenes, the trilogy also contains ironic considerations on the legal profession, as voiced by the protagonist as first-person narrator. Guerrieri moves about Bari and its environs, referring to toponyms and even tracing routes along the city's streets. Furthermore, he comments frequently on the milieu, yet it is worth considering what the author says of the setting of the graphic novel, *Cacciatori nelle tenebre*:

> Yes, it's Bari, the same Bari in which the Guerrieri novels are set. With a few clarifications to be made, however. First of all, it is never named, even if all the frames which depict it are drawings of places in the city. In some cases transfigured and rendered as topoi belonging to a sort of metropolitan literary imaginary, in other cases clearly identifiable as Bari. But the most important thing is that, with the help of the illustrations, I had great fun recounting a city balanced between realistic narration and surreal description of an imaginary and universal place. Above all as far as the undergrounds, both physical and moral, are concerned . . . This city is unequivocally Bari, and at the same time it is all the medium to large cities of the world which harbour unnameable secrets.[38]

Carofiglio's comments refer specifically to the setting as created in collaboration with his brother for the graphic novel. Nevertheless they can be seen as relevant to the Bari of the trilogy, a real city, but also a setting that the author aims to render representative of other cities and defined not so much in terms of southern alterity as of urban normality: its traits are distinctive, but not circumscriptive. So if, in *Ad occhi chiusi*, the second novel of the trilogy, Guerrieri is pitted against the influence and nepotism protecting Gianluca Scianatico, son of one of the most powerful men in the city, president of a section of the court of appeal, the circumstance is not presented as specific to Bari or necessarily to a 'southern' reality.

Carofiglio's first novel had already shown limited dependence on its southern setting, which serves as backdrop for the 'legal thriller'. *Testimone inconsapevole* tells the story of Guerrieri's defence of a Senegalese immigrant charged with the kidnap and murder of a 9-year-old boy. As is to be expected of the genre, the emphasis here is on the techniques and skills employed to prove the innocence of the defendant, rather than a reconstruction by a detective of the crime, so that the outcome of the novel is the desired verdict, while the murder remains unresolved.[39] In the two subsequent Guerrieri novels, however, despite the fact that the trial is still the centre of attention, there is something of a return to the convention of a final resolution, with the guilty parties arrested or about to be arrested in the closing pages.

The emphasis on the trial also underscores the relative importance of the lawyer-protagonist: whereas, for all his or her bravura, and regardless of whatever character traits he or she may have, the focus in the conventional *giallo* tends ultimately to be on what the detective discovers, in the legal thriller, greater significance is attached to how the lawyer achieves a verdict. In Carofiglio's trilogy, this leads to a more direct correlation between the protagonist and the action itself, with a consequent foregrounding of the character.[40] In his personal life, Guerrieri is an ambiguous figure: the novel begins with his account of his separation from his wife, who is no longer prepared to tolerate his frequent infidelities, and of the panic attacks which are brought on by this new situation. Nevertheless, throughout the trilogy, Guerrieri as first-person narrator elicits the reader's sympathy through his sharp-witted observations on the Italian bourgeoisie and, more especially, through the self-awareness he demonstrates in describing his own weaknesses and barely controlled tendency to say the wrong thing or to speak in a ridiculously supercilious manner about the morality and duties of the legal profession. Guerrieri is fully developed as a character with prejudices and failings, but whereas in the case of Camilleri's Montalbano similar traits are not mediated by the narrative voice, Guerrieri's self-conscious reflections have a dual function: while, on the one hand, they do invite a certain complicity on the part of the reader, on the other they oblige the reader to reflect in some way on such attitudes. An example of this ambivalence, more so because used – as in Camilleri – for comic effect, can be seen at the beginning of the second novel, *Ad occhi chiusi*. The protagonist discovers that two lesbian friends of his companion, Margherita, have invited her to do a parachuting course with them:

> They've asked you because they want to fuck you. The lesbian licence, that's what they want you to take. That's it – the flying lesbian licence.

I didn't say that. Obviously. We men of the left don't say things like that, though we might think them. Besides, the two Giovannas looked as if they could easily have ripped my balls off and played pinball with them for a lot less.[41]

On the one hand, Carofiglio attributes to the character homophobia and vulgar stereotype; on the other, a self-deprecating comment on the hypocrisy of a type of political correctness, which nevertheless demonstrates an awareness of the inappropriateness of this kind of discourse: while Guerrieri is not free of socially constructed prejudice or emotional responses, as a left-thinking intellectual he points to them for what they are and obliges the reader to do likewise.

As in Camilleri's *Il ladro di merendine* and *Il giro di boa*, immigration and Italian responses to it are central to *Testimone inconsapevole*.[42] Carofiglio, however, chooses consciously to depict individual immigrants who do not conform to the stereotype of uneducated masses of illegal immigrants working in Italy as drug-dealers or prostitutes (like Fatma in *La forma dell'acqua* and Karima in *Il ladro di merendine*). Carofiglio's immigrants, unlike the anonymous maids who answer Ingrid's phone, have names – rare exceptions in Camilleri's novels are François and his family – and a history, including professional qualifications: Abagiage Deheba (Abajaje in the English translation), the Nubian-Egyptian woman who engages Guerrieri on behalf of her friend, Abdou Thiam, is an agronomist taking a specialization course at an international centre; Abdou himself is a primary schoolteacher, also in Italy legally, selling bags and other articles at Italian beach resorts or on the street because he can earn up to ten times his salary in Senegal. At his first meeting with Abagiage, Carofiglio's first-person narrator underlines the power of stereotype in conditioning our relations with immigrants:

> We all of us go by stereotypes. Anyone who denies it is a liar. The first stereotype had suggested the following sequence: African, precautionary detention, drugs. It is usually for this reason that Africans get arrested.

> But straight away the second stereotype came into play. The woman had an aristocratic look and didn't seem like a drug-pusher's moll.[43]

To reiterate, then: while the character of Guerrieri sometimes displays prejudice and sexist attitudes, the author sometimes introduces an element of critique into the representation, with varying degrees of success. Interestingly, whereas in the first novel, just before Abagiage enters his office, Guerrieri is waiting for a female client accused of physical and mental abuse of her husband and numerous misogynistic observations find their way into this background plot line (pp. 41–9), *Ad occhi chiusi* is centred on a case of severe maltreatment of a woman by her male companion, so that Guerrieri's chauvinism *malgré lui* is brought into perspective in the second novel by his having to confront in a more serious way the more common dynamic of domestic violence.

I will conclude this brief introduction to Carofiglio's work by saying something about the relationship between the author's profession and his legal thriller trilogy. While Carofiglio is a magistrate, his first-person narrator is a lawyer and therefore functions to some extent as an alter-ego to the author. Despite the fact that Guerrieri is depicted in a largely sympathetic fashion (his sense of morality, his humour, even the self-awareness of his less appealing traits and habits), in *Testimone inconsapevole* the author establishes a distance between himself and the character, apparently privileging the point of view of the character.

> I had very little room to move. Very little indeed. So I had to do something, even loose off shots at random, in the hope of hearing some sound, learning if in that direction there might be some way. Some track to follow.
>
> Handbooks for lawyers would have said that this was the wrong way to set about it.
>
> Never ask questions for which you cannot foresee the answer. Never cross-examine blindly, without having a precise object in mind. Your cross-examination must be punctiliously planned, nothing left to improvisation, because otherwise you might even strengthen the position of your adversary. And so on and so forth.
>
> I'd really like to see the fine fellows who write such manuals conduct a damned trial. I'd like to see them in the thick of the noise, the dirt, the blood, the shit of a real trial. I'd like to see them apply their theories then.
>
> Never cross-examine blindly.
>
> I'd like to see them at it! Me, I was forced to go ahead blindly. And not only in the trial either.[44]

This sets Guerrieri as antagonist to Gianrico Carofiglio, author of *L'arte del dubbio* (The Art of Doubt), a manual on cross-examination based on a series of case studies.[45] In the opening chapter of this work, Carofiglio states that the first rule of cross-examination regards not the technique, but the decision of whether to do so or not: 'One should proceed to cross-examination if one has a significant evidential objective and if that objective appears achievable in practical terms.'[46] Later in the manual, when discussing 'fatal errors', the author attributes one such disaster to 'the violation of the rule that advises against asking crucial questions without having at one's disposal elements which allow one in some way to anticipate the responses and, in any case, to avoid undesirable surprises and counter-productive outcomes'.[47] While the title of Carofiglio's first novel contains a reference to a chapter in his manual on the cross-examination of the 'involuntarily false witness', Guerrieri's invocation of the circumstances of a 'real trial', in contrast to the 'theorizing' of the real-life prosecutor Carofiglio based on actual case studies, playfully elicits reflection on the truth claims made by the character.

Crime fictions and the souths of Italy

The three authors examined show how, to some extent, recent Italian crime fiction set in different regions of the south has acted as a form of 'committed writing' and as a witness to its time, with varying degrees of success. In markedly diverse ways, the authors have each engaged with their regional dimension and created a distinctive setting for their works. In the case of Camilleri, despite references to national and international events, that dimension is a distinguishing feature, also because of the nature of the linguistic and media aspects of the representation of Sicily. Fois directly addresses and challenges conventional stereotypes of Sardinia, and presents a region caught between the rock of tradition and the hard place of a modern and homogenized society in decay. Carofiglio, while creating a geographically specific setting for his works with his representation of Bari, is, of the three writers, the one who perhaps resists the regional dimension to the greatest extent. It might be argued that, because of his rejection of 'meridionalist' themes, Carofiglio should not be examined in the context of southern Italian crime fiction, but such an insistence on the specificity of 'the south' is precisely what I have sought to avoid in this chapter. The very 'normality' of the crimes and setting represented in Carofiglio's Bari novels exemplifies a frequently ignored aspect of the multiple realities of those regions traditionally considered to constitute the *Mezzogiorno*. For this reason, an exploration of 'crime and the south' can perhaps be most meaningful if one does include reference to an author such as Carofiglio alongside Camilleri and Fois.

* * *

Extracts from Carofiglio's *Involuntary Witness*

'It is an acknowledged fact – and one of the most important objects of study in modern forensic psychology – that both children and adults make mistakes about the source of their memories and are convinced that they remember contexts, facts and details which have in fact been suggested by others. Deliberately, as in the case of the experiment I have recounted to you. Or involuntarily, as in many situations in everyday life and also, at times, during criminal investigations.

'On the basis of these considerations we can give an answer to the question put by the public prosecutor in the course of his speech, regarding the reliability of the witness Renna. The public prosecutor asked himself, and above all he asked *you*: what reason did Renna have for lying and therefore falsely accusing Abdou Thiam?

'We can answer that question with perfect confidence: no reason at all. And in fact Renna did not lie. Between lying – that is, knowingly uttering falsehoods – and telling the truth – which is giving an account of the facts as they really and truly happened – there exists a third possibility. A possibility which the public prosecutor did not take into consideration, but which you must take into very close consideration. That of a witness who gives a certain version of the facts in the erroneous conviction that it is true.

'We are here concerned with what might be defined as involuntary false witness.'

They seemed interested. Even the judge and the military-looking juryman. The pair who – I was convinced of it – had already decided to find Abdou guilty.

'There are many ways of building up involuntary false witness. Some are deliberate, as in the case of the experiment with children that I told you about. Others are themselves involuntary and often prompted by the best intentions. As in this case.

'Let us together try to reconstruct what happened in the inquiry which led to the indictment of Abdou Thiam, and therefore to this trial. A little boy disappears and two days later his dead body is found. It is a deeply disturbing event, and those whose task it is to put the investigations in hand – the carabinieri, the public prosecutor – feel it is their urgent, their pressing duty to discover the culprits. There is justifiable eagerness to satisfy the demand for justice provoked by such a horrible crime. By questioning the child's relatives, and other persons who knew him well, the carabinieri discover this apparent friendship existing between the boy and this African pedlar. It is something strange, unusual, that arouses suspicions. And also the feeling that perhaps they are on the right track. Perhaps it is possible to satisfy that demand for justice and to placate that anguish. The investigation is no longer groping in the dark; it now has a possible suspect and a theoretical solution. This redoubles the efforts made to find confirmation for this theoretical solution. This is how things stand when the witness Renna is heard for the first time, by the carabinieri. The investigators are understandably excited by the possibility of solving the case, and they realize that the statements of this witness could well constitute a decisive step. It is at this stage that we see the construction of the involuntary false witness.'

> Gianrico Carofiglio, *Involuntary Witness*, trans. Patrick Creagh
> (London: Bitter Lemon, 2005), pp. 247–8.

Notes

1 The concept is most fully articulated in the book-length interview of Sciascia by the French journalist, Marcelle Padovani, in Leonardo Sciascia, *La Sicilia come metafora: intervista di Marcelle Padovani* (Milan: Mondadori, 1979). Translation of *La Sicile comme métaphore: Conversations en italien avec Marcelle Padovani* (Paris: Stock, 1979).

2 Studies that have provided a critique of the naturalization of discourses of or on 'the south' include G. Gribaudi, 'Images of the south', in D. Forgacs and R. Lumley (eds), *Italian Cultural Studies: An Introduction* (Oxford: Oxford University Press, 1996), pp. 72–87, and S. Patriarca, 'How many Italies? Representing the south in official statistics', in J. Schneider (ed.), *Italy's 'Southern Question': Orientalism in One Country* (Oxford: Berg, 1998), pp. 77–97. For a general reappraisal of the notion of 'the south', see also the essays in R. Lumley and J. Morris (eds), *The New History of the Italian South: The Mezzogiorno Revisited* (Exeter: University of Exeter Press, 1997).

[3] Camilleri's first three books, *Il corso delle cose* (The Run of Things), *Un filo di fumo* (A Ribbon of Smoke) and *La strage dimenticata* (The Forgotten Massacre) were originally published in 1978, 1980 and 1984 respectively, but it was after *La stagione della caccia* (Palermo: Sellerio, 1992; The Hunting Season) that the author began to succeed in publishing his books with greater frequency, settling at a rhythm of between three and five titles a year.

[4] While I choose to use the original Italian term, Montalbano's rank of *commissario* is translated in the Garzanti Hazon dictionary as 'inspector' in the collocation 'il commissario Maigret', referring to the character in the detective novels of Georges Simenon. Camilleri refers to his 'debt' to the Belgian writer in an article originally published in *La Stampa* (4 July 1999) and describes how, apart from having been an avid reader of the Belgian author from an early age, he was involved in the production of the 1960s RAI television series based on the Maigret novels ('Il mio debito con Simenon', in A. Camilleri, *Racconti quotidiani* , ed. G. Capecchi (Pistoia: Libreria dell'Orso, 2001; Daily Tales), pp. 66–70).

[5] *Ferro Recente* (Bologna: Granata, 1992; Turin: Einaudi, 1999; Late Iron), *Meglio morti* (Bologna: Granata, 1994; Turin: Einaudi, 2000; Better Off Dead), *Dura madre* (Turin: Einaudi, 2001; Hard Mother): all references are to the Einaudi editions. Fois is also author of a trilogy of detective novels set in late nineteenth-century Nuoro featuring the lawyer-poet, Bustianu Satta: *Sempre caro*, with a preface by A. Camilleri (Nuoro: Il Maestrale, 1998 (*The Advocate*, trans. P. Creagh (London: Harvill, 2003)); *Sangue dal cielo*, with a preface by M. Vázquez Montalbán (Nuoro: Il Maestrale/Milan: Frassinelli, 1999; *Blood from the Skies* (London: Harvill, 2006)); *L'altro mondo* (Nuoro: Il Maestrale/Milan: Frassinelli, 2002; The Other World). The novel *Sheol* (Bresso: Hobby & Work, 1997; Scheol) is set in Rome's Jewish community during the 1993 electoral campaign, and refers back to the anti-Semitic persecutions of fifty years earlier. The novel *Gap* (Milan: Frassinelli, 1999; Partisan Group) also oscillates between the past and present. Fois's involvement with television includes participation in the screenplays of the first three series of the Mediaset series, *Distretto di Polizia* (2000–2) and his storyline for the RAI series *Crimini* of the episode 'Disegno di sangue' (2007; screenplay by Giancarlo De Cataldo; Blood Drawing), featuring *commissario* Giacomo Curreli.

[6] *Testimone inconsapevole* (Palermo: Sellerio, 2002; *Involuntary Witness*, trans. P. Creagh (London: Bitter Lemon, 2005). The other two novels featuring lawyer Guido Guerrieri are *Ad occhi chiusi* (2003; *A Walk in the Dark*, trans. H. Curtis (London: Bitter Lemon, 2006)) and *Ragionevoli dubbi* (2006; *Reasonable Doubts*, trans. H. Curtis (London: Bitter Lemon, 2007)), both also published by Sellerio. Carofiglio is also the author of *Il passato è un paese straniero* (Milan: Rizzoli, 2004; *The Past is a Foreign Country*, trans. H. Curtis (London: Old Street, 2008)), set largely in Bari, which narrates in parallel the story of how card sharp Francesco makes the narrator, Giorgio, his accomplice, and the investigation by a *Carabiniere* lieutenant into a series of rapes. This book won the prestigious *Premio Bancarella* in 2005. In 2007, Rizzoli published the graphic novel, *Cacciatori nelle tenebre* (Hunters in the Shadows), illustrated by Carofiglio's brother, Francesco, and featuring a team led by Inspector Carmelo Tancredi, a minor character from the Guerrieri novels.

[7] In a private conversation cited by Antonio Franchina, Camilleri says of this mixture that it was not his own particular way of telling a story, but simply the way of speaking of the Sicilian petty bourgeoisie, including his own family ('Come l'avevo raccontato a mio padre? Gliel'avevo raccontato in parte in siciliano e in parte in italiano . . . Questo non era un mio peculiare modo di raccontare, era semplicemente il modo di parlare della piccola borghesia siciliana; noi, a casa nostra, parlavamo in quel modo' (A. Franchina,

'Cronologia: Uno scrittore italiano nato in Sicilia', in A. Camilleri, *Storie di Montalbano* (Milan: Mondadori, 2002), pp. ciii–clxix (p. cxlii)). The language of Camilleri's texts is a much debated topic, as is evident from the secondary sources listed in the bibliography to this chapter: see, in particular, A. Sofri, 'La lingua mista di Camilleri', *Panorama*, 38/12 (23 March 2000); N. La Fauci, 'L'allotropìa del tragediatore', in *Il caso Camilleri: Letteratura e storia* (Palermo: Sellerio, 2004), pp. 161–76; M. Arcangeli 'Andrea Camilleri tra espressivismo giocoso e sicilianità straniata. Il ciclo di Montalbano', in G. Marci (ed.), *Lingua, storia, gioco e moralità nel mondo di Andrea Camilleri* (Cagliari: CUEC, 2004), pp. 203–32; and G. Sulis, 'Aspetti stilistici dell'uso del plurilingualismo nella narrativa contemporanea: l'interazione tra italiano, dialetti e lingue straniere nell'opera di Luigi Meneghello e Andrea Camilleri' (unpublished Ph.D. thesis, University of Reading, 2005). In the present context, I will limit myself to the observation that Camilleri's use of dialect or idiolect leads at times to stylistic redundancy, especially in the earlier novels – before the author had 'educated' his readership – as in these examples from *Il ladro di merendine*, in which a gloss (which I have marked with italics) is provided immediately after, either by the narrator for the reader or even by one character when speaking to another for whom, logically, no translation would be necessary: 'Non c'era nel suo gesto il più lontano sospetto di scòncica, *di presa in giro*' (p. 167); 'Gli occhi della fimmina, quando mi taliarono, erano scantati, *spaventati*' (p. 545); 'Ha fatto una trusciteddra, *un fagottino*, e s'è messa a bordo' (p. 555); 'M'avevano garantito che . . . che non avrei avuto camurrìe, *rotture di coglioni*' (p. 561).

[8] A detailed chronology of Camilleri's life and career up to the autumn of 2004, by Antonio Franchini, can be found in the second of the prestigious 'Meridiani' volumes dedicated to the author and containing a selection of his *Romanzi storici e civili* (Historical and Civil Novels), ed. and introduction by S. S. Nigro (Milan: Mondadori, 2004), pp. lvii–cxxvi. The first volume, *Storie di Montalbano* (Montalbano Stories), ed. M. Novelli, introduction by N. Borsellino, was published in 2002 and contains the first six novels in the series, all originally published in Palermo by Sellerio: *La forma dell'acqua* (*The Shape of Water* (New York: Viking Penguin, 2002; cited edition: London: Picador, 2004)), *Il cane di terracotta* (1996; *The Terracotta Dog* (London: Pan, 2004)), *Il ladro di merendine* (1996; *The Snack Thief* (New York: Viking Penguin, 2003)), *La voce del violino* (1997; *Voice of the Violin* (London: Picador, 2005)), *La gita a Tindari* (2000; *Excursion to Tindari* (London: Picador, 2006)), *L'odore della notte* (2001; *The Smell of the Night* (New York: Penguin, 2005), *The Scent of the Night* (London: Picador, 2007)). A selection of the short stories from the collections, *Un mese con Montalbano* (1998; A Month with Montalbano), *Gli arancini di Montalbano* (1999; Montalbano's *Arancini*) and *La paura di Montalbano* (2002; Montalbano's Fear), were first published by Mondadori; all references to the six novels are to this edition. At the time of writing, the other Montalbano novels – all published by Sellerio – are *Il giro di boa* (2003; *Rounding the Mark* (New York: Penguin, 2006; cited edition: London: Picador, 2007)); *La pazienza del ragno* (2004; *The Patience of the Spider* (London: Picador, 2007)); *La luna di carta* (2005; *The Paper Moon* (London: Picador, 2008)); *La vampa d'agosto* and *Le ali della sfinge* (both 2006; *August Heat* (London: Picador, 2009) and *The Wings of the Sphinx* (London: Picador, 2009)); *La pista di sabbia* (2007; *The Track of Sand* (Penguin, 2010)); *Il campo del vasaio* (2008; *The Potter's Field* (Penguin, 2011)); *L'età del dubbio* (2008; The Age of Doubt); *La danza del gabbiano* (2009; The Dance of the Seagull); *La caccia al tesoro* (2010; The Treasure Hunt); *Il sorriso di Angelica* (2010; Angelica's Smile); and *Il gioco degli specchi* (2011; The Game of Mirrors). All the published translations referred to are by S. Sartarelli.

In addition, a further three stories were published by Mondadori in 2004 under the collective title, *La prima indagine di Montalbano* (Montalbano's First Investigation). Further information on Camilleri and his works can be found on the site of the 'Camilleri Fans [*sic*] Club' at *www.vigata.org* (accessed 31 March 2009).

⁹ My translation. 'Tutto ebbe origine da un romanzo "storico" . . ., *Il birraio di Preston*. Mi ero accorto, proprio mentre ero impegnato con questo romanzo, che il mio personale modo di mettere su carta un racconto era, come dire, alquanto disordinato.

'Fu così che mi posi una domanda: ero capace di scrivere un romanzo cominciando dal capitolo primo e proseguendo di seguito, senza salti temporali o logici, sino al capitolo ultimo? Mi risposi che forse ne sarei stato capace se mi fossi auto-imbrigliato all'interno di una struttura narrativa abbastanza robusta.

'Fu a questo punto che mi tornò a mente uno scritto di Leonardo Sciascia sul romanzo poliziesco, sulle regole che un autore di gialli è tenuto a rispettare. E contemporaneamente mi ricordai di un'affermazione di Italo Calvino secondo il quale era impossibile ambientare un romanzo giallo in Sicilia. Così decisi di affrontare una doppia scommessa; con me stesso e con l'inconsapevole Calvino': A. Camilleri, 'I primi tre Montalbano', in *Il commissario Montalbano. Le prime indagini* (Palermo: Sellerio, 2008), pp. 9–12 (p. 9).

¹⁰ Simona Demontis analyses narrative formulae in Camilleri's writing in the chapter, '*Topos* e modelli narrativi', in her book, *I colori della letteratura. Un'indagine sul caso Camilleri* (Milan: Rizzoli, 2001), pp. 117–69. It is worth noting that even the titles of Camilleri's books are highly formulaic, being for the most part noun phrases consisting of a (definite) noun followed by a single modifier: it can be argued that the repetition of the structure constitutes a kind of 'brand identity' of the product.

¹¹ 'I primi tre Montalbano', pp. 11–12. See also the book-length interview of Camilleri by Saverio Lodato, *La linea della palma. Saverio Lodato fa raccontare Andrea Camilleri* (Milano: Rizzoli, 2002): 'He is the character who opened the way to my success. There's no discussion about that . . . But he's also a pain in the neck. In my readers' minds as he is, he ends up conditioning me. Lots of them say: "Okay, so let's read this book while we're waiting for another Montalbano. Speaking of which: when is the next Montalbano?"' ('È il personaggio che ha aperto la strada al mio successo. Su questo non si discute . . . Però è anche 'na camurria. Presente com'è ai miei lettori, finisce col condizionarmi. Molti dicono: "E leggiamo questo libro, intanto che ci arriva un altro Montalbano. A proposito: a quando un altro Montalbano?"' (pp. 382–3; my translation).)

¹² M. Chu, 'Sciascia and Sicily: discourse and actuality', *Italica*, 75/1 (spring 1998), 78–92.

¹³ My translation. 'Montalbano e la realtà, così nascono i miei gialli', now in *Racconti quotidiani*, pp. 71–5 (p. 75).

¹⁴ *La forma dell'acqua*, pp. 5–6. In an ironic note at the end of the first Montalbano novel, the author declares categorically that the novel is not born out of news stories or assembled from real facts and is entirely the fruit of his own fantasy but, given that reality seems these days determined to outdo fantasy or even take its place, he may casually have produced some regrettable coincidence of names or situations ('Ritengo indispensabile dichiarare che questo romanzo non nasce dalla cronaca e non assembla fatti realmente accaduti: esso è, insomma da addebitarsi interamente alla mia fantasia. Poiché però in questi ultimi tempi la realtà pare voglia superare la fantasia, anzi abolirla, può essermi capitata qualche spiacevole coincidenza di nomi o di situazioni' (p. 153)).

¹⁵ Ibid., pp. 6–7.

¹⁶ S. S. Van Dine (Willard Huntington Wright), 'Twenty rules for writing detective stories' (1928), in H. Haycraft (ed.), *The Art of the Mystery Story; A Collection of Critical*

Essays (1946, 1974; New York: Carroll and Graf, 1983), pp. 189–93 (p. 191). The rule –
number 13 – continues: 'A fascinating and truly beautiful murder is irremediably spoiled
by any such wholesale culpability. To be sure, the murderer in a detective novel should
be given a sporting chance; but it is going too far to grant him a secret society to fall
back on. No high-class, self-respecting murderer would want such odds.' Although not
entirely serious, Van Dine's statement is indicative of the aesthetic tendency of the early
detective genre in the anglophone tradition: it is curious that the mafia seems largely
to be excluded from the contemporary *giallo*, with its claims to the status of social and
political commentary; a notable exception in recent Italian crime literature is Roberto
Saviano's genre-defying book *Gomorra. Viaggio nell'impero economico e nel sogno di
dominio della camorra* (Milan: Mondadori, 2006).

17 'If I should write a book with a *mafioso* at the centre? I'd end up enobling him. Because
it may be true that I'm a terrible writer, but the very act of writing enobles. You confer
an identity on these people, a weight which is inevitably your own, and which you end
up transferring into this character' ('Scrivo un libro che abbia al centro un mafioso?
Finirei col nobilitarlo. Perché posso anche essere un pessimo scrittore, ma l'atto stesso
della scrittura nobilita. A questa gente riconosci un'identità, un peso che inevitabilmente
è il tuo, e che finisci col trasferire in questo personaggio'): *La linea della palma*, p. 309.
Interviewed by *il Fatto Quotidiano* on the twentieth anniversary of Sciascia's death,
Camilleri says of *Il giorno della civetta* that 'it is one of those books that I wish had
never been written. I have a personal theory. One cannot make a *mafioso* the protagonist,
because he becomes a hero and is rendered noble by the process of writing. Don Mariano
Arena, the mafia boss in *The Day of the Owl* is a giant. That classification of men of
his – men, half-men, pigmies, arse-crawlers and quackers [from the translation by
Archibald Colquhoun and Arthur Oliver (London: Jonathan Cape, 1963), p. 102] – is
one that we all share. So it ends up being indirectly a sort of positive depiction of the
mafioso and it makes us forget that he is the instigator of murders and other violent
acts. These are the risks one runs when writing about the mafia. The best literature for
speaking of the mafia are police reports and the sentences passed down by judges.
Saviano has managed to show that one can write a book – not a novel, because it is
something different – and show the *camorra* for what it is. But it is an isolated case' ('è
uno di quei libri che non avrei voluto fossero mai stati scritti. Ho una mia personale
teoria. Non si può fare di un mafioso un protagonista, perché diventa eroe e viene
nobilitato dalla scrittura. Don Mariano Arena, il capomafia del *Giorno della civetta*,
gigantéggia. Quella sua classificazione degli uomini – omini, sott'omini, ominicchi,
piglia 'n culo e quaquaraquà [*Il giorno della civetta*, in *Opere, 1956–1971* (Milan:
Bompiani, 1987), pp. 387–483 (p. 466)] – la condividiamo tutti. Quindi finisce con l'essere
indirettamente una sorta di illustrazione positiva del mafioso e ci fa dimenticare che è
il mandante di omicidi e fatti di sangue. Questi sono i pericoli che si corrono quando
si scrive di mafia. La letteratura migliore per parlare di mafia sono i verbali dei poliziotti
e le sentenze dei giudici. Saviano è riuscito a dimostrare che si può scrivere un libro –
non un romanzo perché è una cosa diversa – e mostrare la camorra per quello che è.
Ma è un caso isolato. (Silvia Truzzi, 'Camilleri: Il giorno della civetta "Sciascia non
avrebbe mai dovuto scriverlo"', *il Fatto Quotidiano*, 20 November 2009, *http://www.
ilfattoquotidiano.it/2009/11/20/camilleri-il-giorno-della-cive/12413/* (accessed 27 June
2011)). Camilleri's comments on the 'nobility' of don Mariano echoes earlier criticisms
but, apart from overstating the function in the novel of the antagonist to Carabiniere
Captain Bellodi, seems to be founded on the questionable affirmation that we all

share the character's taxonomy of the human race, whereas Sciascia's text acknowledges Bellodi's fascination with the malignant power of the *mafioso*, but ultimately and unequivocally sides with the rational values of the protagonist.

[18] 'The true relationship between Sciascia and me is that, when my battery is flat, I pick up one of his books, read a few pages and the "motor" starts up again' ('Il vero rapporto tra Sciascia e me è che, quando ho le batterie scariche prendo un suo libro, leggo qualche pagina e il "motore" si riaccende'): 'Sciascia è il mio motore. Intervista ad Andrea Camilleri di Alessandro Eugeni', *La Rinascita della Sinistra*, 14 (2006); now in A. Camilleri, *Vi racconto Montalbano. Interviste* (Rome: Datanews, 2006), pp. 107–12 (p. 110); my translation.

[19] *Il giro di boa*, pp. 12–21, pp. 9–23. All references are to this edition and are included in parentheses in the text.

[20] Ibid., pp. 17–18. While the comments of his deputy, Mimì Augello, who urges Montalbano not to resign, as to do so would be to offend the vast majority of honest policemen, are reassuring and tend to minimize the events of Genova (p. 21), the author's discourse is less conciliatory and aligned more with that of his protagonist: 'In Genova a good part of the police did not behave as we would have expected. Now, to understand this, you don't have to be politically aligned. You see the images. So what did Montalbano see? What did Andrea Camilleri see? They saw the same thing' ('A Genova buona parte della polizia non si è comportata come ci saremmo aspettati. Ora, per capirlo, non occorre essere schierati politicamente. Le immagini le vedi. Quindi cosa ha visto Montalbano? Cosa ha visto Andrea Camilleri? Hanno visto le stesse cose): *La linea della palma*, p. 379; my translation.

[21] *Rounding the Mark*, pp. 75–6. 'La conferma che il suo mondo aveva cominciato ad andare a scatafascio il commissario l'aviva avuta appena una misata appresso il G8, quanno alla fine di una mangiata di tutto rispetto, Calogero, il proprietario-coco-cammareri della trattoria "San Calogero", gli aviva annunziato che, sia pure di malavoglia, si ritirava': *Il giro di boa*, p. 78.

[22] In any case, as Michael Ross has commented on a draft version of this chapter, the francophone François is presented as a highly Europeanized character, a fact underlined heavily by the choice of his name. Furthermore, as a child, he is more readily perceived as not a 'threat'.

[23] *The Shape of Water*, p. 139. '"Ghi è tu ghe palla?" . . . "Ga ora io guarda, tu aspetta"': *La forma dell'acqua*, p. 87.

[24] *Excursion to Tindari*, p. 162. 'Tu palla ki io senta': *La gita a Tindari*, p. 956. 'Ingrid aveva sì cangiato di casa, ma non aveva cangiato d'abitudine per quanto riguardava le cammarere: se le andava a cercare nella Terra del Fuoco, nel Kilimangiaro, nel Circolo polare artico.
"'Montalbano sono."
"Come dikto tu?"
'Doveva essere un'aborigena australiana. Sarebbe stato memorabile un colloquio tra lei e Catarella' (ibid.).
It should be noted that Montalbano's own characteristically Sicilian syntax, involving the postponement of the verb ('Montalbano sono'), disappears completely in the English version ('This is Montalbano'): in any case, the character's self-presentation has been 'normalized' as an endearing and humorous catchphrase, due also to its inclusion in the title sequence of the television series. For more on the inequality of discourses between Italian and non-Italian characters in recent Italian crime fiction, see my article, '*Giallo*

sarai tu! Hegemonic representations and limits of heteroglossia in Carlo Lucarelli', *Spunti e Ricerche*, '*Il Giallo*', 16 (2001), 45–58.

[25] The term 'extracomunitario', meaning literally 'from outside the [European] community [or European Union]', is problematic in that it is almost exclusively applied to non-white, non-EU citizens.

[26] My translation. 'Amo particolarmente questo romanzo, anche se, quasi certamente, ora, dieci anni esatti dopo la sua stesura, lo scriverei diversamente. Nessun pentimento beninteso, la storia è quella che è, e tale resta: il racconto di un posto; il tentativo di stabilire fino a che punto può resistere una cultura millenario di fronte alle malie della modernità. Una storia di terrorismo in Sardegna, a Nuoro. Una storia di generazioni confuse, o, forse, troppo coscienti rispetto a una crisi irreversibile. Una storia di ritardi e eccessi': 'Nota' (March 1999), in *Ferro Recente*, pp. 119–20 (p. 119).

[27] My translation. '"Certo!" aveva risposto Mauro. "Colonialista e manichea. Certa gente si sorprende ancora se arriva in Sardegna e non trova quello che si aspetta, se vede l'industria, la vita cittadina, magari drogati, travestiti, eccetera. Preferisce quella Sardegna che è altrove, posticcia un po' bastarda, come le ghirlande di plastica che si mettono al collo dei turisti all'aeroporto di Honolulu. Ho sentito delle persone parlare dei fatti atroci, come rapimenti, uccisioni, vendette come se si trattasse di un dato costitutivo e indispensabile del territorio, un elemento di fascino. È assurdo"': ibid., pp. 32–3. All references are to this edition and are included in parentheses in the text.

[28] The epigraph (p. 7) to the first part of the novel, citing the guide of the Touring Club, explains that the name refers to the last period of the pre-Roman Sardinian civilization of the *nuraghi* (500–238 BC). Mauro's reflections allude to opposition to NATO bases, the Rome government and the building speculation along the coasts (p. 41).

[29] My translation. 'Restava il folclore, l'esibizione di riti non più rituali, senza significato, restava quel collegamento inconscio con valori estranei e fatali. Restava la violenza' (p. 41).

[30] In a note on the verso of the title page to the 1994 Granata edition of *Meglio morti*, in which he states that the names used in the novel are chance and apologizes for cases of homonymy, Fois thanks the Bolognese writer, Danila Comastri (Montanari), author of the Publio Aurelio crime novels set in ancient Rome, for her permission to use her name for the character. In *Ferro Recente*, on the other hand, *carabiniere* Fois makes an appearance (p. 100).

[31] My translation. 'Ora il commissario cominciò a sentirsi veramente inquieto. "Di noi sardi," ripeté meccanicamente come se ripetersi l'affermazione servisse a renderla più vera.

"Sarebbe un problema regionale dunque?" staffilò senza riguardi. "Signora mia," proseguì con sufficienza, "non le sembra che ne abbiamo avuto già abbastanza di sociologi e antropologi e che sia arrivato il momento di smettere di studiare *noi sardi?*" Avrebbe voluto aggiungere *da quattro soldi, sociologi e antropologi da quattro soldi*' (p. 108).

[32] My translation. '"Roba da non credersi: una dodicenne incinta e una sessantacinquenne illibata. Adoro la Sardegna," commentò d'improvviso senza controllo . . .

"Comunque quella che doveva essere una battuta non sortì il suo effetto. Il commissario e il giudice non parevano essersi divertiti.

"Scusate," tentennò Danila Comastri, sentendo sulla pelle il gelo che era calato nella stanza nonostante il riscaldamento. "Non volevo dire in quel senso. È la stanchezza che mi fa straparlare"' (p. 249).

[33] My translation. '"Comunque non è la prima volta che vengo in Sardegna, ci sono stato cinque o sei anni fa, in vacanza al mare . . . Che razza di posto . . ." commentò entrando nell'androne rustico di un palazzo, "è abitato?" chiese piano, superando la scritta CANTIERE

IN CORSO VIETATO L'INGRESSO AI NON ADDETTI AI LAVORI e constatando che qualche appartamento era già occupato' (p. 12).

34 My translation. '"Mi faccia capire bene: dunque . . .", cominiciò Sanuti radunando le forze con un bel sospiro profondo, "provo a spiegarle cosa ho capito io: voi andate in giro impunemente a dire cose poniamo come il cane di . . ."

'"Fronteddu".

'"Ecco, e fra di voi vi capite al volo? Voglio dire lei cita il cane di questo tizio in un discorso qualunque e i suoi interlocutori la capiscono?"

'"Quelli che conoscono la storia, ma da queste parti la conoscono tutti"' (pp. 41–2).

35 Barbara Pezzotti sees in the collaboration between Sardinians and *continentali* in *Meglio morti* and *Dura madre* a representation by Fois of the possibility of dialogue between two distinct cultural identities ('Risorgimento e identità italiana nel giallo contemporaneo', *Spunti e Ricerche*, 23 (2008), 57–70 (p. 65).

36 My translation. 'Sappiamo che la conoscenza non è di questo mondo. E che le spiegazioni sono voci, voci del luogo. Sono i canti di un coro che modula ai quattro venti.

'Sappiamo che tutta la verità è sulla bocca di tutti' (p. 200).

This echoes Leonardo Sciascia's 1966 novel, *A ciascuno il suo*, in which Professor Laurana conducts his personal investigation into a crime that, the reader discovers at the end of the novel, had not been a mystery for the other, more astute inhabitants of his small Sicilian town.

37 In an article in *The New Yorker*, reference is made to Carofiglio's liking Bruce Springsteen and J. D. Salinger, both cited on various occasions in the novels: L. Collins, 'Mob Appeal', 5 December 2005, *http://www.newyorker.com/archive/2005/12/05/051205ta_talk_collins* (accessed 17 March 2009).

38 My translation. 'Sì, è Bari, proprio la Bari in cui sono ambientati i romanzi di Guerrieri. Con qualche precisazione da fare, però. Prima di tutto non viene mai nominata, anche se tutte le tavole che la descrivono sono disegni di posti della città. In qualche caso trasfigurati e resi come *tópoi* appartenenti a una sorta di immaginario metropolitano, in altri casi chiaramente riconducibili a Bari. Ma la cosa più importante è che, aiutato dal disegno, mi sono divertito moltissimo a raccontare una città in bilico tra narrazione realistica e descrizione surreale di un posto immaginario e universale. Soprattutto per quanto riguarda i sotterranei, sia fisici che morali . . . Questa città è inequivocabilmente Bari, e al tempo stesso è tutte le città medie e grandi del mondo che custodiscono segreti innominabili': 'Elogio della letteratura disegnata. Conversazione di Vincenzo Mollica con Gianrico e Francesco Carofiglio', in G. Carofiglio and F. Carofiglio, *Cacciatori nelle tenebre* (Milan: Rizzoli, 2007), pp. 140–3 (p. 142). The graphic novel develops as its protagonist Inspector Carmelo Tancredi, who appears in the trilogy as a contact of Guerrieri.

39 See B. Pischedda, 'Maturità del poliziesco classico', in Vittorio Spinazzola (ed.), *Tirature '07. Le avventure del giallo* (Milan: il Saggiatore, 2007), pp. 10–19 (pp. 17–18).

40 Although Carofiglio's novels are usually legal thrillers which do not focus on investigations, in *Le perfezioni provvisorie* (Palermo: Sellerio, 2010) – the latest novel with Guerrieri as protagonist – the lawyer investigates a girl's disapperance in order to prevent the dismissal of the inquiry.

41 *A Walk in the Dark*, p. 11. 'Hanno invitato anche te perché ti si vogliono fare. Il brevetto di lesbica, ti vogliono far prendere. Ecco: il brevetto di lesbica volante.

'Non dissi così. Ovviamente. Noi uomini di sinistra non diciamo cose del genere; al massimo le pensiamo. E poi le due Giovanne sembravano capaci di staccarmi le palle e di giocarci a flipper per molto meno': *Ad occhi chiusi*, p. 19.

As a *uomo di sinistra*, Carofiglio was elected to the Italian senate in April 2008 in the Gruppo Partito Democratico.

[42] In his introduction to the anthology *Crimini* ((Turin: Einaudi, 2005 and 2007), pp. v–vii; *Crimini; The Bitter Lemon Book of Italian Crime Fiction*, trans. Andrew Brown (London: Bitter Lemon, 2008)), Giancarlo De Cataldo claims that immigration is one of the key themes of new Italian (and non-Italian) narrative, and that Italian *noir* writers have been among the first and – questionably – the most sensitive observers of the phenomenon (p. vi).

[43] *Involuntary Witness*, p. 33. 'Tutti noi procediamo per stereotipi. Chi dice che non è vero è un bugiardo. Il primo stereotipo mi aveva suggerito la seguente sequenza: africano, custodia cautelare, droga. Gli africani vengono arrestati soprattutto per questo motivo.

'Subito però era entrato in azione il secondo stereotipo. La donna aveva un aspetto aristocratico e non sembrava la donna di uno spacciatore': *Testimone inconsapevole*, p. 43. All references are to this edition and are included in parentheses in the text.

[44] *Involuntary Witness*, p. 151. 'Io avevo poco spazio. Molto poco. E allora dovevo fare qualcosa, anche dei tiri alla cieca, nella speranza di sentire un rumore e capire che da quella parte poteva esserci una strada. Da tentare di percorrere.

'I manuali per avvocati direbbero che questo è un modo sbagliato di procedere.

'Non fate domande di cui non potete prevedere la risposta. Non si controesamina alla cieca, senza avere un preciso obbiettivo da raggiungere. Il controesame deve essere rigorosamente pianificato, senza lasciare nulla all'improvvisazione, perché in caso contrario potrebbe addirittura rafforzare la posizione dell'avversario. Eccetera, eccetera, eccetera.

'Volevo vederli fare un maledetto processo, quei signori che scrivono i manuali.

'Voglio vederli in mezzo al rumore, alla sporcizia, al sangue, alla merda, di un processo vero. E voglio vederli applicare le loro teorie.

'Non si controesamina alla cieca.

'Volevo vederli. Io, alla cieca dovevo andarci per forza. Non solo nel processo': *Testimone inconsapevole*, p. 177.

[45] *L'arte del dubbio* (Palermo: Sellerio, 2007); a revised version of *Il controesame. Dalle prassi operative al modello teorico* (Milan: Giuffrè, 1997).

[46] My translation. 'Si procede al controesame se si ha un obiettivo significativo sotto il profilo probatorio e se tale obiettivo appare praticamente raggiungibile' (pp. 18–19).

[47] My translation. 'La violazione della regola che suggerisce di non rivolgere domande cruciali senza disporre di elementi che consentano in qualche modo di prevedere le risposte e, comunque, di evitare sorprese sgradite ed esiti controproducenti' (p. 115).

Bibliography

Arcangeli, M., 'Andrea Camilleri tra espressivismo giocoso e sicilianità straniata. Il ciclo di Montalbano', in G. Marci (ed.), *Lingua, storia, gioco e moralità nel mondo di Andrea Camilleri* (Cagliari: CUEC, 2004), pp. 203–32.

Camilleri, Andrea, *Il corso delle cose* (Poggibonsi: A. Lalli, 1978; The Run of Things).

——, *Un filo di fumo* (Milan: Garzanti, 1980; A Ribbon of Smoke)

——, *La strage dimenticata* (Palermo: Sellerio, 1984; The Forgotten Massacre).

——, *La forma dell'acqua* (Palermo: Sellerio, 1994).

——, *Il cane di terracotta* (Palermo: Sellerio, 1996).

——, *Il ladro di merendine* (Palermo: Sellerio, 1996).

——, *La voce del violino* (Palermo: Sellerio, 1997).

——, *Un mese con Montalbano* (Milan: Mondadori, 1998; A Month with Montalbano).

——, *Gli arancini di Montalbano* (Milan: Mondadori, 1999; Montalbano's *Arancini*).

——, *La gita a Tindari* (Palermo: Sellerio, 2000).

——, 'Il mio debito con Simenon', in Andrea Camilleri, *Racconti quotidiani*, ed. G. Capecchi (Pistoia: Libreria dell'Orso, 2001; Daily Tales), pp. 66–70.

——, *L'odore della notte* (Palermo: Sellerio, 2001).

——, 'Montalbano e la realtà, cosi nascono i miei gialli', in Andrea Camilleri, *Racconti quotidiani*, ed. G. Capecchi (Pistoia: Libreria dell'Orso, 2001), pp. 71–4.

——, *La paura di Montalbano* (Milan: Mondadori, 2002; Montalbano's Fear).

——, *The Shape of Water* (New York: Viking Penguin, 2002; London: Picador, 2004).

——, *Storie di Montalbano*, ed. Mauro Novelli and introduction Nino Borsellino (Milan: Mondadori, 2002).

——, *Il giro di boa* (Palermo: Sellerio, 2003).

——, *The Snack Thief* (New York: Viking Penguin, 2003).

——, *La pazienza del ragno* (Palermo: Sellerio, 2004).

——, *La prima indagine di Montalbano* (Milan: Mondadori, 2004; Montalbano's First Investigation).

——, *Romanzi storici e civili*, ed. and introduction S. S. Nigro (Milan: Mondadori, 2004; Historical and Civil Novels).

——, *The Terracotta Dog* (London: Pan, 2004).

——, *La luna di carta* (Palermo: Sellerio, 2005).

——, *The Smell of the Night* (New York: Penguin, 2005).

——, *Voice of the Violin* (London: Picador, 2005).

——, *Le ali della sfinge* (Palermo: Sellerio, 2006; The Wings of the Sphinx).

——, *Excursion to Tindari* (London: Picador, 2006).

——, *Rounding the Mark* (New York: Penguin, 2006; London: Picador, 2007).

——, *La vampa d'agosto* (Palermo: Sellerio, 2006; August Heatwave).

——, *Vi racconto Montalbano. Interviste* (Rome: Datanews, 2006).

——, *The Patience of the Spider* (London: Picador, 2007).

——, *La pista di sabbia* (Palermo: Sellerio, 2007; The Sand Track).

——, *The Scent of the Night* (London: Picador, 2007).

——, *Il campo del vasaio* (Palermo: Sellerio, 2008; The Potter's Field).

——, *L'età del dubbio* (Palermo: Sellerio, 2008; The Age of Doubt).

——, *The Paper Moon* (London: Picador, 2008).

——, 'I primi tre Montalbano', in *Il commissario Montalbano. Le prime indagini* (Palermo: Sellerio, 2008), pp. 9–12.

——, *La danza del gabbiano* (Palermo: Sellerio, 2009; The Dance of the Seagull).

——, *Il Sorriso di Angelica* (Palermo: Sellerio, 2010; Angelica's Smile).

——, *La caccia al tesoro* (Palermo: Sellerio, 2010; The Treasure Hunt).

Carofiglio, Gianrico, *Il controesame. Dalle prassi operative al modello teorico* (Milan: Giuffrè, 1997).

——, *Testimone inconsapevole* (Palermo: Sellerio, 2002).

——, *Ad occhi chiusi* (Palermo: Sellerio, 2003).

——, *Il passato è un paese straniero* (Milan: Rizzoli, 2004).

——, *Ragionevoli dubbi* (Palermo, Sellerio, 2006).

——, *A Walk in the Dark*, trans. H. Curtis (London: Bitter Lemon, 2006).

——, *L'arte del dubbio* (Palermo: Sellerio, 2007; The Art of Doubt).

——, *Cacciatori nelle tenebre* (Milano: Rizzoli, 2007; Hunters in the Shadows).

——, *Reasonable Doubts*, trans. H. Curtis (London: Bitter Lemon, 2007).

——, *The Past is a Foreign Country*, trans. H. Curtis (London: Old Street, 2008).

——, *Le perfezioni provvisorie* (Palermo: Sellerio, 2010).

—— and F. Carofiglio, *Cacciatori nelle tenebre* (Milan: Rizzoli, 2007).

—— and ——, 'Elogio della letteratura disegnata. Conversazione di Vincenzo Mollica con Gianrico e Francesco Carofiglio', in G. and F. Carofiglio, *Cacciatori nelle tenebre* (Milan: Rizzoli, 2007), pp. 140–3.

Collins, L., 'Mob appeal', 5 December 2005: *http://www.newyorker.com/archive/2005/12/05/051205ta_ talk_collins*.

Chu, M., 'Sciascia and Sicily: discourse and actuality', *Italica*, 75/1 (spring 1998), 78–92.

——, *'Giallo sarai tu!* Hegemonic representations and limits of heteroglossia in Carlo Lucarelli', *Spunti e Ricerche, "Il Giallo"*, 16 (2001), 45–58.

De Cataldo, Giancarlo, 'Introduzione', in *Crimini* (Turin: Einaudi, 2005 and 2007), pp. v–vii.

——, *Crimini: The Bitter Lemon Book of Italian Crime Fiction*, trans. Andrew Brown (London: Bitter Lemon, 2008).

Demontis, Simona, *I colori della letteratura. Un'indagine sul caso Camilleri* (Milan: Rizzoli, 2001).

Fois, Marcello, *Ferro Recente* (Bologna: Granata, 1992; Turin: Einaudi, 1999; Late Iron).

——, *Meglio morti* (Bologna: Granata, 1994; Turin: Einaudi, 2000; Better Off Dead).

——, *Sheol* (Bresso: Hobby & Work, 1997; Scheol).

——, *Sempre caro, with preface by Andrea Camilleri* (Nuoro: Il Maestrale 1998).

——, *Gap* (Milan: Frassinelli, 1999; Partisan Group).

——, *Sangue dal cielo*, with preface by M. Vázquez Montalbán (Nuoro: Il Maestrale/ Milan: Frassinelli, 1999).

——, *Dura madre* (Turin: Einaudi, 2001; Hard Mother).

——, *L'altro mondo* (Nuoro: Il Maestrale/Frassinelli, 2002; The Other World).

——, *The Advocate*, trans. P. Creagh (London: Harvill, 2003).

——, *Blood from the Skies* (London: Harvill, 2006).

Forgacs, D. and R. Lumley (eds), *Italian Cultural Studies: An Introduction* (Oxford: Oxford University Press, 1996).

Franchina, Antonio, 'Cronologia: Uno scrittore italiano nato in Sicilia', in *Andrea Camilleri, Storie di Montalbano* (Milan: Mondadori, 2002), pp. ciii–clxix.

Gribaudi, G., 'Images of the south', in D. Forgacs and R. Lumley (eds), *Italian Cultural Studies: An Introduction* (Oxford: Oxford University Press, 1996), pp. 72–87.

Haycraft H. (ed.), *The Art of the Mystery Story: A Collection of Critical Essays* (1946, 1974; New York: Carroll and Graf, 1983).

La Fauci, N., 'L'allotropia del tragediatore', in *Il caso Camilleri: Letteratura e storia* (Palermo: Sellerio, 2004), pp. 161–76.

Lodato, Saverio, *La linea della palma. Saverio Lodato fa raccontare Andrea Camilleri* (Milano: Rizzoli, 2002).

Lumley, R. and J. Morris (eds), *The New History of the Italian South: The Mezzogiorno Revisited* (Exeter: University of Exeter Press, 1997).

Marci, G. (ed.), *Lingua, storia, gioco e moralità nel mondo di Andrea Camilleri* (Cagliari: CUEC, 2004).

Padovani, Marcelle, *La Sicile comme métaphore: Conversations en italien avec Marcelle Padovani* (Paris: Stock, 1979).

——, *La Sicilia come metafora: Intervista di Marcelle Padovani* (Milan: Mondadori, 1979).

Patriarca, Silvana, 'How many Italies? Representing the south in official statistics', in J. Schneider (ed.), *Italy's 'Southern Question': Orientalism in One Country* (Oxford: Berg, 1998), pp. 77–97.

Pezzotti, Barbara, 'Risorgimento e identità italiana nel giallo contemporaneo', *Spunti e Ricerche*, 23 (2008), 57–70 (65).

Pischedda, B., 'Maturità del poliziesco classico', in V. Spinazzola (ed.), *Tirature '07. Le avventure del giallo* (Milan: il Saggiatore, 2007), pp. 10–19.

Saviano, Roberto, *Gomorra. Viaggio nell'impero economico e nel sogno di dominio della camorra* (Milan: Mondadori, 2006).

Schneider, J. (ed.), *Italy's 'Southern Question': Orientalism in One Country* (Oxford: Berg, 1998).

Sciascia, Leonardo, *Il giorno della civetta, in Leonardo Sciascia, Opere, 1956–1971* (Milan: Bompiani, 1987), pp. 387–483.

——, 'Sciascia è il mio motore. Intervista ad Andrea Camilleri di Alessandro Eugeni', *La Rinascita della Sinistra*, 14 (2006); now in Andrea Camilleri, *Vi racconto Montalbano. Interviste* (Rome: Datanews, 2006), pp. 107–12.

Sofri, A., 'La lingua mista di Camilleri', *Panorama*, 38/12 (23 March 2000).

Spinazzola, V. (ed.), *Tirature '07. Le avventure del giallo* (Milan: il Saggiatore, 2007).

Sulis, G., 'Aspetti stilistici dell'uso del plurilingualismo nella narrativa contemporanea: l'interazione tra italiano, dialetti e lingue straniere nell'opera di Luigi Meneghello e Andrea Camilleri' (unpublished Ph.D. thesis, University of Reading, 2005).

Truzzi, Silvia, 'Camilleri: Il giorno della civetta "Sciascia non avrebbe mai dovuto scriverlo"', *il Fatto Quotidiano*, 20 November 2009: *http://antefatto.ilcannocchiale.it/glamware/blogs/blog.aspx?id_blog=96578&id_blogdoc=2384413&yy=2009&mm=11&dd=20&title=camilleri_il_giorno_della_cive*.

Van Dine, S. S. (Willard Huntington Wright), 'Twenty rules for writing detective stories', in H. Haycraft (ed.), *The Art of the Mystery Story: A Collection of Critical Essays* (1946, 1974; New York: Carroll and Graf, 1983), pp. 189–93.

www.vigata.org (accessed 31 March 2009).

7

Italian Women Crime Writers

GIULIANA PIERI AND LUCIA RINALDI

In the introduction to their history of women's writing in Italy, Letizia Panizza and Sharon Wood noted bluntly that 'women have not been granted full citizenship in the existing histories of [Italian] literature'.[1] The same could also be said for Italian women crime writers whose contribution to the development of this genre in Italy is still in need of proper assessment. Brief descriptive chapters in Raffaele Crovi and Luca Crovi, though listing a considerable number of women crime writers, have generally favoured a taxonomical approach with lists of writers and novels devoting very limited space to the analysis of their writings.[2] At the turn of the new millennium, in the context of the general critical reappraisal of Italian crime fiction, after the explosive boom of public interest in home-grown talents in the 1990s, a number of important pioneering studies have refocused critical attention on this forgotten area of Italian literary production.[3] The present chapter combines a historical overview of the contribution of women writers to the development of Italian crime fiction with some close textual analysis in order to assess the often considerable contribution of women crime writers to the postmodern reworking of the *giallo*.

In a world dominated by male writers, it is interesting to note that one of the very first proper crime writers in Italy was in fact the popular nineteenth-century writer Carolina Invernizio, whose work was heavily influenced by the tradition of the French feuilleton and who did adopt the new genre in some of her work.[4] Invernizio belongs to the generation of Italian women writers who, in post-unification Italy, started to make a living from contributing to periodicals and found their niche in popular novels and romances written for a female audience. A number of her novels centre on female characters who take on the role of unofficial investigators – see for instance *I ladri dell'onore* (1894), *La sepolta viva* (1896), *La felicità nel delitto* (1907) and, above all, *Nina la poliziotta dilettante* (1909).[5] Invernizio remained, however, isolated and the almost complete lack of women crime writers during the golden age of Italian crime fiction seems to be linked to the difficulties faced by women in the interwar years which, as Maurizio Pistelli rightly noted, 'left women confronted with an ideologically hostile barrage from Church and state alike. Fascism and Catholicism both allowed little space for women outside their traditional domestic and reproductive roles.'[6]

The 1950s and 1960s, which were by and large characterized by the huge success of crime fiction in translation, show an almost complete lack of female crime writers who started to emerge again only in the late 1970s. The only exception is the activity of the doyenne of Italian crime fiction, Laura Grimaldi, one of the most prolific writers of this genre. Grimaldi worked as a writer, translator and editor for the crime fiction series of the publisher Ponzoni, as well as being editor of other popular crime series ('Gialli Canarino', 'Segretissimo'). More importantly, she was chief editor of all detective and crime series of Mondadori between 1983 and 1989 and, in 1989, she founded and ran her own crime publishing house, Interno Giallo, which published amongst others the French polar writer Didier Daeninckx and contemporary Italian crime writers Giancarlo De Cataldo and Pino Cacucci. Grimaldi's interest in *noir* and hard-boiled fiction both as a writer and editor resulted also in her volume for would-be *noir* writers *Il giallo e il nero: scrivere suspense* (1996), a response to the creative and editorial interest in crime fiction in Italy in the 1990s and testimony to her knowledge and passion for the founding fathers of the genre with a special interest in North-American models.[7] Her literary activity started in the 1950s; between 1953 and 1958 she wrote around thirty novels under various pseudonyms – Alfred Grim, Alfred Pomarick, L. D. Grimal and Alfredo Pomarici for the crime series 'I Gialli di Heros' published by the Florentine publisher Sansoni.[8] In 1988, Grimaldi published *Il sospetto*, the first of a trilogy which comprised *La colpa* (1991) and *La paura* (1993) – the trilogy was republished as *Perfide storie di famiglia* by Marco Tropea Editore in 1996.[9] *Il sospetto* is an unsettling crime novel based on a series of brutal sexual murders. The background is the succession of sexually motivated murders of the so-called monster of Florence.[10] Grimaldi's interest in hard-boiled fiction seems to have had an impact on the many graphic descriptions of the killer's assaults and deformations of his victims in the novel which are never gratuitous: they form the backbone of the disquieting account of the story in which Matilde Monterispoli, a 65-year-old widow from the Florentine upper-middle class, starts to suspect that her middle-aged son, Enea, who still lives with her, may be the 'monster'.[11] Enea is a possible suspect because of some pathological behavioural patterns; Matilde becomes convinced of his guilt and eventually kills him by increasing his diabetes medicine, only for the police to inform her that the monster has indeed been apprehended. Carol Lazzaro-Weis interestingly comments on the resemblance of the story to the archetypal myth of Medea.[12] The relationship between guilt and justice, maternal love and the duty to protect other women from depravity, as well as the critique of the social set to which Matilde belongs, in which public scandal is perceived as the most destructive force, are some of the themes of this powerful novel. The whole trilogy is a merciless and devastating analysis of the Italian myth of the family which in these novels is a place of distrust, suspicion, fear and violence and acts as 'a metaphor for the larger social order'.[13] The focus on the family unit, as we shall see, became one of the dominant traits of Italian women crime writers who overall have engaged more fully with this social and cultural institution and have used it very effectively as the microcosm through which they could voice their social critique.

As Lazzaro-Weis had noted, in her study of feminism and Italian fiction between 1968 and 1990, after the radical feminist literature of the 1970s, in the 1980s women writers in Italy returned to already established narrative genres although 'the return to literature . . . [was] informed by their desire both to unmask literature's purported neutral structure and to add their vision to it'.[14] More importantly these writers were 'not retuning to literature to tell the same stories as men, although they may be using common traditions and structures'.[15] The general return to known narrative structures, and in particular to novel writing, created the right conditions for a rebirth of interest in historical and crime novels conceived as tools to explore Italy's recent violent past and some of the most pressing issues in contemporary Italian society respectively. Dacia Maraini's best-selling novel *Voci* (1994; Voices) is one of the first examples of the rebirth of Italian crime fiction in the 1990s. Its open-ended structure places it firmly within the postmodern reworking of this traditional genre. It is, however, in the themes explored by Maraini that one can detect her commitment to a specific feminist perspective. The protagonists of the book are the victims of psychological and physical violence perpetrated on women. Maraini points the finger accusingly towards the patriarchal structure of Italian society and exposes 'another pervasive and equally troubling scourge of contemporary society – the scandalous number of unsolved crimes against women in Italy and in Western society'.[16] In *Voci* there are two female detectives: one a professional and also a lesbian policewoman; the other one an amateur and a radio journalist who is the narrator and who interviews both the primary suspects and witnesses in the novel. The use of the radio is symbolic of the status of women in both the Italian media and society at large: the focus on women's beauty and seductive appearance is turned in the novel into an exploration of the unseen women behind the public personas and their unheard 'voices'. Maraini's *Voci* is a powerful example of how the crime novel could be used by women writers to engage with real and metaphorical questions of justice, the alleged neutrality of justice and the justice system, as well as the themes of female exclusion and isolation in a male-dominated society.

A further thematic and stylistic common denominator amongst Italian women crime writers is the influence of television. As Tiziana Jacoponi has noted, the broadcasting in Italy of the television series *La signora in giallo* (*Murder, She Wrote*) since 1985 influenced a new generation of Italian women crime writers both in terms of the type of female character central to their narratives, the accidental detective á la Miss Marple, but also in terms of narrative and dialogic style: 'fast dialogues, simple and direct language, overt refusal of excessive intellectualisation. The rhythm is almost cinematic, the language is direct and visual, the structure is apparently simple.'[17] These characteristics, which may seem to point in the direction of the writing of crime fiction by women as pure entertainment, are, however, often a deliberate distancing from the social and political engagement practised by their male counterparts who are generally more explicit and direct in their use of this popular genre as a form of indictment of contemporary social mores and politics. As we shall see, especially in the case of Nicoletta Vallorani, Grazia Verasani and Barbara Garlaschelli, the depiction of contemporary Italian society is as socially, politically and culturally acute as that of contemporary male writers;

what does seem to change is the volume of this *impegno*, almost as if a sotto voce had replaced the loudspeaker.

Nicoletta Vallorani

Nicoletta Vallorani (Offida, 1959) is professor of contemporary English literature and cultural studies at the University of Milan, and works as both translator and novelist. Her narrative is characterized by a very original blend of *noir* and crime elements and cyberpunk fiction. *Dentro la notte, e ciao* (1995), her first *noir* novel, focuses on the common denominator of her crime fiction: the protagonists are people at the margins of society who are invisible during the day but populate the city of Milan at night. The crimes committed here, which include the murder of a young drug addict and a tramp, the assault of some prostitutes and transsexuals, also point to another element that Vallorani will explore more fully in later novels: sexual ambiguity, especially transvestism and androgyny, and transgression which are seen as important components of the new urban culture.

The trilogy of detective Zoe Libra, the protagonist narrator, which include *La fidanzata di Zorro* (1996), *Cuore meticcio* (1998) and *Visto dal cielo* (2004), is set in the neighbourhood of Pasteur in Milan, an area in the semi-periphery of the city which has traditionally been associated with both a working-class and a migrant population (this is where the flux of internal migration in the 1950s, at the time of Italy's economic miracle, was directed and where from the late 1980s the new foreign migrants settled).[18] In *La fidanzata di Zorro*, Zoe Libra, who works for the private eye Silvie Dell'Oro, aka Lupin, investigates the death of a research assistant at the University of Milan. The structure and elements of the traditional detective novel are all there (murder, investigation, the detectives, the red herrings and the final return to order) but the novel is characterized by irony and often parody in both thematic and linguistic terms. Zoe's family is a chaotic, dysfunctional but emotionally rich family, reminiscent of Daniel Pennac's characters (Zoe looks after her three nieces since their mother, Zoe's sister, is too busy spending time with her lovers; Zoe's grandmother dresses like a teenager; she has two dogs, Ugo and Cicoria, who are respectively deaf and blind).[19] It is also a family in which men are absent. One cannot fail to notice that male characters in these novels are always the perpetrators of crimes; they are often grotesque, and are portrayed as fundamentally irresponsible. In *Cuore meticcio*, Zoe and Lupin investigate a serial killer of terminally ill patients. The investigative plot here is also a vehicle for the portrayal of other themes such as love, life, illness and death. *Cuore meticcio* still shows an interest in the representation of a multi-ethnic Milan but the main issues are existential themes and typically feminine themes such as the relationship of women with their bodies, love, family and maternity. In the final instalment of the trilogy, *Visto dal cielo*, the co-protagonist is Agata, Lupin's teenage daughter, and the search for a serial killer is a means to explore another area of alternative and marginal culture in Milan, the *centri sociali*, the independently run and originally illegal spaces that came to represent the anarchist and extreme left-wing-inspired counter-culture of the Italian student and workers movement of the 1970s.

Vallorani's characters are the losers of Milan's industrial and post-industrial success history: tramps, prostitutes, drug addicts, transvestites, immigrants, those who live at the margins and are the undesirable side of Milan's slick image. The binary opposition between the bad dangerous city of the night and the good legal city of the day is turned on its head, in a classic *noir* topos: it is the legal city that is crime ridden and violent and the solution will come with the help of the people at the margins of society who populate the metropolis at night. In a revealing passage in *Dentro la notte, e ciao*, Vallorani voices the concerns of one of the apparently respectable members of Milanese society who vents his racist anger:

> What has our Milan changed into? We wanted it to be a beautiful and affluent city, a celebration of art, of hard work and honesty. We have tolerated an unruly immigration of people from the south, of lazy men who have come here to take our jobs away, of women breeding like bitches. And what now? Do we have to accept that a coloured monkey gets the same education that we receive? Somebody must think about how to clean this city up.[20]

If, as Claudio Milanesi has noted, her portrayal of Milanese society, in its inverted polarization, is often too one-dimensional and moralizing – 'this process of reversal becomes sometimes explicit and too didactic'[21] – given that all the positive characters come from the margins of the city, Vallorani's multi-ethnic dream, acted out in the microcosm of Pasteur, is a model community characterized by a strong sense of solidarity which shows her committed exploration of the social and political implication of, arguably, the greatest challenge faced by contemporary Italy: the social and cultural integration of old and new migrants in a true ethnically diverse society.

Eva (2002) is a contamination of *noir* with science fiction, and one of Vallorani's more engaged novels to date. The historical background of this complex narrative is the war in former Yugoslavia, imagined here as a never-ending physical and meta-phorical scar on the bodies and minds of the characters who populate a disquieting Milan in the year 2023. The private eye Nigredo investigates a series of murders perpetrated by a serial killer who displays the corpses in complex visual presen-tations that turn the dismembered bodies into geometrically precise compositions:

> as usual the heart is at the centre of the design. The other pieces are in order and are carefully positioned like rays. First the internal organs, and then the rest in the external section of the circle. A system organized around the heart which mirrors the way we ought to be when we are alive. The design is perfect: precise distances between each piece, creating symmetrical geometries in all directions. A chirurgical operation.[22]

These often resemble art installations: 'rather than a murder it looked like an art installation: a gift of ephemeral art given to the city'.[23] The description of the futuristic Milan of this novel recalls Vallorani's cyberpunk novel *Il cuore finto di DR* (1993). The atmosphere in both novels is reminiscent of *Blade Runner*, Ridley Scott's influential film, which Vallorani mentions explicitly as one of the models for *Eva*: it is a violent, physically and emotionally disfigured city, a bleak place of alienation and loneliness.[24] Nigredo's involvement in the crimes is both an epistemological and ontological quest, an exploration of the real and symbolic significance of war and its consequences. Vallorani focuses on the young victims of radioactive and chemical warfare, whose bodies are the visual embodiment of the fissure caused by war:

> The little girl was new. She was sitting on the kerb, her bare feet plunged into the murky puddle which was rapidly being created by the melting snow. A healthy foot and a deformed one. Her hands: one whole, the other halved. One half of her face was beautiful. A blue eye, a crimson ear lobe. A half-finished person. One half of what she should have been.[25]

Physical and emotional wholeness are replaced emblematically by the mutilated bodies and minds of the characters. The novel's complex symbolism – which encompasses Carl Jung's concept of nigredo, the moment of greatest psychological despair;[26] the link between death, murder and redemption in the figure of Eve; the exploration of life after violence, abuse and deformity – points to the central tenet of the novel, the importance of remembrance and historical memory, as indicated also in the dedication of the book 'for those who have lost their memory, either willingly or by chance'.[27] Vallorani believes that literature is the vehicle through which one can tell stories so that history won't be forgotten and identifies her work as that of a committed writer: 'writing, especially genre, is committed. I don't want my writing to be innocent. I want to commit myself and I want to take a stand.'[28]

Grazia Verasani

Grazia Verasani (Bologna, 1964), actress, musician, playwright, screen writer, journalist as well as crime author, started her career as a writer at the end of the 1980s with the publication of short stories. In 1999, she published her first novel, *L'amore è un bar sempre aperto*; this was followed by several novels, collections of short stories and plays.[29] She gained greater popularity with her first *noir* novel *Quo vadis, baby?* (2004), shortlisted for the Prix SNCF du polar, readily adapted for cinema (Gabriele Salvatores, 2005) and subsequently for a six-episode television drama (Sky, 2008). *Quo vadis, baby?* is the first novel of a series set in contemporary Bologna which features as protagonist the female private investigator Giorgia Cantini. It is an accomplished *noir* story that, whilst following some of Giorgia's investigations, centres around the protagonist's obsessive search for the truth behind her sister's (Ada) suicide, which happened several years before in Rome. *Velocemente da nessuna parte* (2006), the second novel in the series, focuses on Giorgia's investigation into the disappearance of Vanessa (Van), a failed television extra and single mum, who had been making a living as an escort. In the third novel, *Di tutti e di nessuno* (2009), there are two main parallel plots: the story of Giorgia's official investigation into the troubled life of an upper-middle-class girl (Barbara), and her unofficial investigation into the murder of Franca, an eccentric tarot reader and former prostitute, who used to live in Giorgia's neighbourhood.

In Verasani's *noir* novels the writer's real life and eclectic interests, encompassing cinema, music and theatre, as well as her literary preferences play an important role. *Quo vadis, baby?*, for instance, is a line from the highly controversial 1972 film by Bernardo Bertolucci, *Last Tango in Paris*. *Velocemente da nessuna parte*, literally 'nowhere fast', is the title of the anti-royalist song from the album *Meat is murder* (1985) by The Smiths, one of the most important groups to emerge on the British independent music scene in the 1980s. Both references seem to act as pointers to different examples of anti-establishment culture and, together with an array of intertextual and metafictional references to popular culture in the three novels, act as vehicles to guide the readers through a specific social and cultural period in Italian history, which starts with the rebellious and often violent cultural revolution of the 1970s and ends with the new rampant capitalist culture of the 1980s and 1990s.[30] Verasani's own city, Bologna is the co-protagonist of these novels, acting as a cultural and political looking glass to the social and cultural changes in Italian society. The Cantini trilogy is, however, particularly interesting because Verasani re-works the conventions of the *noir* novel through a decisively female perspective.

In these *noir* novels elements of the hard-boiled tradition feature prominently: the solitary private eye, the figure of the femme fatale, the looming obscure past,[31] the importance of the city and its spaces, have all been absorbed and re-adapted. The characterization of her detective figure is remarkably illuminating in this instance. Through the first-person narration, Verasani presents Giorgia as the female version of the private investigator of the hard-boiled school: 'Sitting on a stool in a bar in via Goito I hold the fourth gin lemon of the night . . . My sight is blurred by the alcohol . . . I lean on the door of my old Citroën while I light a Camel.'[32] Giorgia indulges in heavy drinking and smoking, she leads a solitary life characterized by short-term relationships, and she is obsessed with the violence in her past. She clarifies that her job is not as glamorous and exciting as one might expect, and that it was not a choice that she made voluntarily.[33] Although she offers an image of an anti-heroic figure right from the start, Verasani portrays her detective as a strong, emancipated woman who has found her (unconventional) role in a changing world where women seem to have finally acquired independence, as can be seen in the extract from *Quo vadis, baby?* in which Giorgia's curt manner and sarcasm are lost on Dazi's self-centred and blatant male chauvinism.[34] As Giorgia comments mockingly: 'Nobody has ever been surprised by the fact that I am a woman: everybody used to watch *Charlie's Angels*, and many are actually astonished that I don't carry a gun', highlighting with characteristic irony the influence of popular culture in the changing perception of the role of women in Italian society.[35]

Verasani's *noir* novels, however, depart from the traditional *noir* narrative as they do not seem to take on the archetypal notions of law and order, but they engage with questions (and forms) of justice on a more private level. Therefore, widely diverging from the themes advocated by many male Italian crime writers in recent years, no political scandals or notorious cases are exposed and discussed. Verasani focuses instead on social matters with a personal angle, such as infidelities, drug abuse, disappearances, blackmails and sometimes murder. There is no glamorous historical narrative but rather the social and political critique is implicit in the realistic portrayal of the humdrum dimension of ordinary lives and crimes. Verasani's intentions are expressed clearly when Giorgia explains the nature of her job:

> The cases I deal with are mainly love affairs: the majority of my clients are women and ninety-nine percent of them are aware of being betrayed, but they need to hear it clearly and unequivocally . . . Almost no one comes here to attempt to save a marriage: all scream revenge.[36]

Verasani is thus committed to narrate about women's feelings, fears and contradictions and to turn their stories and their desperate search for justice into the protagonists of her novels. Her female characters are often victims of the society that they live in, and while some of them painfully become survivors (such as Barbara), others succumb to its violence. Ada, Vanessa and Franca, who initially are presented as embodiments of the femme fatale because of their uninhibited relationship with the male world, are unambiguous examples of how society so often turns women into victims.

What emerges from Verasani's stories of unhappiness and betrayals is a vivid portrait of contemporary Italian society, a wealthy but decadent world, characterized by alienated and isolated individuals full of regrets, often trapped in dangerous relationships. Giorgia bitterly reflects: 'Certainly when the Agency was founded I was more enthusiastic, maybe because I didn't know yet that I would have been dealing mainly with middle-class dramas, dysfunctional love stories, and love triangles.'[37] Verasani thus questions the values, challenges the nature and exposes the crisis of one of Italian society's key institutions: the family, a recurrent topic in the narrative of other contemporary female crime writers, especially in the work of Barbara Garlaschelli.

Barbara Garlaschelli

Barbara Garlaschelli (Milan, 1965) started her career as a writer in the mid-1990s with the online publication of children's stories. She subsequently published several *noir* novels and short stories, including *Nemiche* (1998) and *Alice nell'ombra* (2002); in 2004 she won the Scerbanenco award for *Sorelle* (2004).[38]

Garlaschelli's *noir* novels are rather unconventional. The typical elements of the traditional formula are missing: there is no investigator or investigation. Her plots are focused on crimes, criminals and revolve especially around the victims. Through an analysis of the dark side of ordinary people, the writer examines the inner self of her characters and depicts sentiments of selfishness, hatred, obsession, regret and revenge, often linking these destructive feelings to past family tragedies and abuses. Her stories explore physical and psychological violence, particularly within the context of the family.[39]

Sorelle, for instance, narrates the story of two sisters, Virginia and Amalia, who kidnap their lodger, Dario, when they discover that he has been having an affair with both of them. Amalia firmly believes he needs to be punished mercilessly because 'he doesn't know the meaning of the word remorse'.[40] The beginning of the story builds up a tense atmosphere of suspense by describing Dario's fear while he is being kept tied to a bed in a dark room and his efforts to understand what is happening to him. The story is narrated from different points of view and focuses on the unusually close relationship between the two sisters, their past of family problems and Amalia's irrationality, bordering on folly, which informs her distorted sense of justice. Betrayal, desertion and emotional emptiness are the key themes in this novel in which feelings of hatred and suffering are explored through the description of the protagonists' psychological processes and inner life. The same elements can be traced in *Alice nell'ombra*, which narrates the story of the pro- tagonist (Alice), who comes to realize that she has been living an empty life, as suggested by the title: in the shadow of her manipulative mother first and then her husband later. When she finds out the truth about the mysterious disappearance of her beloved father when she was a child, she unleashes her dark side and rebels with absolute brutality.

Sorelle and *Alice nell'ombra* present as main characters female figures scarred by a life of oppression, women who undergo the painful transformation from victims of abuse to perpetrators of violence. Garlaschelli summarizes their sentiments with an illuminating sentence: 'sooner or later you need to face up to life'.[41] Although in a different and more violent manner than Verasani's characters, Garlaschelli's figures rise up to violence and set to become avengers in search of an unorthodox, personal form of justice that the social system is unable to grant them. Women are depicted as strong individuals trying to fight against their pre-established roles of victims in a violent, male-dominated world.

Conclusion

Milanesi's contention that, faced with the work of female crime writers, we are confronted with the same questions that fuelled the debate on the *écriture feminine* of the 1980s points to the importance of gender in the analysis of contemporary crime fiction: are there differences in language, themes and general approach in the works of female crime writers which set them apart from their male counterparts;

in the case of such a highly codified genre such as crime fiction, are female crime writers bringing in changes and new perspectives, and do female writers follow the rules of the genre and conform to stereotypes or do they subvert them?[42] Although relevant, these questions could also easily apply more generally to the work of any postmodern writer who approaches this traditional genre. Without wanting to dismiss entirely the question of the *écriture feminine*, in the present analysis we have erred on the side of caution and have sought not to treat these writers as different from their male counterparts in order not to leave a door open to the accusation, which has often been levelled at Italian female crime writers, that they are not really writing crime fiction. For instance, Crovi's otherwise inform-ative and positive appraisal of the contribution of Italian women crime writers in *Tutti i colori del giallo* still betrays the tendency to look at them as separate from the mainstream history of this genre. Their work is not analysed alongside the work of male writers and their difference is further emphasized by the title of the chapter, 'Le dame in nero', which, although a tongue-in-cheek reference to the dark ladies of the detective and *noir* tradition, still carries a semiotic pointer to the idea of a woman crime writer as a genteel amateur.[43]

As this brief analysis has attempted to show, Italian women crime writers are both following the rules of the genre and, when subverting them, they are doing so as much as many other male writers, though the results are distinctive. The case of the social critique which underlies much Italian contemporary crime fiction is particularly instructive. One of the reasons which has often been invoked by commentators for the public success of contemporary Italian crime fiction is that this type of narrative constitutes the new socially and politically motivated literature. Crime writers in the last two decades have often engaged with some of the most pressing problems faced by Italian society and have also been using this genre as a vehicle to explore Italy's recent (and not so recent) troubled past. The tendency, however, has been to see this renewed social and political commitment as a male domain fronted by well-known and outspoken figures such as Lucarelli and Carlotto. As the present analysis has shown, women crime writers are in fact showing the signs of an equally profound engagement with the most pressing issues which Italy is facing in the new millennium with a particular focus on marginal and marginalized characters.

If one were to look for a common denominator in the work of contemporary Italian women crime writers, it would probably be their focus on the family, which is the most striking thematic difference between their work and that of contemporary Italian male crime writers. All the female writers analysed above criticize and expose the contradictions and the dark side of this core social insti-tution in Italy. Within a still male-dominated society, steeped in the ideological legacy of Catholicism, this different and often disquieting portrayal of the Italian family is certainly a provocative and topical theme which finds in the aesthetics and intrinsic violence of the *noir* novel its appropriate narrative form. The family becomes thus a metaphor for patriarchal society at large and violence towards women exposes the inner power dynamics at the core of contemporary Italian society. The attack of the family as a patriarchal construct which supports re-pression and violence towards women acts as the *pars destruens* in the work of Italian women crime writers. The positive counterpart can be found in new ideas of the family, portrayed as a chaotic, non-hierarchical but emotionally rich environment, often devoid of a male (or heterosexual male) presence. The new family is moving away from the nuclear family that has characterized post-war Italy in both the industrial and post-industrial period and which in the novels analysed above often mirrors the oppression and violence of society as a whole. This is a family that reaches out from the shallow confines of blood ties to include strong and unconventional friendships and reflects the desire of women to devote themselves to meaningful relationships of their own choice and to break free from the ties imposed by a traditional male view of this import-ant social and cultural institution.

* * *

Extract from Grazia Verasani's *Quo vadis, baby?*

Dazi looks radiant. He's clean-shaven wearing an Armani suit with a purple and green striped silk tie. 'I'm here because I owe you one.'

'Sure.'

He lights up a Davidoff. 'Can I tell you a secret?'

He doesn't wait for an answer. 'My ex-wife wants to get remarried and it hurt my feelings. It's difficult to think that the women you've had can be with someone else.'

'Do you still love her?'

'I shagged a Nigerian last night.'

'Ah', I say stretching my spine on the back of the office chair.

'I was at a dinner full of beautiful women, there were a couple of them that I could have easily bedded.'

'I'm sure.'

'But dating is such hard work you know.'

'It's easier with Nigerian prostitutes.'

He cracks a smile showing off his perfect teeth. 'I've walked out on loads of women who still ask themselves why.'

'Does it make you proud?'

'Not one bit.'

I look at Dazi with indifferent courtesy, waiting for him to hurry up and tell me what he wants to say.

'Me and my ex-wife were always fighting.'

I light up a cigarette. 'So you were right to get divorced then.'

'Your sister was an actress?'

I nod affirmatively taking a couple of long drags.

'Angela used to organize a lot of parties that were attended by actors and singers . . . Who knows I might have met her.'

I rub my eyes swollen with tiredness. If it were summer I'd switch on the fan and blast it right in his face in the hope of seeing him fly out the door as light as a feather.

'How much do I owe you?' he asks me.

'Just the price of the train ticket.'

'That's all?'

'Yeah, that's all.'

He takes a couple of banknotes out of his wallet and lays them on the table. 'I think I've already asked you but I'll try again. I'd like to take you out to dinner, as a friend.'

I feel as weary as a housewife who's carrying the shopping up five flights of stairs.

'Okay Dazi, call me sometime.'

I see him smile with a hint of satisfaction. 'You're different to all of the other women that I've met.'

'What do you mean?'

'You don't even act like a woman.'

I'm curious. 'What do women act like?'

'What I want to say is that I like talking to you, while normally I only go looking for women to get them into bed.'

I accompany him to the door. 'I'm a little hurt that you don't want to sleep with me.'

'Can I make up for it?' he responds immediately.

Grazia Verasani, *Quo vadis, baby?* (Milan: Mondadori, 2004), pp. 194–5.
Translated by Patrick C. Mcgauley.

Notes

[1] Letizia Panizza and Sharon Wood (eds), *A History of Women's Writing in Italy* (Cambridge: Cambridge University Press, 2000), p. 2.

[2] Raffaele Crovi, 'Le signore del thriller italiano', in *Le maschere del mistero. Storie e tecniche di thriller italiani e stranieri* (Firenze: Passigli Editori, 2000), pp. 171–4, originally published in *Italia Oggi*, 9 September 1988. The book contains a collection of Crovi's reviews of new crime writers dating from the 1970s. There are only three reviews of Italian women crime writers: Gloria Zoff, *Moscacieca col delitto* (1977), set in Milan; Nicoletta Bellotti, *Centro città* (1977), also set in Milan; and Nicoletta Sipos, *Favola in nero* (1989), a thriller that explores industrial espionage and imagines a biological apocalypse. Luca Crovi, 'Le dame in nero', in *Tutti i colori del giallo. Il giallo italiano da De Marchi a Scerbanenco a Camilleri* (Venezia: Marsilio, 2002), pp. 195–217. This is a good overview but given the chronological scope, it is descriptive and there is no space for analysis. Besides, although the intention is to show the considerable number of female crime writers in Italy, the choice of a separate chapter makes it difficult to view their work in the wider context of the development of Italian crime fiction.

[3] Monica Jansen, 'Estrapolare Eva: alla ricerca dell'irriproducibilità tecnica dell'opera d'arte', and Tiziana Jacoponi, 'Detective per caso ovvero donne in cerca di guai', *Narrativa, Trent'anni di giallo italiano. Omaggio a Loriano Macchiavelli e Antonio Perria*, 26 (2006), 69–79 and 111–18; Monica Jansen, 'Un polar métaphysique sans aura: Visto dal cielo de Nicoletta Vallorani', *Cahiers d'études Romanes, nouvelle série*, 15/1 (2006), 239–54; *eadem*, 'Laura Mancinelli e i casi "molto strani" del capitano Flores', *Incontri* (NS), 15/3–4 (2000), 176–82; Mirna Cicioni, 'Loyalties and lesbianism in the novels of Fiorella Cagnoni',

in M. Cicioni and N. Di Ciolla, *Differences, Deceits and Desires. Murder and Mayhem in Italian Crime Fiction* (Newark: University of Delaware Press, 2008), pp. 145–59.

4 On Invernizio and the *giallo* see E. Zanzi, 'La mamma dei "libri gialli", in *Gazzetta del Popolo*, 12 August 1932, also in F. Contorbia, *Il sofista subalpino. Tra le carte di Gozzano* (Cuneo: L'Arciere, 1980); and A. Nozzoli, 'La Invernizio e il "giallo" al femminile', in Carolina Invernizio, *Il romanzo d'appendice*, ed. G. Davico Bonino and G. Ioli (Turin: Gruppo Ed. Forma, 1983), pp. 42–56.

5 Invernizio is mainly known as a writer of *romanzo d'appendice*, which was the Italian response to the French feuilleton. Eugène Sue was one of the most celebrated feuilleton writers. His *Mysteries of Paris* was the inspiration of Francesco Mastriani's *I misteri di Napoli* (1869) and of Invernizio's *Torino misteriosa*. On the fashion for the *Misteri* in Italy see also Maurizio Pistelli, 'I "misteri" e Francesco Mastriani', in *Un secolo in giallo. Storia del poliziesco italiano (1860–1960)* (Roma: Donzelli, 2006), pp. 6–10. Lepschy notes that women characters are always central to her novels and that 'Invernizio's portrayal of a wide social spectrum has the distinctive feature that no behaviour is confined to one class': Anna Laura Lepschy, 'The popular novel', in Panizza and Wood (eds), *A History of Women's Writing in Italy*, pp. 177–89 (p. 178).

6 Pistelli, 'I "misteri" e Francesco Mastriani', p. 7. All translations are by Pieri and Rinaldi unless otherwise stated.

7 It is worth mentioning that Grimaldi's work as a translator included the complete translation, with Sergio Altieri, of Raymond Chandler's novels and short stories for the series I Meridiani by Mondadori in 2005 and 2006.

8 Laura Grimaldi, ad indicem, Roberto Pirani et al. (eds), *Dizionario Bibliografico del giallo*, 1 (Pontassieve: Pirani Bibliografica Editrice, 1996), 735–6. Under the pseudonym Alfred Grim she wrote two successful novels: *Attento poliziotto*, published by Mondadori, and *La collezione del morto*.

9 *Suspicion*, trans. Robin Pickering-Iazzi (Madison, Wisconsin and London: University of Wisconsin Press, 2003).

10 On the mostro di Firenze see Ellen Nerenberg, 'Making a killing: the "Monster of Florence" and the trial(s) of Pietro Pacciani', in S. Gundle and L. Rinaldi, *Assassinations and Murder in Modern Italy. Transformations in Society and Culture* (New York and Houndmills: Palgrave, 2007), pp. 167–79.

11 Di Ciolla-McGowan also noted that 'at the time of these events Grimaldi, as a journalist and a police consultant, was privy to all the documentation relating to the killings, and she conducted a lengthy enquiry on behalf of the magazine *Panorama*, which resulted in the formulation of a psychological profile of the assassin': Nicoletta Di Ciolla-McGowan, 'Society and family politics: Laura Grimaldi's trilogy *Perfide storie di famiglia*', *Spunti e ricerche*, 18 (2003), 77–87 (79).

12 Carlo Lazzaro Weis, '*Cherchez la femme*: feminism and the giallo', in *From Margins to Mainstream: Feminism and Fictional Modes in Italian Women's Writing 1968–1990* (Philadelphia: University of Pennsylvania Press, 1993), pp. 158–79 (p. 174).

13 Di Ciolla-McGowan, 'Society and family politics', 84.

14 Carlo Lazzaro-Weis, '*Cherchez la femme*', p. xv.

15 Ibid.

16 Joann Cannon, 'Voci and the conventions of the giallo', *Italica*, 78/2 (2001), 193–202 (193). See also Bernadette Luciano, 'From novel to film: re-instating patriarchal order to Dacia Maraini's *Voci*', in Cicioni and Di Ciolla (eds), *Differences, Deceits and Desires*, pp. 133–44.

[17] 'Dialoghi veloci, lingua essenziale, rinuncia sfrontata a qualsiasi eccesso di intellettualizzazione. Il ritmo diventa cinematografico, il linguaggio diretto e visivo, la struttura è apparentemente semplice': Jacoponi, 'Detective per caso', p. 112.

[18] Milanesi calls Pasteur 'un quartier representative de la ville et de la société italienne des années 90'. See Claudio Milanesi, 'Les femmes et le *polar* italien. Les trois romans policiers de Nicoletta Vallorani', *Italies*, 3 (January–June 1999), 1–26 (11).

[19] On Pennac see Claire Gorrara, 'Telling tales: Daniel Pennac's *Le Fee Carabine*', in *The Roman Noir in Post-war French Culture: Dark Fictions* (Oxford: Oxford University Press, 2003), pp. 90–106.

[20] 'Cosa mai è diventata la nostra Milano? Volevamo che fosse una città bella e florida, la celebrazione dell'arte, dell'operosità, dell'onestà. Abbiamo saputo tollerare un'emigrazione scriteriata . . . della gente del Sud, degli uomini pigri che sono venuti a rubarci il lavoro e delle donne prolifiche come vacche . . . Ma adesso? Dobbiamo forse accettare che una scimmia colorata riceva la stessa istruzione che riceviamo noi? . . . Qualcuno deve pensare a ripulire questa città': *Dentro la notte, e ciao* (Bologna: Granata Press, 1995), p. 164. All translations into English of the novels cited in this study are by the authors.

[21] 'ce processus de renversement deviant parfois explicite et par trop didactique': Milanesi, 'Les femmes et le *polar* italien', p. 14.

[22] 'come sempre il cuore è il centro del disegno. Gli altri pezzi sono in ordine, sistemati con cura, a raggiera. Prima gli organi interni, poi il resto, nella fascia esterna del cerchio. Un sistema organizzato intorno al cuore, come dovremmo essere noi da vivi. Il disegno è perfetto: distanze precise tra un pezzo e l'altro, simmetrie geometriche in ogni direzione. Un'operazione chirurgica': *Eva* (Einaudi: Stile libero noir, 2002), p. 5.

[23] 'più che un omicidio sembrava un'installazione: arte effimera regalata alla città': ibid., p. 14.

[24] *http://www.nicolettavallorani.com* (accessed December 2010). On the influence of *Blade Runner* see also Monica Jansen, 'Un polar métaphysique sans aura', pp. 239–54.

[25] 'la bambina era nuova. Sedeva sul bordo della strada, con i piedi nudi tuffati dentro un rigagnolo scuro che si stava formando rapidamente dalla neve sciolta. I piedi erano uno sano e uno deforme. Le mani, una intera e una dimezzata. Il viso per metà bellissimo. Un occhio azzurro, un lobo cremisi. Una persona finita a metà: solo un pezzo di quello che avrebbe dovuto essere': *Eva*, p. 67.

[26] For the name of the protagonist, Nigredo, Jansen offers three possible explanations: the novel by Angela Carter, *The Passion of the New Eve*; the *nigredo* of Jung; and the possible echo of Joseph Conrad, *Heart of Darkness*.

[27] 'per chi ha perso la memoria, per volontà o per caso': *Eva*, p. 1

[28] 'La scrittura, soprattutto quella di genere, si compromette . . . Io non voglio che la mia scrittura sia innocente. Io voglio compromettermi, prendere posizione': Jansen, 'Estrapolare Eva', 69–79, (71).

[29] Selected titles: novels: *L'amore è un bar sempre aperto* (Ravenna: Fernandel, 1999); *Fuck me mon amour* (Ravenna: Fernandel, 2001); *Quo vadis, baby?* (Milan: Mondadori, 2004); *Velocemente da nessuna parte* (Milan: Mondadori, 2006); *Tutto il freddo che ho preso* (Milan: Feltrinelli, 2008); *Di tutti e di nessuno* (Milan: Kowalski, 2009); Short stories: *Tracce del tuo passaggio* (Ravenna: Fernandel, 2002); theatre plays: *From Medea* (performed in 2002, published by Sironi in 2004).

[30] See Alessia Risi, 'Donne e contesto storico-sociale: le figure femminili nella scrittura di Grazia Verasani', in Claudio Milanesi (ed.), *Il romanzo poliziesco, la storia, la memoria. Atti del convegno internazionale* (Bologna: Astraea, 2009); and 'Dalle microstorie di

Grazia Verasani alla costruzione del sociale. Analisi delle trame secondarie in *Quo vadis, baby?* e *Velocemente da nessuna parte*', in *Quale memoria per il noir italiano? Un'indagine pluridisciplinare. Atti del convegno* (Brussels : P.I.E.- Peter Lang, 2010), pp. 193–202.

[31] On the negative meaning of the past in *noir* fiction, Giovannini explains: 'Nel noir il passato è il luogo negativo dove sono avvenuti i fatti che conducono al precipitare dei protagonisti . . . Al centro delle storie c'è spesso un destino ossessionante, che agisce in modi misteriosi e irrazionali sugli individui': Fabio Giovannini, *Storia del noir. Dai Fantasmi di Edgar Allan Poe al grande cinema di oggi* (Rome: Castelvecchi, 2000), p. 32.

[32] 'Seduta su di uno sgabello di un bar di via Goito tengo tra le mani il quarto gin lemon della serata . . . Ho la vista appannata dall'alcol . . . Non so come riesco a uscire dal bar. Mi appoggio alla portiera della mia vecchia Citroën e mi accendo una Camel': *Quo vadis, baby?*, p. 7.

[33] 'L'agenzia Cantini mi fu imposta da mio padre per risarcirlo del mio fallimento universitario' (The Cantini Agency was imposed upon me by my father in order for me to compensate him of my failure at university): ibid., p. 43.

[34] 'Giorgia mi consente di raccontare un tipo di donna anti-conformista, che non accetta di adeguarsi ad un modello di femminilità dominante, dove invecchiare è una colpa, non fare figli una mancanza' (Giorgia allows me to talk about an unconventional type of woman who does not accept the traditional notion of femininity which considers ageing as a guilt and being childless as a deficiency): Verasani in Valentina Desalvo, 'Quella Bologna nera e disperata', *La Repubblica, Sezione Bologna*, 6 June 2006, 11.

[35] 'Il fatto che io sia una donna non ha mai sorpreso nessuno: tutti hanno visto le *Charlie's Angels* e tanti si stupiscono addirittura che non abbia una pistola': *Quo vadis, baby?*, p. 39.

[36] 'I casi di cui mi occupo sono per lo più storie di corna: la maggior parte dei miei clienti sono donne e il novantanove per cento sa già di averle, le corna, ma se lo deve sentir dire in modo chiaro ed inequivocabile . . . Quasi nessuno viene qui nel tentativo di recuperare un matrimonio: urlano tutti vendetta': ibid., p. 40.

[37] 'Una cosa è certa quando nacque l'agenzia avevo più entusiasmo, forse perché non sapevo ancora che mi sarei occupata per lo più di drammi borghesi, di amori malati, di triangoli': ibid., p. 41.

[38] Selected titles: *Nemiche* (Milan: Frassinelli, 1998); *Alice nell'ombra* (Milan: Frassinelli, 2002); *Sorelle* (Milan: Frassinelli, 2004); short stories: *O ridere o morire* (Milan: Marcos y Marcos, 1995; repr. Lugano: Todaro, 2005); *L'una nell'altra* (Palermo: Dario Flaccovio Editore, 2006).

[39] On the theme of family in Garlaschelli's works see also Nicoletta Di Ciolla-McGowan, 'Relative values: resisting desire and individuation in Barbara Garlaschelli's *Alice nell'ombra* and *Sorelle*', 21.1 (June 2003), 119–33.

[40] '[Dario] non conosceva il significato della parola rimorso': *Sorelle*, p. 30.

[41] 'La vita prima o poi batte cassa': ibid., p. 131.

[42] Milanesi, 'Les femmes et le *polar* italien', p. 7.

[43] Crovi, 'Le dame in nero', pp. 195–217.

Works cited

Cannon, Joann, 'Voci and the conventions of the giallo', *Italica*, 78/2 (2001), 193–202.

Cicioni, Mirna, 'Loyalties and lesbianism in the novels of Fiorella Cagnoni', in M. Cicioni and N. Di Ciolla, *Differences, Deceits and Desires. Murder and Mayhem in Italian Crime Fiction* (Newark: University of Delaware Press, 2008), pp. 145–59.

Contorbia, F., *Il sofista subalpino. Tra le carte di Gozzano* (Cuneo: L'Arciere, 1980).

Crovi, Luca, 'Le dame in nero', in *Tutti i colori del giallo. Il giallo italiano da De Marchi a Scerbanenco a Camilleri* (Venezia: Marsilio, 2002), pp. 195–217.

Crovi, Raffaele, 'Le signore del thriller italiano', in *Le maschere del mistero. Storie e tecniche di thriller italiani e stranieri* (Firenze: Passigli Editori, 2000), pp. 171–4.

Desalvo, Valentina, 'Quella Bologna nera e disperata', *La Repubblica, Sezione Bologna*, 6 June 2006.

Di Ciolla-McGowan, Nicoletta,'Society and family politics: Laura Grimaldi's trilogy *Perfide storie di famiglia*', *Spunti e ricerche*, 18 (2003), 77–87.

——, 'Relative values: resisting desire and individuation in Barbara Garlaschelli's *Alice nell'ombra* and *Sorelle*', 21.1 (June 2003), 119–33.

Garlaschelli, Barbara, *Nemiche* (Milan: Frassinelli, 1998).

——, *Alice nell'ombra* (Milan: Frassinelli, 2002).

——, *Sorelle* (Milan: Frassinelli, 2004).

——, *O ridere o morire* (Milan: Marcos y Marcos, 1995; repr. Lugano: Todaro, 2005).

——, *L'una nell'altra* (Palermo: Dario Flaccovio Editore, 2006).

Giovannini, Fabio, *Storia del noir. Dai Fantasmi di Edgar Allan Poe al grande cinema di oggi* (Rome: Castelvecchi, 2000).

Gorrara, Claire, 'Telling tales: Daniel Pennac's *Le Fee Carabine*', in *The Roman Noir in Post-war French Culture: Dark Fictions* (Oxford: Oxford University Press, 2003), pp. 90–106.

Grimaldi, Laura, *Il sospetto* (Milan: Mondadori, 1988).

——, *Suspicion*, trans. Robin Pickering-Iazzi (Madison, Wisconsin and London: University of Wisconsin Press, 2003).

Jacoponi, Tiziana, 'Detective per caso ovvero donne in cerca di guai', *Narrativa, Trent'anni di giallo italiano. Omaggio a Loriano Macchiavelli e Antonio Perria*, 26 (2006), 111–18.

Jansen, Monica, 'Laura Mancinelli e i casi "molto strani" del capitano Flores', *Incontri* (NS), 15/3–4 (2000), 176–82.

——, 'Estrapolare Eva: alla ricerca dell'irriproducibilità tecnica dell'opera d'arte', *Narrativa, Trent'anni di giallo italiano. Omaggio a Loriano Macchiavelli e Antonio Perria*, 26 (2006), 69–79.

——, 'Un polar métaphysique sans aura: Visto dal cielo de Nicoletta Vallorani', *Cahiers d'études Romanes, nouvelle série*, 15/1 (2006), 239–54.

Lazzaro Weis, Carlo, '*Cherchez la femme*: feminism and the giallo', in *From Margins to Mainstream: Feminism and Fictional Modes in Italian Women's Writing 1968–1990* (Philadelphia: University of Pennsylvania Press, 1993), pp. 158–79.

Lepschy, Anna Laura, 'The popular novel', in Letizia Panizza and Sharon Wood (eds), *A History of Women's Writing in Italy* (Cambridge: Cambridge University Press, 2000), pp. 177–89.

Luciano, Bernadette, 'From novel to film: re-instating patriarchal order to Dacia Maraini's *Voci*', in M. Cicioni and N. Di Ciolla (eds), *Differences, Deceits and Desires. Murder and Mayhem in Italian Crime Fiction* (Newark: University of Delaware Press, 2008), pp. 133–44.

Maraini, Dacia, *Voci* (Milan: Rizzoli, 1994).

Milanesi, Claudio, 'Les femmes et le *polar* italien. Les trois romans policiers de Nicoletta Vallorani', *Italies*, 3 (January–June 1999), 1–26.

Nerenberg, Ellen, 'Making a killing: the "Monster of Florence" and the trial(s) of Pietro Pacciani', in S. Gundle and L. Rinaldi, *Assassinations and Murder in Modern Italy. Transformations in Society and Culture* (New York and Houndmills: Palgrave, 2007), pp. 167–79.

Nozzoli, A., 'La Invernizio e il "giallo" al femminile', in Carolina Invernizio, *Il romanzo d'appendice*, ed. G. Davico Bonino and G. Ioli (Turin: Gruppo Ed. Forma, 1983), pp. 42–56.

Panizza, Letizia and Sharon Wood (eds), *A History of Women's Writing in Italy* (Cambridge: Cambridge University Press, 2000).

Pirani, Roberto et al. (eds), *Dizionario Bibliografico del giallo* (Pontassieve: Pirani Bibliografica Editrice, 1996).

Pistelli, Maurizio, 'I "misteri" e Francesco Mastriani', in *Un secolo in giallo. Storia del poliziesco italiano (1860–1960)* (Roma: Donzelli, 2006), pp. 6–10.

Risi, Alessia, 'Donne e contesto storico-sociale: le figure femminili nella scrittura di Grazia Verasani', in Claudio Milanesi (ed.), *Il romanzo poliziesco, la storia, la memoria. Atti del convegno internazionale* (Bologna: Astraea, 2009).

——,'Dalle microstorie di Grazia Verasani alla costruzione del sociale. Analisi delle trame secondarie in *Quo vadis, baby?* e *Velocemente da nessuna parte*', in *Quale memoria per il noir italiano? Un'indagine pluridisciplinare. Atti del convegno* (title tbc) (Brussels : P.I.E.-Peter Lang, 2010).

Vallorani, Nicoletta, *Dentro la notte, e ciao* (Bologna: Granata Press, 1995).

——, *La fidanzata di Zorro* (Milan: Marcos y Marcos, 1996).

——, *Cuore meticcio* (Milan: Marcos y Marcos, 1998).

——, *Eva* (EinaudiStile libero noir, 2002).

——, *Il cuore finto di DR* (Milan: Mondadori, 1993; and Lugano: Todaro, 2003).

——, *Visto dal cielo* (Turin: Einaudi Stile Libero, 2004).

Verasani, Grazia, *L'amore è un bar sempre aperto* (Ravenna: Fernandel, 1999).

——, *Fuck me mon amour* (Ravenna: Fernandel, 2001).

——, *Tracce del tuo passaggio* (Ravenna: Fernandel, 2002).

——, *From Medea* (Milano: Sironi, 2004).

——, *Quo vadis, baby?* (Milan: Mondadori, 2004).

——, *Velocemente da nessuna parte* (Milan: Mondadori, 2006).

——, *Tutto il freddo che ho preso* (Milan: Feltrinelli, 2008).

——, *Di tutti e di nessuno* (Milan: Kowalski, 2009).

Zanzi, E. 'La mamma dei "libri gialli", in *Gazzetta del Popolo*, 12 August 1932.

Websites

http://www.nicolettavallorani.com.
http://www.graziaverasani.it

8

Milano nera: *Representing and Imagining Milan in Italian* Noir *and Crime Fiction*

GIULIANA PIERI

Since the unification of Italy, Milan has occupied a special place in the country's economic development, history and imagination. This is reflected in the various labels which have been attached to this city: the moral capital, the business and industrial capital since the very first Italian industrial revolution in the early twentieth century and especially during the years of the economic miracle and, more recently, the fashion and finance capital of Italy. All these identities have shaped the image of the city and, alongside the place occupied by Milan in the social and economic history of Italy since the 1950s, have resulted in Milan's special position in the *noir* imaginary of the Italians.[1]

Several novelists since the 1950s have represented the changing face of Milan during and in the aftermath of the economic miracle – they comprise Luciano Bianciardi's *La vita agra* (1962) and the series of novels by Giovanni Testori, which go under the collective title of *The Secrets of Milan*, set in the new periphery of the city created by the boom.[2] Yet, as John Foot has pointed out, 'almost as soon as it had begun, the boom came to an end', and Milan 'was faced with a yet more painful process of de-industrialisation',[3] which coincided with the social and political unrest brought about by the students and workers movement which, in Italy, lasted well beyond the initial outburst in 1968. The change from an industrial to a postindustrial city in the 1970s was followed by a second transformation, in the 1980s, when Milan became the city of service industries, fashion, stock market, investment banking, private television and advertising. These are the years that go under the label *Milano da bere* (an advertising slogan, which literally means 'Milan is good enough to drink') which symbolized the new values of the decade: Milan was the city of the yuppies and the nouveau riche, of political and economic corruption, and the stronghold of Bettino Craxi, the Milanese Socialist leader, who made the city his political and economic power base. In 1992, with the judicial scandals of bribesville (Tangentopoli), there began a new phase in the city's political, social, and cultural life. From the mid-1990s Milan became the city of Silvio Berlusconi, who had already made a mark on the city's physical landscapes in the 1980s with his two large housing developments, Milano 2 and Milano 3, and who 'then remoulded the cultural landscape through private television and advertising' and gave strong foundations to the launch of his political career at national level.[4]

The aim of this study is to discuss the way in which Milan has been represented and imagined by successive generations of Italian *noir* and crime writers who, as I shall argue, have transformed the city into a more complex metaphor for the changing Italy. The tension between local or regional identity and national identity has a particular resonance and meaning in Italy given the complex, and some would argue flawed, nature of the unification of the country. The regional versus national is also an issue that has resurfaced in the 1990s, in the context of a renewed debate over national identity after the country faced the scandals and investigations that brought down the old post-war political class and saw the emergence of new political forces. It is also notable that this new cultural and socio-political phase should coincide with an unprecedented success of Italian crime and *noir* fiction. In particular, the new postmodern *noir* writers, some of whom display and openly declare their social engagement, have again chosen Milan as the signifier for the whole country. Although Bologna, thanks to the work of Macchiavelli and Lucarelli, as has been discussed in chapter 5, has also become a *noir* city in the Italian imaginary, its crimes are often fashioned in ways which recall closely the model established by Scerbanenco, the father of the Italian *noir*, thus reinforcing the idea that the *Milano nera* is the ideological mirror of the whole country.

One of the most striking elements in the recent history of Milan is the fact that, since the economic miracle, the periphery of the city has started to dominate the historic centre. This, as we shall see, is a central theme for crime writers who, through their detectives, who during their investigations cross the real and imaginary boundaries of the different spaces of the city, have engaged with the spatial and social geography of the industrial and post-industrial city.[5]

When, as Chandler pointed out in his classic critique of British Golden Age detective fiction, 'Hammett gave murder back to the kind of people that commit it for reasons, not just to provide a corpse', and the 'realistic mystery novel' was born, Italy did not have a tradition of home-grown crime writers.[6] However, the very beginnings of Italian crime fiction coincided with the representation of Milan, the city where, with a few exceptions, Augusto De Angelis's Commissario De Vincenzi is based.[7] De Angelis and Scerbanenco are crucial to understand the particular place of Milan in what Luca Crovi has called 'the mythology of crime Milan-style'.[8] Although De Angelis's works are not *noir* novels, since the first Italian *giallisti* preferred the classic detective formula, and descriptions of the ambience are kept to a minimum, the way in which he portrays Milan is nevertheless interesting and seems to have had an impact on Scerbanenco, who also started his literary career during the interwar years. De Angelis's characteristically enclosed spaces of the murder and investigation, which are imported directly from the Anglo-American tradition of the classic detective novel, have however a special connotation. Luca Somigli has argued that 'they seem to provide an alternative to the metropolis that surrounds and encroaches on them [i.e. the enclosed spaces] like a suspension fluid'.[9] These spaces also seem to shelter both Commissario De Vincenzi and his suspects from the cold and unforgiving city that surrounds them whilst also acting as a claustrophobic container for the psychologies of the characters, which are ultimately the focus and most innovative element in De Angelis's narrative.

Any analysis of Italian *noir* fiction, as Jennifer Burns has argued in chapter 3, and the depiction of Milan are inextricably linked to the work of Scerbanenco. Carloni viewed Milan in Scerbanenco's novels as: 'a city symbol of Italy's socio-economic reality, eroded by wild industrialization, rampant consumerism and by a widespread criminality generally condoned by sociological analysis'.[10] He also rightly pointed out that the most important legacy of Scerbanenco for Italian crime and *noir* fiction is the 'relationship between crime and urban reality',[11] and, I would add, his vision of Milan as the first proper Italian capital of crime which could compete with its foreign counterparts; this being particularly important for Italian crime writers who, until that time, had suffered from the esterophilia of the genre. Carloni has also suggested that Scerbanenco's vision is fundamentally Manichean with a clear distinction between honest people and dishonest criminals.[12] As I have argued elsewhere, this dualism between good and evil is actually more complex than it first seems when one takes into account Scerbanenco's ideological ambiguity.[13] However, Scerbanenco's portrayal of Milan does feature a strong emphasis on the dialectic between centre and periphery. The lumpenproletarian zones of the city are captured by Scerbanenco as they shift from the city centre to the new peripheries, which became the perfect setting for the new violent and often pointless crimes of the new industrial city. Interestingly, this representation of the tension between centre and periphery and their changing faces following the industrial boom has been recurrently echoed by later generations of Milanese *noir* writers. Scerbanenco portrays this tension under different guises. There is a strong emphasis on the scale of the space of the periphery with its characteristically large empty open spaces that highlight the sense of isolation of the characters.[14] In his critique of the loss of identity of the historic city, there are several ironic references to the treatment of the city's cultural and historic heritage,[15] and the dubious architectural aesthetics that underpins the lack of interest in the historic and social fabric of the city's spaces and buildings.[16]

The 1970s and 1980s saw a sharp decline in the production of home-grown crime and *noir* fiction in Italy. However, at least in Milan, the legacy of Scerbanenco guaranteed the survival and growth of the 'delitto alla Milanese'. Antonio Perria, a former journalist like Scerbanenco, published three novels between 1974 and 1975 set in the response unit of the police headquarters of Milan: *Incidente sul lavoro*, *Delitto a mano libera* and *Giustizia per scommessa*. A similar setting is chosen by Secondo Signoroni in his 1976 novel *Qui commissariato di zona*. Both Perria and Signoroni are indebted to Scerbanenco for their portrayal of the new post-economic miracle Milan: a place of isolation, crime and de-socialization.

Renato Olivieri's highly successful series with Commissario Ambrosio also have an important place in the representation of Milan in Italian crime fiction. Olivieri was a prolific writer: his series started in 1978 and continued throughout the 1980s and early 1990s.[17] As Crovi has observed: 'Ambrosio's Milan is a sophisti-cated and fashionable city, inhabited by well-bred ladies and gentlemen who behind their honest façade hide morbid and criminal impulses.'[18] Olivieri's background – he was a columnist for women's magazines – is similar to Scerbanenco's as they both often cross the boundaries between different popular narrative genres. Olivieri's novels are set in the historic centre of the city, in elegant apartment blocks and houses, amongst the aristocracy and the bourgeoisie whose habits and rituals, despite hiding a dark side, are untouched by the crimes committed which are always of a personal nature and never the result of the corruption of social mores. The geography, both social and physical, of the city is central to these novels that, with no hint of criticism, portray a city which is no more, and in reality probably never was, which has its boundaries well within the old nineteenth-century city walls. It is the stereotype of the sophisticated wealthy city ruled with confidence by its social elite who never set foot in the new peripheries of the industrial and post-industrial real city, which are central to all recent *noir* novels set in Milan.

When Carloni published his study of the geography of Italian crime fiction in 1994, he claimed that after 1978 the regional identity of the genre became less relevant.[19] This study was, however, published before the emergence of the new wave of talents, such as Lucarelli, Camilleri, Fois, Carlotto, Carofiglio and Santo Piazzese, who have shown how the regional model is indeed still central to Italian crime writers. Although the explosion of public interest in Italian crime and *noir* fiction dates to the second half of the 1990s, already in the early part of the decade Milan saw a resurgence of interest in the *roman noir*. Andrea G. Pinketts, one of the most interesting Italian postmodern crime authors, whose narrative is character-ized by an irreverent and ironic mix of different styles and narrative techniques borrowed from different types of popular fiction, attributes this rebirth of *noir* fiction in Milan – and I would suggest that this date is significant for the rest of the country – to the immediate aftermath of the Tangentopoli scandals, the Milanese inquest which began the tidal wave of the greatest political scandal in post-war Italy, and which, albeit a local event, profoundly shook Italy's social and political fabric. Pinketts observed that the so-called hard-boiled school of Milanese writers:

> Was born in 1993. Milan was facing the full force of Tangentopoli. The fog, which was being lifted, uncovered the problems of years of corruption. Stripped of its designer clothes and its corrupt administration, Milan, now 'naked', could not be the 'moral' capital anymore.[20]

Once Milan had lost its veneer of fashionable respectability and alleged moral façade, it could more easily become the new postmodern capital of crime, and hard-boiled Milanese writers in recent years have once again helped redefine the country's geo-social map of crime.

Piero Colaprico's *Kriminalbar* (1999) is a collection of ten short stories that are interconnected but can also be read individually. Crovi has rightly pointed out the many similarities between Colaprico's collection and Scerbanenco's works.[21] Although Colaprico often infuses his stories with irony, as Crovi has underlined, overall his portrayal of Milan and its criminal underworld, albeit less violent than

Scerbanenco's short stories collected in *Milano calibro 9*, is equally disheartening and morally squalid. His characters comprise a policeman turned private eye with a penchant for unorthodox methods of investigation and interrogation, bosses of criminal organizations, racketeers and young small calibre criminals who dream of a future of easy money against the backdrop of the *Milano da bere* of the 1980s and early 1990s, the wealthy elegant city of fashion, business and hard drugs.[22] Cynicism, desperation and anger fill the lives of the characters. The many references to Milanese and Italian political events and in particular to Tangentopoli reflect the writer's social and political interests.[23] The Milan of *Kriminalbar* is a city seen through the eyes of its bad guys, who drive along the seemingly infinite and monotonous ring roads, and fight or kill in the *aree dismesse* (the former industrial districts awaiting redevelopment). The use of different narrative voices and focalizers enables Colaprico to avoid the nostalgic view of Milan which surfaces at times in Scerbanenco's and in other contemporary writers' work. Genito, the former policeman who is present in many of these stories, is the only character able to visualize a different image of the city, a long-lost Milan tinged with nostalgia:

> The tarmac was wet, gleaming like a sou'wester, and I thought that Milan must have been wonderful, a mere century ago, when the canals glittered in the night . . . A city without peripheries and high-rise blocks, in which you could see the mountains all round, green in spring, yellow in the autumn, and white and crystal in winter. Now all I can see are cars, street lights, and hypermarkets.[24]

This vision of the pre-industrial city with its shimmering canals, still dominated by the natural landscape and its colours, is set in stark oppositional contrast to the industrial cityscape of the new peripheries and their housing estates.

The urban peripheries are a particular focus of Colaprico's stories. They are portrayed as places that breed small crime.[25] Most images emphasize the periphery as a deserted place,[26] which bears the visible scars of de-industrialization.[27] The pervading feeling is that of isolation both in the deserted roads of the periphery or the protected walled spaces of the rich bourgeoisie.[28] The only instance of a more positive portrayal of the periphery is linked significantly to the mythology of the old working-class peripheral districts. Genito meets old partisans and survivors of concentration camps at Bovisa, a working-class housing district to the northeast of the city centre that provided housing for factory workers during Italy's first industrial revolution in the early twentieth century and in the years of the miracle and that suffered years of neglect during the years of de-industrialization. The people here are the only moral individuals in Colaprico's otherwise bleak vision of contemporary Milan; they are the people who remained true to their values and principles whilst Milan and Italy were embracing uncontrollable changes: 'during the war they did what they had to do and at the end of the Resistance they went back to do what they used to do before . . . They saw the Italy of their dreams morphing into the cesspool we know.'[29]

Milan in *Kriminalbar* is also more than in any other Milanese *noir* writer the city of non-places (in the Augé sense).[30] They are the neglected service stations – glimpsed 'past trucks, lorries and sodden rubbish balls swirled by the wind'[31] – and peripheral train stations. Interestingly, Milan Central Station, the Stazione Centrale which featured so prominently in Scerbanenco's short stories and which, thanks to writers and film-makers in the 1950s and 1960s became an emblem of the new process of industrialization of the country and mass internal emigration, is here substituted by the smaller, more peripheral Stazione Garibaldi, placed in an area that is still awaiting a process of urban regeneration.

Colaprico's interest in the representation of Milan continued through his collaboration with Pietro Valpreda (1933–2002), the Milanese anarchist who, in December 1969, was charged – and eventually acquitted some sixteen year later – with one of the most horrendous crimes of Italy's post-war period, the bombing of Piazza Fontana.[32] The protagonist of these '*noir* tinged with humour',[33] is Pietro Binda, a retired low-ranking officer in the Carabinieri. Despite the many references to Italy's post-war troubled history, overall the novels weave a nostalgic and reassuring fiction of Milan as a city in which the old popular culture is still alive, where people still speak their native dialect – for instance the first two novels have subtitles that translate the titles in the dialect of Milan, *Quarter gott d'aqua piovanna* and *La fioccada del 85* – and eat traditional dishes, a city where even the thick fog envelops the characters in its evocative mantle. This nostalgic view is, however, very different from other writers, and especially Olivieri. It is first linked to the focalizer of the narrative, Pietro Binda, but above all its *raison d'être* seems to be the portrayal of the quasi-mythical Milan of strong working-class values, solidarity and sense of community, which seems to stem principally from Valpreda's anarchist ideals and way of life.

One of the characteristics of Milan that has fascinated Italian *noir* and crime writers is the city's weather: *la nebbia*, the fog in the winter, the *afa* (sultry weather) in the summer are linked inextricably with Milan in the public mind. The meteorological observations are linked to the inhospitable and invisible quality of the city, a factual and metaphorical condition of this city. The greyness of the city, its colourless quality, as well as its extreme urban environment, which does not bear any traces of the natural world, are emphasized by many writers. Giuseppe Genna's first novel *Catrame* (1999) begins with a characteristic description of the sultry weather in Milan: 'that sweltering and white afternoon in Milan. The milky-white light of the heat which came into the office.'[34] The protagonist, police Inspector Guido Lopez, looks at 'the searing hot cobble stones, the deserted tarmac, the glowing grey sky of the sultry Milanese summer'.[35] This is contrasted with the nostalgic memories of a cold, crisp winter morning in the Brera quarter, where the police station is situated:

> To wander through the cold and solitary roads of Brera, filled with the metallic morning light of Milan, inhaling the fragrance of warm bread from the back door of the bakery in via Pontaccio; to stretch in the icy atmosphere; and to hear

the crunching sound of one's heels on the paving stones damp with pollution and rust.[36]

Brera is one of the old inner city districts. Now an elegant bourgeois area, it used to be a working-class neighbourhood with very poor housing and slums until, in the 1960s, its inhabitants were transferred to new council houses in Quarto Oggiaro, the notorious crime-ridden neighbourhood, conveniently freeing up space in an area located in very close proximity to the much sought after 'cerchia dei Navigli' – the inner circle of canals that used to surround the historic centre of the city. Brera was subsequently sanitized and suitably gentrified. It is also interesting that the novel sets from the very beginning Milan as a city of stark contrasts. The warmth of the nostalgic view of Lopez's early days in the Questura is contrasted with the perception that the climate in Milan is changing.[37] The novel is in fact also a condemnation of the role of the secret services in Italy in the anni di piombo and the lack of transparency of Italy's most recent national past. The strong social and political critique is accompanied by some of the bleakest portrayals of the Milanese periphery, which emphasize the extent of the process of urban degeneration:

> The crumbling paint of the large council blocks was falling off along with fragments of stone from the balconies, mixing with tattered plastic bags, empty and worn out by dust and pollution, left outside the empty flats. In the streets one could see dark liquids, oily and of unclear origin. Hanging from the filthy clothing lines, garments that had turned a shade of grey or yellow were fading in the heat . . . From the cellars came the humid and pungent smell of soil and mouse droppings . . . The big council estate in via Tommei on the inside was not dissimilar from the one that Lopez had hurriedly glimpsed at when he arrived. The large courtyard, with an unkempt flower-bed in the middle in which only bleached grass was growing, was filled with fragments of chipped plaster . . . surrounded by a busy jumble of washing, hanging haphazardly everywhere.[38]

There are no redemptive qualities here: the faceless housing conglomerates in the periphery of Milan are squalid, deserted, decrepit, forgotten by social services and crime-ridden. The few vestiges of the natural landscape – the sterile trees and bleached grass – underline even further the dehumanizing conditions of life.

A topos of Milanese crime fiction since Scerbanenco's first description of it, Milan's outer ring road – the Tangenziale – has been used by many contemporary *noir* writers to reinforce the image of Milan as a sprawling metropolis, but also as a means to visualize the social geography of the city. The Tangenziale separates both physically and symbolically the centre and the new periphery. Milan's city plan is still indebted to the medieval concentric geometry. Radiating from Piazza Duomo, Milan has four distinct concentric corridors – the cerchia dei navigli, circonvallazione interna, circonvallazione esterna and the Tangenziale – which measure both physically and metaphorically the distance from the city centre constructing thus also a social geometry of the city. The Tangenziale is the gateway to the new periphery and an almost imperative journey for the detectives who move between the visible and invisible boundaries of the different spaces of the city. It is also the point of contact with the undesirable face of the postmodern metropolis with its faceless anonymous buildings which are never experienced but only glanced at from a safe distance during the seemingly endless car journeys: 'a *blackened* landscape. Houses with tightly closed shutters which overlook the bypass: *silent boxes, charred, deserted.*'[39] The Tangenziale, with its elevated position, emphasizes the physical and metaphorical barrier between the city and the indistinct sprawl of the periphery: 'he was driving through the dark city . . . The outskirts were sprawling in the direction of the granite-like mass of the council estates, which looked like sleeping giants in the mechanic rustling noise of the urban night.'[40] Genna's portrayal of the periphery is as a non-city, kept at a safe distance from the viewer in order to emphasize further its isolation and alienation. In fact it illustrates a fundamental lack of understanding of the changes brought about in Milan – and in many other Italian cities – by the new postmodern and post-industrial model of the *città diffusa*, which is both policentric and less preoccupied with the dualism centre-periphery. This very negative stereotyping of the spatialization of the city and framing of the problem of urban expansion is presented in a more balanced and ironic manner by the final two authors, who will be analysed below and who are amongst the most representative new Milanese *noir* talents.

Sandrone Dazieri's hard-boiled novels present a critical, but more unprejudiced and above all humorous, image of Milan.[41] Crovi described it: 'a city viewed through the eyes of those at the margins: beggars, punks, and extreme radicals'.[42] In his debut novel, *Attenti al Gorilla*, Dazieri presents Milan as a city of extreme opposites, of great wealth,[43] underground movements, 'paria milanesi',[44] and *centri sociali* – the most notorious of all in Milan and Italy is the Centro Sociale Leoncavallo which was the hub of the anarchist and left-wing movements post-1978 and which features prominently in the novel. Dazieri's activity as a journalist for the socialist daily *Il Manifesto* and his interest in Italian counter-culture movements and contemporary postmodern narrative are clearly visible in the themes and style of the novel.

Despite its division between the space of the rich and the mean streets, Milan is also presented as a city where the old political and social divisions are failing – this is particularly visible in the description of the crowd at a hip-hop gig at the Leoncavallo, shown here as a melting pot of different city tribes and social classes and a tangible symbol of the less radicalized culture of Milan in the 1990s.[45] One should also note that the geographical location of this space of socialization – 'the area is the heavy-industrial type'[46] – helps to construct a new and more positive image of the periphery. Although peripheral areas are still realistically portrayed as areas that lack basic amenities and opportunities for leisure and socialization, the emphasis in Dazieri's works shifts away from the traditional idea of the isolated, crime-ridden and squalid spaces.[47] Most importantly, Dazieri's Milan is also a city where the new foreign immigrants have found their own space:

> Viale Tunisia is normally called the Kasbah because of the high percentage of Arab immigrants and ethnic shops. It is an area I know well. I used to go there to eat couscous and zigni in small cheap eateries which had sprung up everywhere, among the spice and ethnic food shops, shops selling brightly coloured garments, wooden objects and oriental music.[48]

This is one of the very few positive portrayals of the multicultural and multi-ethnic new face of Milan in the new millennium. The immigrants appear harmoniously integrated in the fabric of the city, with thriving businesses and, most importantly, they occupy a dignified – and incidentally relatively central – space in the city. This contrasts very strongly with Genna's bleak view of Milan city council's lack of policy towards immigration resulting in degrading living conditions in an already marginal and marginalized area of the city's periphery.[49]

Gianni Biondillo, architect, essayist and novelist, set his debut novel, *Per cosa si uccide* (2004), in the police station of Quarto Oggiaro, arguably the most notorious Milanese peripheral quarter.[50] The novel follows Inspector Ferraro's activities over the course of the four seasons weaving into the narrative different stories that all focus on the relationship between the characters and the city spaces that they inhabit.

Schmid, in his analysis of the contribution of crime fiction to perceptions of the city as a violent and dangerous place, highlighted how this is a particularly crucial issue in the postmodern city, which is viewed as an eminently divided city in which the levels of tension between centre and periphery worsen and give rise to violence. Schmid is particularly interested in the spatialization of violence – a central concern for all the *noir* writers who have chosen Milan as their protagonist – and how violence can interconnect with other levels of space in the city. In most of the writers analysed so far, the detective crosses the boundaries of the city and comes into contact with the periphery which is the space of violence par excellence. However, Biondillo – similarly to Dazieri – in a postmodern twist, often reverts this trajectory. Inspector Ferraro, born and bred in Quarto Oggiaro like the author himself, investigating the assassination of two members of the Donnaciva family, a rich bourgeois family, has to travel to an area of Milan which exists in the public imaginary but which, as Biondillo's narrator observes, very few Milanese do ever encounter in the course of their lifetime. It is the mythical 'hidden' Milan:

> There are areas in Milan where you are not in Milan; you are in a different city, in a different world. Uncontaminated places, where there are no cars, full of green spaces for the children to play . . . In those streets it looks like you are walking in a small provincial town. People all know one another; the local baker delivers your bread, the mothers on their bicycles go on their errands.[51]

This idyllic inner sanctum, sheltered and protected, is the social and geographical central core of the city. Its reassuring size and space, which turn it into a familiar back garden or drawing room, also emphasize the binary oppositions between personal/impersonal and centre/periphery. The issue of accessibility to the city spaces and factual and symbolic mobility within these spaces is further reinforced by the ironic observation about the means of transport available to different people when experiencing the city spaces:

> Note this: a rich Milanese member of the bourgeoisie goes around the city centre on her bike and uses the city as if it were her own courtyard. Try and imagine a girl who comes from Gratosoglio [an area to the estreme periphery of the city] doing her shopping in via della Spiga [this is part of the famed Golden Block in the fashion district of Milan] and you'll see the difference.[52]

A description of the aftermath of a heavy snowfall in Milan plays with the image of the concentric spatial and socio-economic geometry of the city:

> Whilst inside the inner ring of the city centre, snow had been carefully stacked on the side of the road which was more convenient for shopping, once you moved towards the outer city ring road the snow had covered in white the pathetic areas of urban green . . . On the other side of the outer ring road only the main access routes and a handful of other roads of strategic importance were swept by the snowplough. In the periphery it was worse than in Siberia and all relied on the survival instinct.[53]

The periphery may be the forgotten land that surrounds the city, but Biondillo does not portrays it as a space of loneliness and desocialization. Its problems are highlighted in order to draw attention to the failure of the city's government. Ultimately Biondillo's most stringent critique is levelled against Milan's ruling classes who are portrayed as fundamentally unprincipled and opportunistic.[54]

During the first industrial revolution in the late nineteenth and early twentieth century, the periphery of Milan saw the growth of the first Italian working-class neighbourhoods. These areas in the years of the miracle were surrounded by the public and private housing projects that changed the landscape of the city completely and which in the next twenty years would continue to grow to create the *città diffusa*. As Foot pointed out: 'throughout this whole period, the periphery has largely been seen as a problem, as a crisis, in negative terms',[55] as we have seen the way in which the city and its periphery is represented is particularly central in crime and *noir* fiction. What all the writers analysed above have done is to map out a socio-economic geography of the city with a clear distinction between the space of the rich and the mean streets.

When Foot analysed the spatial location of the periphery, he noticed how this is not fixed but moves as new areas adjacent to the city centre are gentrified, thus becoming central and not peripheral anymore. Furthermore, many isolated peripheral areas are now part of the urban sprawl and have easy accessibility to the centre of Milan in contrast with the enduring perception of the periphery as far and isolated from the centre. The periphery, as we have seen, is both a geographical and anthropological entity which helped shape the imagery associated with Milan and, in particular, reinforced the dichotomy between a nostalgic old world and the new industrial and post-industrial condition.[56] The periphery as Other is a powerful physical, real, but also a 'visual' phenomenon.[57] The most striking feature of the representation of Milan in its *noir* writers is the use of oppositional and binary categories that include certain keywords: centre/periphery; golden age/ modern era; order/disorder; planned/non-planned; monuments/non-places; social peace/crime; poverty/wealth; colour/black-and-white; light/dark; full/ empty; accessible/isolated; and socialization/de-socialization. These are consistent with other writings on the city and, as Foot observed, stem ultimately from 'the hegemonic "model" of the old city, the historic city',[58] which depicts the old city centre as the ideal walled space, a medieval commune with well-defined boundaries, which allows its inhabitants to know its streets and spaces intimately. In all the works analysed above, this is still the space occupied by Milan's upper classes who enjoy a sense of visual and physical possession of the city space that is lacking in the new cities and their urban sprawls and that is presented as the cause of the disorientation, isolation and ultimately alienation which breed crime. Yet, at least in the case of Dazieri and Biondillo, contemporary writers are also showing signs of a new acceptance and understanding of the new ways of urban life which are being fostered by the peripheries. They acknowledge that the centre, in the new post-industrial era, has become the exception and the periphery is the norm. The urban sprawl now extends to the entire Milanese region; there are no more visual boundaries that mark the end of the city and its periphery and the beginning of the countryside:

> Milan is now one big city until Como and beyond. However, between the two poles . . . it is an indistinct forest of little villas, tiny villas, ugly villas, rustic villas, little houses, garages, basement extensions, loft extensions, Doric temples, Snow Whites with their seven dwarves, lions rampant, concrete eagles, shopping centres, car parks, asphalt, tarmac, briars, rubbish. It is the paradise of the near-architect, the delirium of engineers, the triumph of postmodern, pre-modern, post-postmodern, super-modern, hyper-modern, neo-Gothic, New Romantic, pseudo-country, space-age UFO style; the triumph in one word of the *Brianza style* . . . a true work of art of the territory, *land art*, a sublime monument to Lombard kitsch and productivity.[59]

Milan extends nowadays to a very large section of Lombardy. Although this is still disorienting and strong criticism is levelled at its aesthetics, the often mordent irony which pervades the descriptions of the architectural failings of the *città diffusa* are increasingly becoming an indictment of the city's planners rather than a bleak reflection of the periphery itself. The *città diffusa* is still portrayed as a labyrinth (*indistinta*) but it is also a *selva*, a modern-day enchanted forest.[60] Scerbanenco was the first to engage with the new aesthetics of the periphery, which in the industrial period was dominated by the modernist style of the new housing blocks, characteristically presented as the new isolated cathedrals in the desert. Biondillo's periphery is the post-postmodern triumph of kitsch.

The new *città diffusa* encompasses classical architecture, Snow White and her little companions, and non-places. The faceless space of anonymity has been transformed into its own work of art. It is a deeply ironic move away from the overall simplistic and desolate view of the periphery as non-city or anti-city towards an image of Milan and its *periferia diffusa* as a large-scale monument to a new aesthetics and way of life.

* * *

Extract from Sandrone Dazieri's *Attenti al Gorilla*

The house at number 4 Viale Tebaldi appeared before me with a grey and anonymous façade, its three floors wedged between a pair of much taller and equally colourless buildings. But pressing my eye against the crack that separated the two leaves of the wooden and wrought iron front door I could make out a small park hidden in the internal courtyard. A stone fountain, green with moss, flowed happily as a pair of swans strolled across the perfectly manicured lawn. Climbing vines blocked the rest of the view but I had no doubt that there was a small lake in there somewhere: maybe the owner was windsurfing at that very moment. I mechanically brushed my best suit in a vain attempt to dispel the feelings of inadequacy that were tormenting me . . .

A few hours earlier, having just woken up, I had found an order in the daily report (stuck to the fridge by my business partner) to put on my Sunday best and meet Vale in the usual place to talk about work. After a quick check of my scant finances I had decided to heed the request and headed to Bar Motta in Piazza Duomo to wait for the fair maiden dressed in my fashionable brown and off-green mismatched suit. None of the passing models turned to check out how great I looked . . .

Vale was late as usual, so with nothing better to do I warmed myself in the faint Milanese September sun and watched the various passers-by make their way through the square . . .

Hardly anyone who lives in Milan likes the city. They hate its pace which drives them to be eternally hurried; they have stomach problems from eating toasted sandwiches and side orders of vegetables. Nor can they stand the smell of piss from the underpasses; the stench of vomit left by junkies; the alleyways paved with condoms; the carpet of dog shit. While they dream of green spaces they find only a few dying trees as well as parks full of police ready to tell you that you can't sit on the meagre grass minding your own business. They are disorientated by the lack of landmarks; by the handful of squares without benches; by the jumble of architectural styles and its oddly shaped houses resembling squares, pineapples, or pinecones; the fake rococo and fake gothic. They fail to understand that Milan isn't a city, rather it's a lump of lava that has suffered the wrath of the gods. It's barren like a desert and you need to be properly equipped to live there. It's ill-suited to amateurs. That's why I love it . . .

Sandrone Dazieri, *Attenti al Gorilla* (Milan: Mondadori, 1999).
Translated by Patrick C. Mcgauley.

Notes

[1] 'Milano, alla fine degli anni '60, costituisce la città-pilota di tutto il processo di trasformazione economica e sociale che l'Italia sta vivendo': Massimo Carloni, 'La geografia metropolitana del giallo italiano contemporaneo: Roma e Milano', *Letteratura italiana contemporanea*, 11 (1984), 250. See also by the same author: *L'Italia in giallo. Geografia e storia del giallo italiano contemporaneo* (Reggio Emilia: Diabasis, 1994).

[2] See Giovanni Testori, *I segreti di Milano. 1, Il ponte della Ghisolfa* (Milan: Feltrinelli, 1959a); *I segreti di Milano. 2, La Gilda del Mac Mahon* (Milan: Feltrinelli, 1959b); *I segreti di Milano. 3, La Maria Brasca: quattro atti* (Milan: Feltrinelli, 1960a); *I segreti di Milano. 4, L'Arialda: due tempi* (Milan: Feltrinelli, 1960b); *I segreti di Milano. 5, Il fabbricone* (Milan: Feltrinelli, 1961).

[3] John Foot, *Milan since the Miracle. City, Culture and Identity* (Oxford; New York: Berg, 2001), p. 1.

[4] Ibid., p. 2. See also 'From boomtown to brisbesville: the images of the city, 1980–2000', in Foot, *Milan Since the Miracle*, pp. 157–80. On Italian recent history see also: Stephen Gundle and Simon Parker (eds), *The New Italian Republic: from the Fall of the Berlin Wall to Berlusconi* (London: Routledge, 1996); and Paul Ginsborg, *Italy and its Discontents: Family, Civil Society, State 1980–2001* (London: Allen Lane, 2001).

[5] David Schmid, 'Imagining safe urban space: the contribution of detective fiction to radical geography', *Antipode*, 27/3 (1995), 242–69.

[6] Raymond Chandler, *The Simple Art of Murder* (London: Hamish Hamilton, 1950), p. 234.

[7] Several novels by Augusto De Angelis have now been republished by the Italian publisher Sellerio. They comprise: *Il mistero delle tre orchidee* (Palermo: Sellerio, 2001); *L'albergo delle tre rose* (Palermo: Sellerio, 2002); *La barchetta di cristallo* (Palermo: Sellerio, 2004); and *Il candelabro a sette fiamme* (Palermo: Sellerio, 2005). De Angelis, *Il commissario De Vincenzi*, ed. Oreste Del Buono (Milan: Feltrinelli, 1963) was the first post-war anthological republication of De Angelis's works.

[8] 'la mitologia del "delitto alla Milanese"': Luca Crovi, *Tutti i colori del giallo. Il giallo italiano da De Marchi a Scerbanenco a Camilleri* (Venice: Marsilio, 2002), p. 106. See in particular 'Le città del delitto', pp.101–64.

[9] Luca Somigli, 'The realism of detective fiction: Augusto De Angelis. Theorist of the Italian *Giallo*', *Symposium*, 59/2 (2005), 77.

[10] 'Una città simbolo per la nostra [italiana] realtà socio-economica, erosa da un'industrializzazione selvaggia, da un consumismo rampante, da una diffusa criminalità analizzata da una sociologia ampiamente assolutoria': Carloni, *L'Italia in giallo*, p. 17. His analysis is however restricted to the years 1966–78.

[11] 'rapporto tra crimine e realtà metropolitana': ibid., p. 22.

[12] Ibid., p. 18.

[13] Giuliana Pieri, 'Crime and the city in the detective fiction of Giorgio Scerbanenco', in Robert Lumley and John Foot (eds), *Italian Cityscapes. Culture and Urban Change in Contemporary Italy* (Exeter: University of Exeter Press, 2004), pp. 144–55.

[14] 'Sola nello smisurato piazzale all'estrema periferia di Milano': Giorgio Scerbanenco, *Traditori di tutti* (Milan: Garzanti, 1998), p. 15.

[15] 'Tutta la cerchia della semiantica Milano coi pezzi ancora residui e architettonicamente conservati o spesso ricostruiti, per i turisti, dei bastioni dai cui spalti, un tempo, pare, vigilavano prodi armigeri': ibid., pp. 53–4.

16 'Ed eccola lì, apparentemente innocua, folcloristica, architettonicamente orrenda per quel miscuglio di stile tra la cascina della Bassa Lombarda e la chiesa protestante svedese': ibid., p. 99.

17 The novels comprise among others: *Villa Liberty* (Milan: Rusconi, 1985); *Maledetto Ferragosto* (Milan: Rizzoli, 1988b); *Largo Richini* (Milan: Rizzoli, 1987a); and *Hotel Mozart* (Milan: Mondadori, 1990). There are also various collections of short stories: Olivieri, *Le inchieste del commissario Ambrosio* (Milan: Rusconi, 1987b); *Ambrosio indaga* (Milan; Rizzoli, 1988a); *Ambrosio ricorda* (Milan: A. Mondadori, 1992); and *99 casi di ordinaria criminalità* (Milan: Interno giallo, 1994).

18 'la Milano di Ambrosio è una città raffinata, à la page, abitata da signori e dame perbene che dietro la loro apparente facciata onesta nascondono passioni morbose e criminali': Crovi, *Tutti i colori del giallo*, p. 111.

19 See in particular 'Diaspora del giallo italiano contemporaneo', Carloni, *L'Italia in giallo*. The second part of the study focuses on the years 1979–94.

20 'È nata nel 1993. Milano stava affrontando in pieno gli effetti di Tangentopoli. La nebbia si era diradata rendendo visibili le magagne di anni di corruzione. Spogliata degli abiti firmati dagli stilisti, spogliata dalle amministrazioni Levantine. Milano in quanto "nuda", non poteva più essere capitale "morale"': Andrea G. Pinketts in Crovi, *Tutti i colori del giallo*, p. 122. The three major writers connected to this school are Sandro Ossola, Andrea Carlo Cappi and Raoul Montanari. All translations are my own.

21 'Molte sono le affinità che legano la Milano nera di *Kriminalbar* alla *Milano calibro nove* di Giorgio Scerbanenco: ma a un sentimento disperato come la rabbia Colaprico preferisce sostituire l'ironia, consapevole che i personaggi da lui descritti non sono che burattini di una grande commedia umana': ibid., p.120.

22 Motozappa, a petty criminal, dreams of a better life full of easy money in an attempt to escape from the honest but hard and unmerciful life of the working classes that offers no real social and economic advancement: 'Uno arranca da quando nasce, si alza presto, fa tardi, traffica, si sbatte, e ha sempre quei bastardi venti milioni sul conto in banca. Compra la casa e la casa fa schifo. Si sposa e la moglie fa figli, che costano altri soldi': Piero Colaprico, *Kriminalbar* (Milan: Garzanti, 2000), p. 164.

23 Colaprico, who has worked as a journalist for the Italian daily *Repubblica*, has published a number of essays on the scandals of Tangentopoli: *Duomo Connection* (Siena: Sisifo, 1991); Colaprico and Luca Fazzo, *Manager calibro 9* (Milan: Garzanti, 1995); and, again with Fazzo, *Capire Tangentopoli* (Milan: Il saggiatore, 1996).

24 'C'era l'asfalto bagnato, lucido come un impermeabile, e pensavo che Milano doveva essere stata splendida, anche solo un secolo fa, quando c'erano i navigli a luccicare nella notte . . . in una città senza periferie e palazzoni, si vedevano le montagne tutt'intorno, il verde a primavera, il giallo in autunno, il bianco e il cristallo della neve, mentre ora vedo solo macchine e luci e supermercatoni': Colaprico, *Kriminalbar*, p. 47.

25 'Una di quelle creature prodotte dal calderone della periferia Milanese, periodicamente obbligate a spostarsi dalle vie lunghissime e costeggiate da fabbrichette e condomìni, spacciatori e mercatoni': ibid., p. 65.

26 'Per strada, poche donne con la borsa della spesa, tre ragazzi con un motorino, buste di cellophane e foglie a mezz'aria': ibid., p. 94.

27 'In via Scarsellini, davanti a una tetra sfilata di capannoni chiusi': ibid., p. 127.

28 'Il quartiere delle ville blindate': ibid., p. 104.

29 'durante la Guerra hanno fatto quello che dovevano, alla fine della Resistenza sono tornati a fare quello che facevano prima. Non sono entrati in politica, non hanno rubato

. . . Hanno visto l'Italia che sognavano trasformarsi nella fogna che noi conosciamo': ibid., p.136.

[30] Marc Augé, *Non-places. Introduction to an Anthropology of Supermodernity*, trans. John Howe (London: Verso, 1995).

[31] 'passando tra camion, Tir e spazzatura fradicia appollottolata dal vento': Colaprico, *Kriminalbar*, p. 139.

[32] There are four novels in the series: Colaprico and Pietro Valpreda, *La nevicata dell'85* (Milan: Marco Tropea, 2001a); *Quattro gocce di acqua piovana* (Milan: Marco Tropea, 2001b); *L'estate del mundial* (Milan: Marco Tropea, 2002a); and *La primavera dei maimorti* (Milan: Marco Tropea, 2002b).

[33] 'noir velati di umorismo': Carloni, *L'Italia in giallo*, p. 120.

[34] 'quel pomeriggio afoso e bianco di Milano . . . La luce lattiginosa dell'afa che entrava nell'ufficio': Giuseppe Genna, *Catrame* (Milan: Arnoldo Mondadori, 1999), p. 7. Genna's series with Inspector Guido Lopez continued with *Non toccare la pelle del drago* (Milan: Mondadori, 2003) and *Grande madre rossa* (Milan: Mondadori, 2004).

[35] 'al pavé rovente, all'asfalto deserto, al cielo grigio e fosforescente della cappa milanese': Genna, *Catrame*, p. 8.

[36] 'Girare per le vie di Brera fredde e solitarie, invase dalla luce metallica del mattino di Milano, farsi attraversare dal profumo caldo del pane dietro il forno di via Pontaccio, stirarsi nel gelo, e fare scricchiolare le suole sulle mattonelle umide di smog e ruggine': ibid.

[37] 'Quel tempo era terminato . . . Invecchiavano, aumentavano il cinismo e i silenzi, le energie erano calate, improvvisamente. Chiunque era più scettico di un tempo. Tutto era molto cambiato': ibid.

[38] 'Le incrostazioni di vernice dei grandi casamenti dell'Istituto Autonomo cadevano insieme ai frammenti di tufo dei balconi, ai sacchetti di cellophane strausati messi fuori dagli alloggi, vuoti e consumati dalla polvere e dallo smog. Per strada si vedevano macchie di liquidi oscuri, oleosi, di natura incerta. Stese su appendipanni luridi, maglie grigiastre o ingiallite impallidivano nel caldo . . . Dalle cantine usciva un odore umido, intenso, di terra e di escrementi di topo . . . La grande casa popolare di via Tommei, all'interno, non era diversa da quelle che Lopez aveva spiato di sfuggita arrivando. Il cortile, molto ampio, con un'aiuola desolata al centro, in cui cresceva in disordine un'erba biancastra, era invaso da pezzi di vernice scrostata . . . panni stesi ovunque, ma in maniera casuale e affollata, fastidiosa': ibid., pp. 21–3.

[39] 'paesaggi *anneriti*. Case dalle tapparelle *serrate*, che sporgono sulla tangenziale: *scatole mute, abbrustolite, lasciate deserte*': ibid., p. 65. My emphasis.

[40] 'Guidava, per la città oscura . . . La periferia . . . si allargava in direzione dei . . . quartieri popolari, fitti e granitici, [che] sembravano colossi addormentati nell'enorme fruscio meccanico della notte cittadina': ibid., pp. 149–50.

[41] Sandrone Dazieri, *Attenti al Gorilla* (Milan: Mondadori, 1999) and later titles: *La cura del Gorilla* (Turin: Einaudi, 2001); *Gorilla Blues* (Milan: Mondadori, 2003); and *Il karma del Gorilla* (Milan: Mondadori, 2005).

[42] 'una Milano vista con l'occhio degli emarginati, dei barboni, dei punk a bestia, degli autonomi': Carloni, *L'Italia in giallo*, p. 121. The 'autonomi' are members of Autonomia Operaia (Workers' Autonomy), an extreme radical group of the left.

[43] There are many descriptions of the town and country houses of the Gardoni family, the wealthy bourgeois family whose daughter is assassinated at the beginning of the novel. The description of the Gardoni's country house is typical of the mordent irony

of the novel: 'built in a style which recalled the American mansions at the time of the Civil War . . . you could almost see Scarlett O'Hara wafting around looking for her Rhett; that would have made the picture perfect' ('costruito in uno stile che richiamava le magioni americane pre guerra civile . . . mancava solo che spuntasse Rossella O'Hara, cercando il suo Rhett, e il quadro sarebbe stato completo'): Dazieri, *Attenti al Gorilla*, p. 33.

44 Ibid., p. 222. The novel focuses on a small but highly visible Milanese urban tribe, the 'punkabbestia', an evolution of the punk movement, who are characteristically always accompanied by numerous dogs and in their refusal of any involvement with capitalism, beg and live in squats.

45 The new crowd of the *centro sociale* is an excellent portrayal of the new Milan of the 1990s: 'There were maybe about five thousand people, without any special look. Nowadays punks have laid down their arms and the young Heavy Metal followers are nearing their fifties. The most common look was looney left shabby-chic complete with trainers and leather jackets, but there were also some well-dressed people and ordinary family men.' ('ci saranno state circa cinquemila persone, senza look particolari. Ormai i punk sono in disarmo e i giovani metallari sfiorano la cinquantina. La divisa più diffusa era quella rifondarola [Rifondazione Comunista], scarpe da ginnastica e giubbotto, ma non mancavano i benvestiti e i padri di famiglia'): ibid., p. 104.

46 'la zona è industriale spinta': ibid., p. 103.

47 'Gratosoglio is one of the areas of the periphery which is generally considered by both upright citizens and the press as the hub of every possible wrongdoing and the war zone for drug dealing. As far as I could see, it was simply a decaying periphery, with very little to do in the evening except getting high' ('Gratosoglio, zone dell'hinterland generalmente considerate da stampa e cittadini per bene covo di ogni nequizia e zona di Guerra del narcotraffico. Per quello che ne sapevo io, era solo una periferia degradata, con poche possibilità serali di fare qualcosa di diverso che spararsi una pera'): ibid., p. 122.

48 'Viale Tunisia, zona comunemente chiamata la Casbah per l'alta percentuale di immigrati arabi e locali etnici. È una zona che conosco bene. Una volta ci andavo a mangiare il cuscus e lo zicnì nelle piccole trattorie a buon mercato che spuntano da ogni via, tra i negozi di spezie e cibi, di abiti coloratissimi, oggetti in legno e musica orientale': ibid., p. 85. Zigni is a traditional Ethiopian dish.

49 The periphery in Genna is shown as the space of containment of the new immigrants. An area behind some faceless housing blocks has become a characteristically illegal but tolerated refuge for new immigrants: 'qui svernavano romeni e marocchini, c'era questa intesa con le forze dell'ordine (la strategia di "contenimento" di Santovito), era come un campo d'accoglienza privo di tutto': Genna, *Catrame*, p. 29.

50 Biondillo's debut novel, *Per cosa si uccide* (Parma: Guanda, 2004), was followed by *Con la morte nel cuore* (Parma: Guanda, 2005). His essays comprise studies on Pasolini, Carlo Levi and Elio Vittorini. His professional and academic interest in architecture and the city is linked with the sociopolitical engagement of his creative writings.

51 'Ci sono zone di Milano dove non sei a Milano, sei in un'altra città, in un altro mondo. Luoghi incontaminati, dove non passa una macchina, pieni di verde per i bambini che giocano . . . Per quelle strade sembra di camminare in un paese, o tutt'al più in una piccola capitale di provincia. Tutti si conoscono, si salutano, il panettiere ti porta la spesa a casa, le mamme vanno in bicicletta a fare le loro commissioni': Biondillo, *Per cosa si uccide*, p. 33.

[52] 'Fateci caso: una ricca borghese Milanese gira per il centro in bicicletta, usa la città come fosse il cortile di casa sua. Provate ad immaginare una ragazza che viene in bici da Gratosoglio, per fare le compere in via Spiga, e capirete la differenza': ibid., p. 39.

[53] 'Mentre dentro la cerchia dei Navigli la neve appariva a sprazzi ben accatastata sul lato più comodo per lo shopping, già verso la circonvallazione esterna inbiancava indistintamente tutti i patetici slarghi di verde urbano . . . Oltre la cerchia della 90-91 [circonvallazione esterna] solo i grossi assi di penetrazione urbana e qualche strada strategica alla circolazione venivano battuti dagli spazzaneve. In periferia era peggio della Siberia. Il tutto era affidato allo spirito di sopravvivenza': ibid., p. 91.

[54] See for instance this very critical statement against Italy's ruling and political class and their faux political stances which encompass communism, Opus Dei and extreme liberalism: 'il mangiabambini [i.e. communist] che pontificava contro la stampa di regime nel frattempo era caduto da cavallo sulla strada di Damasco e si era convertito all'*Opus Dei* . . . quando fu scaricato dai sacri banchieri, fece un nuovo salto della quaglia e divenne un puttaniere libertario e liberista. Insomma la strada era segnata: gli mancava ancora di essere liberale e un liberticida e Montecitorio gli avrebbe sicuramente aperto le porte' (the Communist who used to preach against the regime press in the meantime had fallen off his horse on his way to Damascus and had converted to *Opus Dei* . . . when he was dumped by the sacred bankers, he jumped on a new bandwagon and became a libertarian and liberalistic whoremonger. In short, his path was marked out: he only needed to become a liberal and an opponent of liberties and the palace of Montecitorio [the Italian Chamber of Deputies] would have opened its doors to him): Biondillo, *Per cosa si uccide*, p. 217.

[55] Foot, *Milan since the Miracle*, p. 135.

[56] Foot noted how the old periphery of 'hard work, honesty, simplicity and thrift' is contrasted with the new peripheries as spaces of 'desocialization, emptiness, unemployment, crime': ibid., p. 137.

[57] Ibid., p. 139, *passim*.

[58] Ibid., p. 146.

[59] 'Milano è ormai un'unica città fino a Como e oltre. Ma fra i due poli . . . è una selva indistinta di villette, villucce, villacce, rustici, casette, box, tavernette, mansarde, templi dorici, Bianchenevi, sette nani, leoni rampanti, aquile di cemento, centri commerciali, parcheggi, asfalto, bitume, rovi, cartacce. Il paradise del geometra, il delirio dell'ingegnere, il trionfo del postmoderno, del premoderno, del post postmoderno, del supermoderno, dell'ipermoderno, del neogotico, del newromantic, dello pseudocascinale, dell'uforobot, del, in una parola, *Brianza style* . . . vera e propria opera d'arte a livello territoriale, *land art*, monumento sublime del kitsch Lombardo e produttivo': Biondillo, *Per cosa si uccide*, p. 223.

[60] Giuseppe Petronio, who was the first to champion the cause of popular literature in Italy in the late 1970s, saw crime fiction as a modern form of epic and considered the city in this type of narrative as the new jungle or enchanted forest. See his study *Letteratura di massa. Letteratura di consumo. Guida storica e critica* (Bari: Laterza, 1979).

Bibliography

Augé, Marc, *Non-places. Introduction to an Anthropology of Supermodernity*, trans. John Howe (London: Verso, 1995).

Bianciardi, Luciano, *La vita agra* (Milan: Rizzoli, 1962).

Biondillo, Gianni, *Per cosa si uccide* (Parma: Guanda, 2004).

——, *Con la morte nel cuore* (Parma: Guanda, 2005).

Carloni, Massimo, 'La geografia metropolitana del giallo italiano contemporaneo: Roma e Milano', *Letteratura italiana contemporanea*, 11(1984), 247–52.

——, *L'Italia in giallo. Geografia e storia del giallo italiano contemporaneo* (Reggio Emilia: Diabasis, 1994).

Chandler, Raymond, *The Simple Art of Murder* (London: Hamish Hamilton, 1950).

Colaprico, Piero, *Duomo Connection* (Siena: Sisifo,1991).

——, *Kriminalbar* (Milan: Garzanti, 2000).

—— and Luca Fazzo, *Manager calibro 9* (Milan: Garzanti, 1995).

—— and ——, *Capire Tangentopoli* (Milan: Il saggiatore, 1996).

—— and Pietro Valpreda, *La nevicata dell'85* (Milan: Marco Tropea, 2001a).

—— and ——, *Quattro gocce di acqua piovana* (Milan: Marco Tropea, 2001b).

—— and ——, *L'estate del mundial* (Milan: Marco Tropea, 2002a).

—— and ——, *La primavera dei maimorti* (Milan: Marco Tropea, 2002b).

Crovi, Luca, *Tutti i colori del giallo. Il giallo italiano da De Marchi a Scerbanenco a Camilleri* (Venice: Marsilio, 2002).

Dazieri, Sandrone, *Attenti al Gorilla* (Milan: Mondadori, 1999).

——, *La cura del Gorilla* (Turin: Einaudi, 2001).

——, *Gorilla Blues* (Milan: Mondadori, 2003).

——, *Il karma del Gorilla* (Milan: Mondadori, 2005).

—— (ed.), *Italia overground: mappe e reti della cultura alternative* (Roma: Castelvecchi, 1996).

De Angelis, Augusto, *Il commissario De Vincenzi*, ed. Oreste Del Buono (Milan: Feltrinelli, 1963).

——, *Il mistero delle tre orchidee* (Palermo: Sellerio, 2001).

——, *L'albergo delle tre rose* (Palermo: Sellerio, 2002).

——, *La barchetta di cristallo* (Palermo: Sellerio, 2004).

——, *Il candelabro a sette fiamme* (Palermo: Sellerio, 2005).

Foot, John, *Milan since the Miracle. City, Culture and Identity* (Oxford; New York: Berg, 2001).

Genna, Giuseppe, *Catrame* (Milan: Arnoldo Mondadori, 1999).

——, *Non toccare la pelle del drago* (Milan: Mondadori, 2003).

——, *Grande madre rossa* (Milan: Mondadori, 2004).

Ginsborg, Paul, *Italy and its Discontents: Family, Civil Society, State 1980–2001* (London: Allen Lane, 2001).

Gundle, Stephen and Simon Parker (eds), *The New Italian Republic: from the Fall of the Berlin Wall to Berlusconi* (London: Routledge, 1996).

Olivieri, Renato, *Villa Liberty* (Milan: Rusconi, 1985).

——, *Largo Richini* (Milan: Rizzoli, 1987a).

——, *Le inchieste del commissario Ambrosio* (Milan: Rusconi, 1987b).

——, *Ambrosio indaga* (Milan; Rizzoli, 1988a).

——, *Maledetto Ferragosto* (Milan: Rizzoli, 1988b).

——, *Hotel Mozart* (Milan: Mondadori, 1990).

——, *Ambrosio ricorda* (Milan: A. Mondadori, 1992).

——, *99 casi di ordinaria criminalità* (Milan: Interno giallo, 1994).

Perria, Antonio, *Delitto a mano libera* (Milan: Longanesi, 1974a).

——, *Incidente sul lavoro* (Milan: Longanesi, 1974b).

——, *Giustizia per scommessa* (Milan: Longanesi, 1975).

Petronio, Giuseppe, *Letteratura di massa. Letteratura di consumo. Guida storica e critica* (Bari: Laterza, 1979).

Pieri, Giuliana, 'Crime and the city in the detective fiction of Giorgio Scerbanenco', in Robert Lumley and John Foot (eds), *Italian Cityscapes. Culture and Urban Change in Contemporary Italy* (Exeter: University of Exeter Press, 2004), pp. 144–55.

Scerbanenco, Giorgio, *Traditori di tutti* (Milan: Garzanti, 1998).

Schmid, David, 'Imagining safe urban space: the contribution of detective fiction to radical geography', *Antipode*, 27/3 (1995), 242–69.

Somigli, Luca, 'The realism of detective fiction: Augusto De Angelis. Theorist of the Italian *Giallo*', *Symposium*, 59/2 (2005), 70–83.

Testori, Giovanni, *I segreti di Milano. 1, Il ponte della Ghisolfa* (Milan: Feltrinelli, 1959a).

——, *I segreti di Milano. 2, La Gilda del Mac Mahon* (Milan: Feltrinelli, 1959b).

——, *I segreti di Milano. 3, La Maria Brasca: quattro atti* (Milan: Feltrinelli, 1960a).

——, *I segreti di Milano. 4, L'Arialda: due tempi* (Milan: Feltrinelli, 1960b).

——, *I segreti di Milano. 5, Il fabbricone* (Milan: Feltrinelli, 1961).

9

Annotated Bibliography

LUCIA RINALDI

This bibliography provides selected secondary sources devoted to the study of Italian crime fiction.

Full-length studies and selected articles

Ania, Gillian and Ann Hallamore Caesar (eds), *Trends in Contemporary Italian Narrative, 1980–2007* (Cambridge: Scholars Publishing, 2007): This volume contains three essays on Italian crime fiction. In the first, Luca Somigli examines crime novels dealing with recent history. In the second, Nicoletta McGowan discusses the particular case of a *noir* by Claudia Salvatori. In the third, Monica Jansen and Inge Lanslots focus on the 'Young Cannibals' and their non-literary language and orientation towards cinema, pop music and slang.

Ascari, Maurizio (ed.), *Two Centuries of Detective Fiction: a New Comparative Approach* (Bologna: Cotepra, University of Bologna, 2000). A comparative study of English, American and Italian crime fiction of the nineteenth and twentieth centuries.

Bacchereti, Elisabetta, *Carlo Lucarelli* (Fiesole: Cadmo, 2004): A brief monograph on Carlo Lucarelli which summarizes his work as a television presenter and novelist; it includes a short analysis of his work and an interview with the writer.

Bini, Benedetta, 'Il poliziesco', in Asor Rosa, Alberto (ed.), *Letteratura italiana. Storia e geografia* (Torino: Einaudi, 1989), pp. 999–1026: A brief overlook of the history of Italian crime fiction.

Bonina, Gianni, *Il carico da undici: le carte di Andrea Camilleri* (Siena: Barbera, 2007): A detailed study of Camilleri's work. This comprehensive volume, in which each chapter is dedicated to a group of texts, is organized chronologically, and includes a lengthy interview with the writer and useful summaries of the plots.

Buttitta, Antonino (ed.), *Il caso Camilleri, letteratura e storia* (Palermo: Sellerio, 2004): This collection of essays, stemming from a 2002 conference, comprises several studies on Camilleri's writing as well as articles and notes by his translators.

Capecchi, Giovanni, *Andrea Camilleri* (Fiesole: Cadmo, 2000): One of the earliest studies on Camilleri's writing which briefly describes the writer's life, discusses the literary influences on his work, and includes comments on his distinctive language. It also comprises an interview with the author.

Capozzi, Rocco (ed.), *Reading Eco: an Anthology* (Bloomington: Indiana University Press, 1997): This collection of essays provides an introduction to Umberto Eco's writing and thinking.

Carloni, Massimo, *L'Italia in giallo. Geografia e storia del giallo italiano contemporaneo* (Reggio Emilia: Diabasis, 1994): One of the few critical studies dedicated to the history of Italian crime fiction. It applies an interesting geographical approach while offering a historical perspective to the development of crime fiction in Italy.

Cazzato, Luigi, *Generi, recupero, dissoluzione: l'uso del giallo e della fantascienza nella narrativa contemporanea* (Fasano: Schena, 1999): Cazzato applies a postmodern approach to his study of contemporary fiction (not only Italian) by discussing the deconstruction and use of crime and science fiction genres by mainstream authors such as Umberto Eco and Italo Calvino.

Cicioni, Mirna and Nicoletta Di Ciolla (eds), *Differences, Deceits, and Desires. Murder and Mayhem in Italian Crime Fiction* (Cranbury, NJ: University of Delaware Press, 2008): This is a collection of essays arising from an international conference which brings together a selection of studies on contemporary Italian crime fiction by dealing with the work of prominent authors such as Leonardo Sciascia and Antonio Tabucchi, as well as the work of less known writers such as Gianni Farinetti and Fiorella Cagnoni.

Crovi, Luca, *Tutti i colori del giallo. Il giallo italiano da De Marchi a Scerbanenco a Camilleri* (Venezia: Marsilio, 2002): A comprehensive history of Italian crime fiction which offers an insight into the development of different forms of crime narrative in Italy, such as literature, cinema and comics while examining their circulation, fruition and critical response.

Crovi, Raffaele, *Le maschere del mistero. Storie e tecniche di thriller italiani e stranieri* (Firenze: Passigli Editori, 2000): A vast collection of Crovi's brief, heterogeneous essays, articles and notes on Italian and foreign crime fiction appeared on a number of newspapers, journals and books.

Demontis, Simona, *I colori della letteratura, un'indagine sul caso Camilleri* (Milano: Rizzoli, 2001): A well-researched study, supported by a number of citations and examples from texts, devoted to Andrea Camilleri's work which examines themes, characters and writing style.

Farrell, Joseph, *Leonardo Sciascia* (Edinburgh: University of Edinburgh Press, 1995): An excellent, informative study on Sciascia's work. Detective and historical novels, novellas and essay-investigations are thoroughly examined.

Giovannini, Fabio, *Storia del noir. Dai Fantasmi di Edgar Allan Poe al grande cinema di oggi* (Roma: Castelvecchi, 2000): A brief history of *noir* fiction which contextualizes Italian crime narrative within British and American *noir* literature and film.

Gundle, Stephen and Lucia Rinaldi (eds), *Assassination and Murder in Modern Italy*, (Basingstoke: Palgrave, 2007): A wide-ranging collection of essays which explore notorious true cases and their representation(s) in Italian culture. It includes essays on Leonardo Sciascia and Carlo Lucarelli.

Lodato, Saverio, *La linea della palma. Saverio Lodato fa raccontare Andrea Camilleri* (Milano: Rizzoli, 2000): A lengthy interview with Camilleri in which the writer narrates episodes of his childhood, his experience with television and theatre, his career as a novelist, and discusses his views on Italian politics.

Lombard, Laurent (ed.), *Massimo Carlotto: interventi sullo scrittore e la sua opera* (Roma: Edizione e/o, 2007): A collection of articles, stemming from a symposium on Carlotto's work, which includes a variety of essays dealing with different aspect of his narrative, but especially focusing on his political commitment and representation of violence.

Lucamante, Stefania, (ed. and trans.), *Italian Pulp Fiction, the New Narrative of the Giovani Cannibali Writers* (Madison, NJ: Fairleigh Dickinson University Press; London: Associated University Presses, 2001): A collection of studies which explore various aspects of the writing of the 'Young Cannibals' and which also includes translations into English of four of their short stories.

Mullen, Anne and Emer O'Beirne (eds), *Crime Scenes. Detective Narratives in European Culture since 1945* (Amsterdam, Atlanta: Rodopi, 2000): A valuable collection of essays which examine crime fiction in Europe and includes essays on Leonardo Sciascia and Antonio Tabucchi.

Padovani, Gisella and Rita Verdirame (eds), *L'almanacco del delitto* (Palermo: Sellerio, 1996): An interesting anthology of crime stories published in the 1930s, accompanied by an introduction and an appendix which examine the rise of Italian crime fiction during the Fascist period.

Petronio, Giuseppe (ed.), *Il giallo degli anni Trenta* (Trieste: Lint, 1988). A collection of essays, stemming from a conference on mass literature, which focuses on the inception and flourishing of mystery fiction in Italy during the interwar period.

Petronio, Giuseppe, *Sulle tracce del giallo* (Roma: Gamberetti, 2000): This volume collects Petronio's most significant essays which focus, in particular, on the debate on the literary merits of crime literature.

Pieri, Giuliana, 'Crime and the city in the detective fiction of Giorgio Scerbanenco', in Robert Lumley and John Foot (eds), *Italian Cityscapes. Culture and Urban Change in Contemporary Italy* (Exeter: University of Exeter Press, 2004), pp. 144–55: A valuable essay on the representation of Milan in the novels of Giorgio Scerbanenco.

Pistelli, Maurizio, *Un secolo in giallo. Storia del poliziesco italiano (1860–1960)* (Roma: Donzelli, 2006): A comprehensive history and analysis of the origins and development of different forms of Italian crime fiction, from the early mystery and adventure stories in the nineteenth century to *noir* narrative in the 1960s. It encompasses an examination of forms of crime narrative for radio, theatre, comics and television.

Rambelli, Loris, *Storia del giallo italiano* (Milano: Garzanti, 1979): A seminal study on Italian crime fiction: through a historical perspective, it examines in detail the birth and development of crime fiction in Italy from the end of the nineteenth century until the 1970s. Up to now, this is the most valuable study on Italian crime fiction.

Rinaldi, Lucia, 'Bologna's *noir* identity: narrating the city in Carlo Lucarelli's crime fiction', *Italian Studies*, 64/1 (2009), 120–33: A study of the representation of the city (Bologna) in Carlo Lucarelli's earlier crime novels and in his most successful *noir* novel, *Almost Blue*.

Ross, Charlotte and Rochelle Sibley (eds), *Illuminating Eco: on the Boundaries of Interpretation* (Aldershot: Ashgate, 2004): A collection of essays on the prolific literary and theoretical work of Umberto Eco which include a contribution by the author.

Sangiorgi, Marco and Luca Telò (eds), *Il giallo italiano come nuovo romanzo sociale* (Ravenna: Longo Editore, 2004): A collection of essays by critics and writers dealing with different aspects of Italian crime fiction, and which also includes works on crime fiction by secondary-school pupils.

Spinazzola, Vittorio (ed.), *Tirature '07. Le avventure del giallo* (Milano: Il Saggiatore, 2007): An interesting volume consisting of several brief articles which consider reception and fruition of crime fiction in Italy in the last decades.

Tani, Stefano, *The Doomed Detective* (Carbondale and Edwardsville: Southern Illinois University Press, 1984): A study which investigates the influence of postmodernism on detective fiction in the writing of mainstream authors such as Eco and Sciascia.

Wren-Owens, Elizabeth, *Postmodern Ethics* (Newcastle: Cambridge Scholars, 2007): This volume examines the ways in which Leonardo Sciascia and Antonio Tabucchi make use of their narrative to engage with their socio-political environment.

Selected specialist journals and special issues

Delitti di carta (Pistoia: Libreria dell'Orso): A six-monthly journal, founded in the early 1990s, entirely dedicated to crime fiction, especially Italian. It offers critical studies, essays, short stories, books reviews and lists of events devoted to crime narratives. Further details: *http://www.libreriadellorso.it/coll_ddc/leuscite.htm* (accessed 10 December 2009).

Narrativa, 26 (2006). *Trent'anni di giallo italiano. Omaggio a Loriano Macchiavelli e Antonio Perria*: A wide-ranging special issue devoted to Italian crime fiction of the last two decades which includes valuable essays by scholars as well as crime writers.

Narrativa, 29 (2007). *Letteratura e politica*: A special volume devoted to politics in literature which includes several essays on representation of political issues in contemporary Italian crime fiction.

Romance Studies, 25/2 and 4 (2007). Noir *Cityscapes*: Two special numbers dedicated to the representation of the city in *noir* fiction, which include articles on the representation of Milan and Rome in Italian crime fiction.

Spunti e ricerche, (2001). Pagliaro, Antonio (ed.), *Il giallo*: A special issue which consists of a collection of articles engaging with several aspects of Italian crime fiction and encompasses essays on Scerbanenco, Lucarelli and Camilleri.

Symposium, 59/2 (2005). Somigli, Luca (ed.), *Form and ideology in Italian detective fiction*: A special issue consisting of four essays which explore the writing of Augusto De Angelis, Carlo Emilio Gadda, Umberto Eco and Leonardo Sciascia.

Main websites

A selection of useful websites dealing with Italian crime fiction active in 2010:

Andrea Camilleri: *http://www.vigata.org*: An extremely useful and detailed website primarily devoted to Andrea Camilleri's work, but which includes links to and information on other crime writers.

Giallo web: *http://ww.gialloweb.net*: An Italian website devoted to crime fiction which features lists of events, interviews, book reviews and bibliographies of Italian and foreign crime writers.

Europolar: *http://www.europolar.eu.com/*: A European website dedicated to *noir* fiction, translated into five languages, which offers scholarly essays and more generic information and discussion on crime narratives.

MissFatti: *http://missfatti.wordpress.com*: A website run by Italian female crime writers which offers information on their activities and publications.

Index

Agostinelli, Maria 77
Alinovi, Francesca 79
Allain, Marcel 7
Allingham, Margery 9
Almanzi, Ventura 8
Ambroise, Claude 64
Ambrosiano, L' 16
Aquinas, Saint Thomas 56, 57
Ariosto, Ludovico 57
Aristotle 54, 58
  Poetics 58
Auden, W. H. 2
Augé, Marc 137

Bacchereti, Elisabetta 80
Baldini, Erasmo 74
Balzac, Honoré de 51
Beckett, Samuel 61
Bennett, Arnold 50
Berlusconi, Silvio 93, 132
Bertolucci, Bernardo 121
Bianciardi, Luciano 132
  vita agra, La 132
Biondillo, Gianni 140–2
  Per cosa si uccide 140
Bologna school 4, 90
Borges, J. L. 2, 59
Borsellino, Paolo 92
Bosch, Hieronymus 62
Brancati, Vitaliano 65
Burns, Jennifer 18, 44, 134

Cacucci, Pino 80, 83–4, 116
  Punti di fuga 84
Calvino, Italo 3, 53, 91
Camilleri, Andrea 3, 61, 73, 89, 90–4, 99, 100, 102, 135
  ali della sfinge, Le 94
  birraio di Preston, Il 91
  cane di terracotta, Il 91, 92
  corso delle cose, Il 90

filo di fumo, Un 90
forma dell'acqua, La 90–1, 92, 100
giro di boa, Il 92, 94, 100
ladro di merendine, Il 93–4, 100
Salvo Montalbano 61, 90–4, 99
strage dimenticata, La 90
Capozzi, Rocco 56
Carloni, Massimo 74, 134, 135
Carlotto, Massimo 73, 80, 124, 135
Carofiglio, Gianrico 4, 73, 89, 90, 98–102, 135
  Ad occhi chiusi 99, 100
  arte del dubbio, L' 101
  Cacciatori nelle tenebre 98
  Testimone inconsapevole 90, 99, 100–1, 102–3
Cervantes, Miguel de 63
Chandler, Raymond 133
Chesterton, G. K. 2, 14, 17, 49
Chiara, Piero 73
Christie, Agatha 9, 49, 51
  Murder on the Orient Express 60
Colaprico, Piero 83, 135–7
  Kriminalbar 135–7
  see also Colaprico and Valpreda
Colaprico and Valpreda 137
  Quarter gott d'aqua piovanna 137
  fioccada del 85, La 137
Cold War 56
Collins, Wilkie 7, 59
  Moonstone, The 59
Comastri Montanari, Danila 82–3
  campana dell'arciprete, La 83
  Giallo Antico. Come si scrive un poliziesco storico 82
  Mors tua 82
  strada giallo sangue, Una 83
Comez, Armando 11
Conan Doyle, Arthur 7, 51, 52, 53, 57, 58, 59, 79
Conrad, Joseph 59, 60

Lord Jim 59
Corriere della Sera 7, 13
Craxi, Bettino 132
Creagh, Patrick 103
Cremante, Renzo 2
Croce, Benedetto 81
Crovi, Luca 42, 115, 124, 134, 135
Crovi, Raffaele 115

Daeninckx, Didier 116
Dazieri, Sandrone 139–40, 142, 143
  Attenti al gorilla 139, 143
De Angelis, Augusto 7, 16–18, 20, 133, 134
  albergo delle tre rose, L' 17
  barchetta di cristallo, La 16, 20
  candeliere a sette fiamme, Il 16
  do tragico, Il 16
  impronta del gatto, L' 16
  mistero delle orchidee, Il 16
  mistero di Cinecittà, Il 17
  Sei donne e un libro 16
  sette picche doppiate, Le 17
De Cataldo, Giancarlo 83, 116
  Romanzo criminale 83
De Marchi, Emilio 48
  Priest's Hat, The 48
De Stefani, Alessandro 11
D'Errico, Ezio 7, 15–16, 17, 20
  famiglia Morel, La 15
  fatto di Via delle Argonne, Il 15
  naso di cartone, Il 15
  notte del 14 luglio, La 15
  Qualcuno ha bussato alla porta 15
  quaranta, tre, sei, sei non risponde, Il 15
  uomo dagli occhi melanconici, L' 15
Del Buono, Oreste 77
Dolfi, Anna 61
Dombroski, Robert 55
Domenica del Corriere, La 7
Doninelli, Luca 32
Dostoevsky 48, 51
  Crime and Punishment 48
Dunnett, Jane 3, 20
Dürer, Albrecht 66
Dürrenmatt, Friedrich 61

Easton Ellis, Bret 82
  American Psycho 82
Eastwood, Clint 75, 81
Eco, Umberto 2, 48, 49, 50, 51, 52, 54, 56–8, 73, 82
  Foucault's Pendulum 56, 57

Name of the Rose, The (or *Il nome della rosa*) 2, 51, 56–8, 73, 82
economic miracle 33, 41, 75, 78, 118, 132, 133, 134, 136, 141
Eliade, Mircea 60
Enna, Franco 75

Falcone, Giovanni 92
Faletti, Giorgio 82
  Io uccido 82
Faulkner, William 63
Fascist regime 6, 8, 10, 16, 18, 19, 28, 33, 52, 78, 80, 81
  censorship 10
Farrell, Joseph 67
Felisatti, Massimo 75
  Violenza a Roma (with Pittorru) 75
Ferretti, Giancarlo 55
Fois, Marcello 4, 73, 80, 89, 90, 94–8, 102, 135
  Dura madre 95, 97–8
  Ferro Recente 95
  Meglio morti 95–6
  Piccole storie nere 98
Foot, John 132, 141, 142
Fra Dolcino 56
Freeman, Richard A. 2
Freud, Sigmund 16
Fruttero e Lucentini 73, 89
  donna della domenica, La 73

Gaboriau, Émile 7
Gadda, Carlo Emilio 2, 3, 6, 27, 48, 49, 50, 51, 52–5, 65
  Quer pasticciaccio brutto de Via Merulana 6
  Second Novella 53
  That Awful Mess on Via Merulana 52–3, 55
Gallimard 13
Gardner, Erle Stanley 51
Garlaschelli, Barbara 117, 122–3
  Alice nell'ombra 122–3
  Nemiche 122
  Sorelle 122–3
Genna, Giuseppe 137–9, 140
  Catrame 137
Giuliani, Carlo 93
Gramsci, Antonio 2, 50–1
Green, Anna Katherine 8
Grim, Alfred *see* Laura Grimaldi
Grimal, L. D. *see* Laura Grimaldi

Grimaldi, Laura 116
  colpa, La 116
  giallo e il nero, Il 116
Grim, Alfred 116
Grimal, L. D. 116
  paura, La 116
  Perfide storie di famiglia 116
Pomarici, Alfredo 116
Pomarick, Alfred 116
  sospetto, Il 116
Gruppo 13, 79–80, 81
  delitti del Gruppo 13, I 79
Guccini, Francesco 79

Heidegger, Martin 51
Hess, Herman 59
Holmes, Sherlock 7, 14, 16, 50, 53, 55,
  57, 59

impegno 1, 3, 4, 94, 118
Invernizio, Carolina 115
  felicità del delitto, La 115
  ladri dell'onore, I 115
  Nina la poliziotta dilettante 115
  sepolta viva, La 115

Jacoponi, Tiziana 117
James, P. D. 49
Jansen, Monica 62
Jung, Karl 120

Kant, Immanuel 54
Kerouac, Jack 59
  On the Road 59
Kipling, Rudyard 60

Lanocita, Arturo 13
  Otto ore di angoscia 13
  Quaranta milioni 13
  Quella maledettissima sera 13
Lazzaro-Weis, Carol 116
Le Rouge, Gustave 8
Leaden Years (also anni di piombo) 4, 76,
  138
Leibnitz, Gottfried 54
Leoncavallo (Centro Sociale) 139
Leoni, Giulio 83
  delitti della Medusa, I 83
Lucarelli, Carlo 73, 80–2, 84, 85, 89, 124,
  133, 135
  Almost Blue 81–2, 84–5
  Blu Notte-Misteri italiani 80

Carta Bianca 80–1
estate torbida, L' 81
Falange armata 81
isola dell'angelo caduto, L' 80
Lupo mannaro 81
Via delle Oche 81

McBain, Ed 75
Macchiavelli, Loriano 3, 74–80, 82, 89, 133
  Coscienza sporca 79
  Cos'è accaduto alla signora perbene 78
  Fiori alla memoria 78, 81
  Funerale dopo Ustica (as Jules Quicher)
    79
  Macaronì (with Francesco Guccini) 79
  piste dell'attentato, Le 74–5, 78
  Sequenze di memoria 78
  Sergeant Sarti Antonio 76, 79, 81
  Stop per Sarti Antonio 79
  Strage (as Jules Quicher) 79
  triangolo a quattro lati, Un 79
Mcgauley, Patrick 126, 143
mafia 4, 29, 64–5, 80, 85, 91, 92, 93, 98
Malraux, André 63
Mani Pulite see also Tangentopoli 4
Manifesto, Il 139
Maraini, Dacia 55, 117
  Voci 117
Mariotti, Vasco 11
Marzaduri, Lorenzo 80
Masella, Maria 89
Mason, Alfred E. W. 9
Matrone, Maurizio 83
  Erba alta 83
Maugham, Somerset 60
Meirs, George 7
Milanesi, Claudio 119, 123
Mondadori 1, 8, 9, 10, 11, 12, 13, 15, 19,
  82, 116
  cerchio verde, Il 15
Montano, Lorenzo 9, 10, 11, 12, 13, 19
Morchio, Bruno 89
Mussolini, Benito 55, 80

Olivieri, Renato 134–5, 137

Panizza, Letizia 115
Paoli, Marco 37, 42
Pasolini, Pierpaolo 80
Pessoa, Fernando 61
Perria, Antonio 75, 134
  Delitto a mano libera 134

Giustizia per scommessa 134
Incidente sul lavoro 134
Petronio, Giuseppe 2
Pezzin, Claudio 59
Piazzese, Santo 135
Pieri, Giuliana 33
Pinketts, Andrea G. 80, 135
Pirandello, Luigi 61, 63, 64, 65
Right You Are (If You Think So!) 63
Pirani, Roberto 73
Pistelli, Maurizio 12, 115
Pittorru, Fabio 75
Violenza a Roma (with Felisatti) 75
Plato 16
Poe, Edgard Allan 7, 13, 17
Storie incredibili 7
Pomarici, Alfredo *see* Laura Grimaldi
Pomarick, Alfred *see* Laura Grimaldi
Ponson du Terrail 7
Ponzoni 116
Prohibition era 14

Queen, Ellery 9, 13
Quicher, Jules *see* Macchiavelli, Loriano

Rambelli, Loris 2, 11, 12, 13, 15
Resistance 28, 78, 81, 136
resto del Carlino, Il 16
Rusca, Luigi 9

Saint Paul 16
Epistles, The 16
Salazar, António de Oliveira 58
Salvatores, Gabriele 120
Sansoni 116
Sartarelli, Stephen 94
Savinio, Alberto 6
Sayers, Dorothy 51
Scajola, Claudio 93
Scerbanenco, Giorgio 3, 7, 18–19, 20,
    27–42, 43, 73, 75, 89, 122, 133, 134,
    135, 136, 137, 138, 142
antro dei filosofi, L' 18
bambola cieca, La 18
cane che parla, Il 18
Duca Lamberti 27, 28–31, 32, 34, 36,
    37, 38, 39, 40, 41, 42, 43
Milan (in Scerbanenco's work) 31–3
milanesi ammazzano al sabato, I 27, 29,
    34, 35, 37
Milano calibro 9 136
Nessuno è colpevole 18

ragazzi del massacro, I 27, 28, 30–1, 34,
    37, 39, 40
Sei giorni di preavviso 18
Traditori di tutti 27, 28, 33, 37, 39
Venere privata 27, 28, 30, 31, 32, 34, 35,
    36, 37, 38, 39, 40, 41, 42, 43–4
Schmid, David 140
Schopenhauer, Arthur 51
Sciascia, Leonardo 2, 3, 27, 34, 48, 49, 50,
    51, 52, 55, 61, 63–6, 67, 73, 89, 90, 91,
    92, 93
1912 +1 64, 66
Brief History of the Detective Novel 48,
    65
*Day of the Owl, The (Il giorno della
    civetta)* 64–5, 93
Equal Danger 64, 65
inchiesta 63, 64
Knight and the Death, The 64, 66–7
One Way or Another 63, 64, 65
Open Doors 55, 64, 66
Parishes of Regalpetra, The 63
Straightforward Tale, A 64, 66
To Each His Own 63, 64, 65
Scott, Ridley 120
Scott, Walter 56
Rob Roy 56
secolo XIX, Il 16
Sellerio, Elvira 90
Sellerio (publisher) 90, 92
Signoroni, Secondo 134
Qui commissariato di zona 134
Simenon 12, 15, 17, 59, 75
Soldati, Mario 48, 73
Somigli, Luca 133
Souvestre, Pierre 7
Spagnol, Tito Antonio 13–15, 19, 20
bambola insanguinata, La 14
griffe di lion, La 13
Sotto la cenere 15
unghia del leone, L' 14
Uno, due, tre 14
Spinoza, Baruch 54, 61
Stampa, La 16
Stevenson, Robert Louis 8
Moby Dick 52
Stout, Rex 9
Stransky, Oonagh 85

Tabucchi, Antonio 3, 48, 49, 50, 51, 52,
    58–62
Declares Pereira 58

Indian Nocturne 58, 59, 61, 62
Requiem 62
Vanishing Point 61, 62
Taibo II, Ignacio Paco 84
Tangentopoli 4, 132, 135, 136
Tasso, Torquato 57
Testori, Giovanni 132
secrets of Milan, The 132
Todorov, Tzvetan 2, 3
Turchetta, Gianni 83

'Uno bianca' 79, 81, 83

Vailati, Franco 11
Vallorani, Nicoletta 117, 118–20
cuore finto di DR, Il 120
Cuore meticcio 118
Dentro la notte e ciao 118, 119
Eva 119–20
fidanzata di Zorro, La 118
Visto dal cielo 118
Valpreda, Pietro 83, 137
see also Colaprico and Valpreda
Van Dine, S. S. 8, 9, 13, 17, 51, 92
Varaldo, Alessandro 7, 11–12
avventure di Gino Arrighi, Le 11
Casco d'oro 11, 12
Circolo chiuso 11

gatta persiana, La 11
scarpette rosse, Le 11, 12
scomparsa di Rigel, La 11
segreto della statua, Il 11
sette bello, Il 11, 12
signor ladro, Il 11
tesoro dei Borboni, Il 11
Tre catene d'argento 11
trentunesima perla, La 11
Vassalli, Sebastiano 65
Verasani, Grazia 117, 120–2, 126
amore è un bar sempre aperto, L' 120
Di tutti e di nessuno 121
Quo vadis baby? 120–2, 125–6
Velocemente da nessuna parte 120–2
Voltaire 54, 63
Candide 54
Traité sur la tolerance à l'occasion de la mort de Jean Calas 63

Wallace, Edgar 8, 9, 12
Wilde, Oscar 16
De Profundis 16
Wills Crofts, Freeman 9
Wilson, Edmund 2
Wood, Sharon 115

Zingaretti, Luca 91